Welcome to the EVERYTHING® series!

These handy, accessible books give you all you need to tackle a difficult project, gain a new hobby, comprehend a fascinating topic, prepare for an exam, or even brush up on something you learned back in school but have since forgotten.

You can read an *EVERYTHING*® book from cover to cover or just pick out the information you want from our four useful boxes: e-facts, e-ssentials, e-alerts, and e-questions. We literally give you everything you need to know on the subject, but throw in a lot of fun stuff along the way, too.

We now have well over 100 *EVERYTHING*® books in print, spanning such wide-ranging topics as weddings, pregnancy, wine, learning guitar, one-pot cooking, managing people, and so much more. When you're done reading them all, you can finally say you know *EVERYTHING*®!

E FACTS
Important sound bytes of information

ESSENTIALS
Quick handy tips

ALERT
Urgent warnings

QUESTIONS?
Solutions to common problems

THE
EVERYTHING®
Series

Dear Reader,

I've had the good fortune of working in a variety of business environments, including retail and a couple of entrepreneurial endeavors of my own. Along the way, I witnessed manager-employee relations ranging far and wide. What I gleaned from my diverse experiences was learning there's a right way to manage people and a wrong way. And I suspect you're interested in the right way.

I discovered that premium employee performances didn't result from a lot of yelling and threats from managers' mouths, but just the opposite. People performed best in environments where they were respected and challenged. Coaching and mentoring are revolutionizing management-employee relationships in so many places and in so many ways. Their varied tools and techniques transcend the office environs and are relevant, too, in retail and service businesses, not to mention outside of business altogether.

Simply put, it's a managerial methodology rooted in forward movement and positive outcomes. And I don't think I'm being presumptuous when I say that's what we all want.

Straight Ahead,

Nicholas Nigro

Nicholas Nigro

THE
EVERYTHING®
COACHING
AND
MENTORING
BOOK

How to increase productivity, foster
talent, and encourage success

Nicholas Nigro

Adams Media Corporation
Avon, Massachusetts

EDITORIAL
Publishing Director: Gary M. Krebs
Managing Editor: Kate McBride
Copy Chief: Laura MacLaughlin
Acquisitions Editor: Bethany Brown
Development Editors: Michael Paydos
                        Tere Drenth
Production Editor: Khrysti Nazzaro

PRODUCTION
Production Director: Susan Beale
Production Manager: Michelle Roy Kelly
Series Designer: Daria Perreault
Cover Design: Paul Beatrice and Frank Rivera
Layout and Graphics: Brooke Camfield,
Colleen Cunningham, Rachael Eiben
Michelle Roy Kelly, Daria Perreault

An Everything® Series Book.
Everything® is a registered trademark of Adams Media Corporation.

Published by Adams Media Corporation
57 Littlefield Street, Avon, MA 02322 U.S.A.
www.adamsmedia.com

ISBN: 1-58062-730-7
Printed in the United States of America.

J I H G F E D C B

Library of Congress Cataloging-in-Publication Data
Nigro, Nicholas J.
The everything coaching and mentoring book / Nicholas Nigro.
     p.   cm.   —(An everything series book)
     Includes bibliographical references and index.
     ISBN 1-58062-730-7
1. Mentoring in business. I. Title. II. Everything series.
     HF5385 .N54 2002
     658.3'124–dc21
                                                    2002009979

This publication is designed to provide accurate and authoritative information with regard to the subject matter covered. It is sold with the understanding that the publisher is not engaged in rendering legal, accounting, or other professional advice. If legal advice or other expert assistance is required, the services of a competent professional person should be sought.
—From a *Declaration of Principles* jointly adopted by a Committee of the American Bar Association and a Committee of Publishers and Associations

Illustrations by Barry Littmann.

This book is available at quantity discounts for bulk purchases.
For information, call 1-800-872-5627.

Visit the entire Everything® series at everything.com

Contents

109879

Introduction

MANAGING PEOPLE SUCCESSFULLY ISN'T EASY. Whether you're managing a Little League baseball team or twenty- and thirty-something grownups ensconced in corporate office cubicles, managing is an involved responsibility that requires healthy doses of patience, foresight, and—above all else—empathy and appreciation of individual personalities and people's unique and varying abilities.

Successful managing is, in fact, an art form. These days in particular, managing demands a great deal more than mere technical know-how and a loud, booming voice. Managers have to fully understand the depth and breadth of human behavior, if they seriously hope to secure peak performance from the players on their teams. A one-size-fits-all approach to managing people just doesn't make sense anymore, whether on the sports field, in the home, or in the workplace. In fact, it never really did do the job, and that's what people are at long last coming to grips with today.

To maximize the performance of your team—on the baseball diamond, in business, or wherever—you have to determine what makes each and every one of your players tick. You've got to locate the keys that unlock their drive to succeed. And the only way you can possibly make this amazing discovery is by closely working with every person in your charge—on an individual basis. From the many on your team, you can achieve one satisfying result, if you always remember to faithfully tend to each individual's essential role in contributing to the final product—whatever that may be.

This is precisely where coaching and mentoring come in. Exiting the Little League field for the time being and focusing our discussion solely on the business world, you find that this spanking new methodology of managing people has taken the corporate world by storm.

Nothing in life is perfect. Coaching and mentoring as managerial disciplines aren't either, simply because people are a very imperfect lot. Ironically, though, this is an essential tenet of coaching and mentoring. Imperfection! Yes, you heard it right. Coaching and mentoring sharply focus their lenses on people—warts and all. Their managerial formulas are firmly rooted in fashioning a contented and personally nourishing work atmosphere, while simultaneously making employees more productive.

This resourceful approach to managing people fully realizes and appreciates that these two positive results are not mutually exclusive.

In managing men and women, coaching and mentoring readily accept the reality that people will stumble on occasion. The practice of coaching and mentoring not only wholeheartedly embraces this "to err is human" fact of life, but it boldly goes that extra mile by acknowledging that individuals require guidance—coaching—to augment their knowledge base, grow their skills, and enhance their overall work performance. And when employees—from executives to middle managers to supervisors, and so on—maximize their performances, companies maximize their bottom lines. And the bottom line is still the bottom line in the corporate world. Never lose sight of this truth.

In fact, the chief reason that coaching and mentoring in management are becoming more widespread as an accepted business approach is precisely because the practice is proving highly effective in spurring employees to produce favorable results for the companies that implement these forward-looking managerial tools and techniques. Companies that employ coaches as managers, bring in external coaches as consultants, or utilize mentors are not motivated by mere altruism. As sitcom character Gomer Pyle might say, "Surprise . . . surprise . . . surprise!" Companies exist to make money. They have to realize profits or they will find themselves in the ash heap of corporate history before you can say "Jack the Ripper."

The exact reason coaching and mentoring are fast becoming the choice managerial practice in many companies is not important. Because regardless of whether or not it's solely the profit motive, or something more magnanimous at work, the coaching and mentoring methodology delivers results. When properly executed, its management ways benefit one and all—the companies, the coaches, the mentors, and the employees.

Coaches in management seek to amplify the human possibilities in the workplace. By recognizing the existence of an unalterable connection between employee job satisfaction and overall performance and level of productivity, coaching and mentoring present new ways of managing people. The practice moves away from the longstanding directive-style of managing and embraces a more pliable approach, reflective in nature and always searching for solutions to positive outcomes. This is the foundation upon which coaching and mentoring rest.

CHAPTER 1

The Brave New World of Coaching and Mentoring

Before getting into the specific tools and techniques of coaching and mentoring, it's important to understand the basic foundation of this intriguing managerial method. This introductory chapter reveals the benefits of coaching and mentoring and explains why they're the right fit for managing people in the twenty-first century.

Establishing a Coaching Vocabulary

There are coaches who operate as independent consultants (and rather high-paid ones at that). These are men and women who are brought into companies from the outside to solve specific problems ranging from the highly technical to the more abstract, like communication deficiencies and morale issues. And then there are mentors within companies (usually highly regarded top managers) who take selected subordinates "under their wings" and groom them for "bigger and better things" in a rather informal, open-ended relationship.

The thrust of this book is on coaching and managing. That is, the ABCs of what distinguishes coaching from more traditional managing. Coaching and day-to-day managing are no longer strangers, but a very compatible, happy couple. Why manage when you can coach and get better results?

So, from this point forward, sole references to "coaches," without any qualifiers, will refer to the managers who are employing—or wish to employ—this sound and fast-spreading managerial methodology on an everyday basis. As a matter of fact, coaching requires that it be done on a continual basis. A manager who says to an employee, "Let's have a coaching session now" is not employing the art of coaching.

FACTS

The English word "mentor" is derived from Homer's *Odyssey*. In this literary classic, Odysseus goes off to war and turns the guidance of his young son Telemachus over to his friend Mentor. In the absence of his father, the boy is "mentored" by Mentor in the ways of the world.

In addition, there will be endless references to "coaching and mentoring" to describe the overall managerial discipline, even though "coaching" and "mentoring" are not exactly the same thing (see Chapter 4).

Understanding the Benefits of Coaching

What are the benefits of being a manager and a coach all rolled into one? For one, coaches who get the utmost out of their employees achieve the personal and professional satisfaction of seeing their managerial talents bear real fruit. Additional benefits to successful coaches include a pat on the head from the executive class (nice), financial remuneration (nicer still), and, sometimes even a promotion (how sweet it is!).

And, if none of these things comes the coach's way, the tested and proven coaches can always take their formidable track records of managerial achievements somewhere else. For talented managers, with tried-and-true results on their resumes, are highly coveted in the overall corporate picture—rare birds indeed. Essentially, you can write your own career ticket when you demonstrate that you can manage people with self-assurance and get results on top of that.

ESSENTIALS

If New York is the "city that never sleeps," then coaching and mentoring are the managerial methods that never sleep. Their tools and techniques are rooted in continuous learning. And continuous learning asks that coaches, mentors, and employees alike view the workplace as a learning center without knowledge boundaries.

The icing on the cake of good coaching is that high-performing employees are similarly put on the fast track of personal growth and career advancement. Coaches, who delegate real responsibilities and genuinely challenge their employees to better themselves, grow their staff members' skills and make them more self-sufficient and productive workers. Thus, employees who respond favorably to a coach's guardianship are destined to rise in the company or—perhaps—in another company that is on the prowl for self-motivated, solid talent.

In the big picture, coaching and mentoring are all-encompassing. Their learning tree avails its fruit to all who are willing to taste it. And it's not Adam's apple—so don't worry about taking a hearty bite. Good coaches, and those on the receiving end of their wise, devoted leadership, are always poised to move on to the next level of learning and of skills. The coach-employee relationship, and the learning environment that's all a part of it, embodies not only career growth and a fatter paycheck, but a rewarding interior journey as well, where all concerned feel better about themselves and what they do. And this job satisfaction cuts across their professional lives and into their personal lives as well. The bottom line: Reliable, results-oriented coaches can always take pride in the knowledge that they inspired people to perform at higher levels than they otherwise would have if left to their own devices. And that they accomplished this feat without a horn and bullwhip, but instead with the guiding principle that employees are not automatons to be used and abused, but real people with unique temperaments and abilities.

Coaching and Mentoring as Teaching

Coaching and mentoring are essentially about teaching. And good teaching entails more than just imparting facts and figures, although that's very important. Inspired teaching is all about stimulating students to crave learning on their own. The best educators—whether in the classroom or in the workplace—plant the seed of learning and hope that it gets enough water and sunshine over time to grow into a tree of knowledge—and not a spindly stinkweed of ignorance.

FACTS

Coaching and mentoring continually seek to expand everyone's knowledge base and skill levels. Knowledge is the ability to organize information into a context and put it in a workable perspective. Skills embody the application of this knowledge in performing a task or job.

However, where coaching and mentoring break new ground in the twenty-first century is in business circles—and most notably, the corporate world. Until relatively recently (before 1990), the workplace was clearly delineated from "home sweet home." It was rigidly structured and rather antiseptic. Generally speaking, the boss was the boss and you did what you were told to do. You performed your daily tasks and functioned in your jobs and went home. And maybe—in time—you became the boss.

Times have certainly changed. For the greater part of the twentieth century, it was not unusual for men and women to labor in one job—and one job only—for their entire working lives. Countless young adults graduated from high school or college, went to work for a company, and were still around for their retirement parties forty or fifty years later. And for their extensive efforts on the job, they received engraved wristwatches and pensions to live on until the Grim Reaper paid them a visit. These hearty folks, who stayed put in one job from beginning to end of their working years, were once upon a time lauded for their steadfastness and loyalty to the companies that employed them. And many of the companies, in turn, reciprocated the favor by not casting them aside when they sprouted their first gray hairs or liver spot.

Solving Today's Unique Challenges

It's a new millennium. And it's counterproductive to debate whether the sedentary but stable old business world was somehow better than the more dynamic and unstable new business world of today. We are living in the here and now, and—last we checked—no time machine's been invented to take us all back to the days when everything, it seemed, cost a nickel.

ESSENTIALS The days of moving up the corporate ladder in the same company, while not completely history, are fast becoming the exception rather than the rule. Today, employee advancement is more often a lateral movement. Moving on up, yes, but in different companies, in a zigzag rather than a straight line.

Technological Competency

There may be no time machines, but there are these curious contraptions called computers that are omnipresent in the business sphere (and everywhere else for that matter). And courtesy of this technological marvel that has spawned the sprawling Internet, the corporate world is in a constant state of flux. The information age makes it altogether more imperative that businesses never rest on their laurels. To put it bluntly, every business, great and small, must adapt to perpetual and rapidly changing market conditions, or wither and die.

ESSENTIALS

To err is human; to forgive is being a coach. Forgive, yes, but don't ever overlook performance lapses! You must always identify mistakes and performance lapses immediately and at the source. You don't do this to embarrass anyone, but to impart valuable lessons on avoiding similar slips in the future.

So, what exactly does this new business-world order mean for you, a manager or manager of tomorrow? Essentially it means that you must be a sponge for learning with an insatiable capacity for absorption. The necessary new skills required to keep up with all these technological advances must become your skills.

Continuous Growth

Nowadays, developing new skills throughout your entire work career is not only recommended, it is indispensable. College knowledge is merely the beginning, not the end of the learning curve. By keeping up with the times, you will be prepared to effortlessly slide into another position if and when a job termination occurs (voluntarily or involuntarily). And not only that, your new job will be a better one because your knowledge base and skill level will be in such great demand.

Coaching and mentoring in today's corporate environs endeavor to counterbalance, as much as humanly possible, the sometimes very unpleasant twenty-first-century realities. As a coach, your predominant mission is to always broaden your own competencies along with those of your employees. To accomplish this, you must ply your people with substantive responsibilities, genuine challenges, and ceaseless opportunities for growth and development.

Preparing for the Future

The Boy Scouts' motto is "be prepared." That is, don't go out into the wilderness without the accouterments of survival (food, bandages, mosquito spray, snake bite kit, and so on). And it's an adage worthy of the coaching and mentoring approach to managing. Because, in this modern-day working world, you had better be prepared to one day lose your job or change jobs by choice—in a heartbeat. Now that sounds rather scary! But follow along and you'll see how the benefits of the coaching and mentoring methodology can turn seemingly negative work circumstances into very positive ones.

ESSENTIALS
Coaches understand that employee turnover is a fact of life in today's workplace. This sober reality, however, makes it even more vital that they create a work environment full of genuine challenges and opportunities for advancement, to keep solid employees in the fold and encourage outsiders to want in.

If you haven't been "downsized," "rightsized," gotten laid off, or been handed a pink slip yourself (whatever you want to call it), you've perhaps witnessed what happens to some of the terminated minions on the corporate landscape these days. They're often given no warning at all, their computers are unplugged, and they're instantly and unceremoniously escorted out of the workplace by dour-faced security guards. ("We'll mail you your personal effects—now beat it!")

A rather humiliating affair all around. Some of the dismissed employees depart with a quiet dignity; some leave the premises with tears freely flowing; and still others part in a pique of rage, threatening retaliation against the ax-wielding company or a particular manager or executive. It's the complete human spectrum of personalities and emotions revealed in a moment of crisis.

Fashioning Resilient Workers

The practice of coaching and mentoring strives to fashion an army of resilient workers capable of quickly getting up off the ground when they get knocked down. In the final analysis, coaching and mentoring tools and techniques are all about entrusting people to move forward—to take the knocks and disappointments of life on the job without looking back and without launching debilitating recriminations.

Empowering Employees with Knowledge and Skills

Coaching and mentoring in management afford recipients a cornucopia of knowledge and skills that those without such managerial tutoring just don't get. Why? Because those who work with a coach or mentor more fully understand and appreciate the ways of the twenty-first-century working world, its trials and tribulations, and what is required of them to succeed. Softly wallowing and lumbering about may work well for manatees in the wide-open ocean. However, it doesn't do the trick for employees in the demanding, results-oriented, and often very stressful workplace in today's business world.

ESSENTIALS   In order to consider yourself a coach in good standing, you must lead by example, delegate important responsibilities, listen to and freely communicate with your staff, and treat each and every one of your employees as individuals with distinct personalities and unique competencies.

Setting Out the Welcome Mat

Men and women on the move reign supreme in the work force these days, assuring that the labor pool is in a perpetual state of motion. Thus, coaching and mentoring seek to fashion, as much as is humanly possible in this mobile climate, work environments that encourage employees to stay put—that is, stay put in the companies that put a premium on learning. When companies offer employees training in cutting-edge skills, challenging jobs, and promotion opportunities, relative stability is the result. Vague promises to employees of what may, might, or could be don't cut it anymore. While it's inevitable that there will be many changes in personnel in the overall long haul of any company, this isn't to suggest that fast-paced employee turnover is a positive thing and welcomed in any way. Hardly! Both the retention and the attraction of the best and the brightest from the employee pool are coaching and mentoring's desired results. Good management breeds loyalty by fashioning a work environment that is a magnet for employees with solid skills, self-motivation, and a hearty appetite for career growth and development. A business atmosphere that genuinely appreciates and rewards achievement is where all of us want to be, whether in managerial jobs or in fledgling employee positions looking to latch onto the bottom rung of a corporate ladder.

FACTS

Coaching and mentoring are not mushy managerial styles based on cheerleading. They are action-oriented approaches to managing employee performance. They take the tested managerial model of plan, do, check, act, and raise it to a higher level by focusing on maximizing individual productivity.

There is one bromide that certainly rings true, now more than ever, and that's "Good help is hard to find." So, when you, as a coach, find employees who are producing for you, you want to keep them in your fold for as long as possible. And, simultaneously, you always want to be—in fact, you have to be—on the lookout for new and energized talent. A wise coach always keeps one eye focused on today's work situation and the other eye on tomorrow's. Put out the welcome mat, and remember to dust it off from time to time.

Why Coaching and Mentoring Pay Off

Why are coaching and mentoring managerial methods achieving positive results? Why are they becoming increasingly the rule and not the exception in work environments? There are some very significant reasons worth mentioning.

Technology

As already intimated, technological advancement is moving faster than a speeding bullet. This means that required job skills are constantly changing, the natural byproduct of these fast and furious advances in computer programming and other information technology. Your technical proficiency today may well be obsolete tomorrow. And then there's the flip side to this technological progression: Computers and machines are eliminating many jobs and performing many tasks formerly the sole province of the living.

Mergers and Acquisitions

It seems that almost every minute of every day you hear about one company buying out another, or merging with another, to maximize their profitability by combining their resources and know-how. This invariably leads to serious streamlining. That is, elimination of human resources— real people's jobs.

Investors

More and more public companies these days have more and more antsy investors needing constant reassurance that they've made the right financial moves. Quite often shareholder pressure results in cost cutting, which sometimes includes layoffs to sweeten the bottom line and placate apprehensive investors.

ESSENTIALS

Delegating important job responsibilities is key to good coaching. It's the best evidence there is that you believe in your employees' talents and abilities. It also means that you, the coach, are maximizing your resources—your people—while simultaneously maximizing the company's bottom line.

CHAPTER 2

Coaching and Mentoring as Art, Not Science

This chapter introduces you to the key principles that make coaching and mentoring more of a managerial art form than a dry science. This chapter also delves into the significance of respect and trust in the workplace and explores coaching and mentoring's emphasis on character and virtue, establishing ethical boundaries, and leadership by example.

Distinguishing Coaching from Therapy

There's a lot of psychobabble today, and in some circles, coaching and mentoring are somehow thought to be about corporate managers and consultants acting more like psychotherapists than business men and women. This misconception has coaches and mentors handling questions and dispensing advice far afield from job-related concerns.

Well, if that's what you think coaching and mentoring in business is all about, it's time to disabuse yourself of the notion. It's not a paint-by-numbers, rigid style of managing. Rather, it traverses the borders of traditional managerial ways by recognizing individuals as unique persons with unique talents and abilities who require coaching on a one-by-one basis to maximize their potential both on and away from the job. This people-oriented managerial methodology is a far cry from managing with a couch in the office. The rest of this chapter explains exactly what it really is.

Coaches and mentors are not psychotherapists and should be careful not to go down that analytical path. Even a management style that emphasizes a people approach should leave severe emotional and behavioral problems to those professionals specifically trained in handling them.

Results Matter

One obvious difference between coaches in business and licensed therapists is that coaches have to produce results. Managers who don't produce positive performance results will be out of a job in short order. With all due respect to the honorable profession of psychiatry, therapists do not have to realize any kind of quantifiable results to get paid for their services. Patients can be in therapy for years—even decades—and still be struggling with the same issues. In business situations, however, answering the "what do we do now?" question is the key to managers' long-term successes, whether they are more traditional dinosaur managers or cutting-edge coaches.

Coaching is all about now, but it's also about tomorrow. It's about powerful job performance driven by the emancipation of human potential. But aren't all managerial methods committed to top performance and getting the best possible productivity out of employees? A fair and very relevant question. The answer is "yes," but it's the avenues to positive outcomes that put coaching and mentoring on a much higher plane. For instance, you can travel long distances in your car via the back roads in small towns, twisting and turning, encountering endless stoplights, getting lost, and eventually running out of gas. Or you can take the interstate. You'll get to your destination more rapidly using the interstate. Coaching and mentoring are the interstates of managing—fast and focused on the final destination.

ESSENTIALS

Coaching and mentoring are all about self-development, and that includes the coaches and the mentors, too. Coaches should be coachable. The best and the brightest coaches and mentors don't ever put a cork on their thirst to acquire more knowledge and new skills.

Coaching Helps You Focus on the Work at Hand

So yes, coaching and mentoring are firmly committed to grappling with human behavior and understanding what motivates people, but decidedly not about getting employees' romantic lives in order, dealing with their eating disorders, forging close personal friendships, and such. That said, coaching and mentoring fully appreciate that dissatisfaction in employees' personal lives directly impacts their professional performance. Many managerial tools and techniques applied by coaches seek to increase employees' insight into themselves, and by osmosis strengthen their personal wellness by making their job experiences very satisfying ones. Nevertheless, the coach or mentor always—with no exceptions—operates within the parameters of the business environment. Performance on the job is job one.

Coaching Helps You Focus on Results

You will be judged by the overall performance of your employees and the results that they ultimately deliver. In the end, the buck stops on your desk. Coaching, and the delegating of responsibilities that goes with it, doesn't mean distancing yourself from the final results. You have to "be" for your employees in the following ways:

Be aware. Be aware of precisely what you've got to accomplish and what you have to work with in both personnel and time.

Be fair. Be fair with your employees at all times, never losing sight of the fact that things don't always run as planned and that individuals are unique personalities who work at different paces and sometimes in very distinct ways.

Be there. Be there for them in the work environment—from point A to point Z—of any office task or project.

Your aim is to secure peak performance from your employees by nudging them to realize their full potential. Sometimes you walk a fine line between offering support and encouragement and pushing a bit. When appropriate, don't be afraid to prod and shove a little.

You're Not a Neutral Observer

Okay, that's a relief. You're not expected to imitate Dr. Ruth, Dr. Joy, or even Oprah, as a coach or mentor. But you're expected to maintain very high ethical standards, which is often one of the most difficult of seas to navigate. If you think that kids get all kinds of mixed messages from the political establishment, mass media, and entertainment, you are absolutely on the money—but don't factor adults out of this addled equation. Today's societal mores are caught between a rock and a hard place. They seem to implore us to be value-neutral in judging most kinds of behavior. This nonjudgmental mindset blurs the age-old line between right and wrong. But in business, like everywhere else, there are clearly defined rights and wrongs. The ethical baby has been thrown out with the judgment-free bathwater in all too many instances.

Today we're also witnessing a counterproductive war on setting standards—in education, particularly, which translates into a diminished pool of genuinely qualified help in the business sector. When remedial reading and writing courses are offered in colleges, a red flag goes up—make that a sea of red flags! The obvious questions are: How do students make it to college without mastering basic reading and writing skills? And how on earth do they earn high school diplomas? The answers are obvious. They don't "earn" anything and are merely pushed along by hapless bureaucrats and their politician enablers. This is bad for society as a whole and very tough on business in general. This is why it's absolutely crucial that coaches always insist on raising the standard's bar and never lowering it.

FACTS

Coaching and mentoring are fast supplanting the more traditional, directive-style management. Coaches are replacing doer managers, sometimes referred to as dinosaur managers, who are still utilizing the day-to-day task approach to managing.

Coaches, make no mistake about it, do not practice "social promotion" with their employees. A coach presides over a staff of people who must earn their stripes by working hard and producing strong results.

Virtue Matters Most

If you've had the good fortune of working alongside a manager with undeniable integrity, you noticed it, appreciated it, and in all likelihood respected that person. Respect breeds respect. And those whom you respect, you trust. When you place your trust in a manager, you generally want to please him or her. Respect and trust are the two best motivating factors in town. Conversely, if you've worked in an office or on a team run by a less than stellar individual, you've no doubt experienced the complete opposite feeling. When working for a manager whom you hold in utter contempt, there's no warm, fuzzy feeling in the air. Managers who are not respected by their employees invariably preside over an office rife with dissension and assembly-line personnel turnover.

You're Not Mother Teresa

This little discourse on virtue does not mean you, as a coach and manager of people, need be an ethical Mother Teresa to pass muster. Many managers have topsy-turvy personal lives for one reason or another, and this shouldn't come as any big shock to you. Indeed, we are all human beings walking around with our various faults. And, if you haven't noticed, not many of us are sporting halos. But the fact remains, morally bankrupt persons away from the job are not about to find their morals in a desk drawer at the office. Shallow and insincere individuals, without the capacity to grasp the interior needs of their fellow human beings, always come up short and lack the necessary interpersonal skills required of good coaches and mentors.

You're Also Not an Actor

Granted, there are a lot of great actors on the business stage. Men and women who can fool us all for a time by achieving positive results in their managerial roles. But in the long run, their acts invariably wear thin, and the real personalities must, sooner or later, show their faces. And when those faces resemble the murderous Freddie Krueger, their managerial gigs are up.

You Have Ethical Boundaries

The two examples of dysfunctional managers in this section make a case that respect and trust in a positive workplace environment are absolutely crucial if employee satisfaction and company profits are to be maximized. And this cannot be stressed enough. The ethical standard you set as a coach—by both your words and deeds—sets the overall tone for your employees. In the common parlance, it's known as leadership by example and tone setting.

At some point, some of you may have worked for the dreaded "Manager from Hell." (And if you haven't yet, your day may well come.)

Here's an illuminating case study of one such manager named Andy. Andy was a marketing whiz with an undeniable creative streak. He was charming and quite ambitious—a man destined to "go places," people said. And Andy did indeed go places. He was a very successful salesperson, a high-paid consultant, and finally a manager of a sales division with a large staff in a very big company. Andy fancied himself the right man for the job, properly schooled and highly experienced, who knew by heart all those managerial textbook bullets on how to get the most out of people. He could recite backwards and forwards all the conventional techniques to motivate people. And merely increasing his team's productivity wasn't Andy's only goal. Are you kidding? Andy desired increasing sales by leaps and bounds and smashing all kinds of company records. He viewed his managerial moment as a chance to get the biggest feather yet in his career cap.

The trouble with Andy, aside from his inflated opinion about himself and runaway hubris, was that his personal life was a total shambles. To put it nicely, he lived life in the fast lane. And that's fine, until you come to a sharp curve. Andy lived a swinging bachelor's life, but was married with an infant son. His frenzied lifestyle dazzled his subordinates at first, most of who were young and, more or less, in sync with him in letting the good times roll in the after hours. Gradually, though, Andy's personal peccadilloes severed the umbilical chord of trust between him and his staff. Ultimately, his employees perceived him as a man who looked out for number one only. On the occasions that his wife and child would come to the office, ol' Andy boy would play the part of doting husband and father, while his staff looked on aghast, knowing full well their leader was insincere and downright disreputable. They began to see Andy as not the Man Without a Face, but the Man with Two Faces. Two heads may be better than one in many instances in life; but two faces on a manager never are!

The larger point here is not to condemn Andy to eternal damnation. The particulars of Andy's personal life are not a business concern. What is, however, a business concern in this case is Andy's utter lack of discretion. His personal behavior led directly to a breakdown of respect and trust at the office, the two cornerstones of a manager-employee relationship, and predictably shattered his ability to lead effectively and get the positive outcomes that he so desperately wanted from his people. And when he didn't get all that he wanted, Andy lashed out at his employees, blaming them entirely for their less than brilliant performances.

One more from the case files—a short one in a similar vein. This brash young supervisor named Ted actually bragged to his staff about how he regularly switched price tags on department store merchandise. Ted reasoned that this conduct somehow enhanced his reputation as a crafty doer willing to do "whatever it takes" to get the job done. Needless to say, it achieved just the opposite effect. Trying to elevate your stature by boasting about stealing—committing a criminal act—is the wrong road to go down to uplift your standing as a leader of people (unless you're a member of the Soprano family). And, by the way, it's not part of the coaching and mentoring doctrine either.

ESSENTIALS   If you are successful as a coach, you've pulled off the coaching and mentoring trifecta: managing people by understanding them, solving problems without getting sidetracked, and achieving positive results pleasing to both your employees and the company.

Maybe you've had the displeasure of working for an Andy or Ted type. If you have, it's a safe bet that the office atmosphere was absent of the respect and trust that is essential in any productive and healthy working environment. Without respect and trust emanating from the manager's office, you can, rest assured, predict there will be day-to-day bedlam with fast and furious turnover in the staff, until the day comes when the Andys and the Teds themselves are turned over.

Use an Ethical Framework for Coaching

But what about the flip side of this ethical coin? How do you as a coach confront the ethical conundrums that arise from the employee side of the office? And where exactly do you fix these moral and ethical boundaries? What do you believe you, as a coach and a leader of men and women in a business setting, are responsible for—and not responsible for—regarding your staff's on-the-job behaviors? Here's a guiding framework for you to operate within, which should assist you in establishing such boundaries, and in walking that sometimes very fine line between respecting people for who and what they are and demanding that your employees respect what you are trying to accomplish.

You are not required to manage as an equalizer. You are not expected to parcel out your time on an equal basis. Some employees need more counsel and more of your time than others do. Knowing who needs a little extra attention is an important part of a coach's job.

The Three Ps

First and foremost, never lose sight of coaching and mentoring and their three Ps: people, performance, and positive outcomes. Give your employees as much latitude—responsibilities and challenges—as possible, but never cut them adrift. Pay careful attention to them! Keep a watchful eye on their individual progress in all jobs and office projects, while wholly accepting that specific talents and temperament vary widely from person to person.

Differentiating Between Values and Virtue

Scrupulously differentiate between values and virtue. Very often these two words are used interchangeably, but they do not mean the same thing! You may have a completely different set of values than one of your employees. Respect this chasm. But don't ever confuse values with virtue, which is something you must possess and insist that all of your employees likewise uphold. Virtue is integrity; it's honesty. Virtue on the job means, among many things, reliability. And employee reliability is what you need—always—to achieve positive outcomes. For instance, you may disapprove of how an employee on your staff disciplines her children away from the job. (You heard it in the gossip mill.) That's a completely different kettle of fish than the same employee covering up her mistakes in her job with lies and distortions, or shifting the blame onto others. Values versus virtue.

Make Your Expectations Realistic

Make certain you have realistic expectations for your employees on a personal basis. John may thrive in a pressure cooker. Melanie, on the other hand, may be productive in a more sanguine setting. Recognize and reward progress, not just results. By offering positive feedback along the way, you will ensure positive results.

As a coach, you've been conferred the imposing responsibility to shape a work environment to a great extent in your own image. And so it's your job—and duty—to forge a workplace with high morale and a highly motivated staff of people. This doesn't mean that you are a people pleaser come hell or high water. It's not part of your job description to give the office the feel and flavor of a Madonna concert. It is, however, your obligation as a coach to construct a work setting that's most conducive to heightened productivity.

Make Adjustments—But Not to Ethical Standards

Impressive results more often than not come out of a contented, galvanized group of people. A bunch of malcontents is not ordinarily a very productive group (unless they're in a band or are comedy writers). So this may require that you, from time to time, make adjustments to various employee performance plans, and even some concessions on occasion to the disparate idiosyncrasies in your employees' personalities. However—and this is a biggie—no adjustments or concessions should ever be made to the core ethical standards that you lay down. You must insist that each and every member of your staff respect these ethical boundaries, and that you yourself painstakingly abide and live within them.

ALERT

If you thought mind-melding was the sole province of Vulcans and Mr. Spock, you were wrong. Coaches and mentors, too, have the involved task of performing a mind-meld. They have to make employees' personal and career goals jibe with the company's priorities (profits)—and this isn't always easy.

CHAPTER 3

Motivating Employees

This chapter examines the ways and means to motivate your employees to deliver the goods. Put away that managerial cookie cutter and allow each member of your staff the space to do his or her job within the ethical boundaries that you've established.

Being All That You Can Be

Motivation is a fashionable word today. In fact, it's a whole lot more than just a word; it's an industry unto itself. Turn on your TV at any time of day and you are sure to see someone peddling motivational books, cassettes, or videotapes. There are legions of people making big bucks "motivating" you to reach for the stars or whatever you're supposed to be reaching for. But what are these self-proclaimed motivators actually doing?

First of all, what they are really purporting to do is "inspiring," not "motivating," others. There's a difference. They are hoping to inspire people to motivate themselves to do certain things. And some people are motivated to do so many things at the drop of a hat, while others are immovable lumps of humanity. Why the disparity? Because it's entirely up to the individual to be motivated or not. You are the one who motivates you, not a coach or mentor at the office, or Tony Robbins on QVC. In your own coaching efforts, you are not there to motivate your employees per se, but, hopefully, to inspire them to motivate themselves.

You are—believe it or not—on the same plane as the aforementioned motivational big-shot Tony Robbins. Granted, you probably aren't as wealthy, but you are entrusted, nevertheless, to inspire your employees to motivate themselves to grow their skills and competencies, just as Robbins's materials are expected to inspire his customers, many of whom dole out big dollars for his rakish form of coaching. If Tony Robbins can make it as an inspirational cult figure, you too can make it as a coach adept at inspiring your employees to motivate themselves. And in your case, you'll be producing quantifiable, that is, measurable, results. You have to—that's what you're hired to do. Robbins established a bond of trust with people and it took hold. But in the end, a person can buy every book, cassette, and videotape in the Robbins self-help arsenal and still have the get-up-and-go of a Pet Rock.

This isn't meant to discourage you, but it's pretty much the same scenario that you're up against as a coach in a business setting. There are some employees you won't succeed in inspiring to motivate themselves. If everyone motivated him- or herself with unrestrained abandon, the labor market would look a whole lot different than it presently does.

Essentially, your job as a coach is to apply a cattle prod—metaphorically speaking, that is—to the dormant motivation percolating in the hearts and souls of your employees. What is this metaphorical cattle prod? What is it exactly that motivates workers to motivate themselves? Personal gain of some kind, be it financial or in relationships; a quest for an overall richer and better life is what motivates people. These are the same broad reasons why so many people buy Tony Robbins's stuff; and this is the all-important starting point for your coaching efforts to begin in inspiring your employees to motivate themselves.

FACTS

Renowned football coach Lou Holz had an interesting view of self-motivation. He once said: "My task is not to motivate people to play great football. They are already motivated when they come to me. My challenge is simply not to demotivate them."

Employees must adopt the notion that their productivity on the job benefits them in a uniquely personal way; that their job performance—up to the hilt—makes their lives better in many ways. In ways, by the way, beyond the workplace corridors and immediate paychecks. Sure, a lot of employee self-motivation revolves around money. And this isn't some greedy capitalistic tenet. It's merely that money translates into so many things, not the least of which is the freedom to pursue interests and hobbies outside work and career. Freedom from worry about mortgage payments and credit card bills. Money makes the world go around.

Inspiring Commitment

You must aim the cattle prod carefully or it will do more harm than good. You want to inspire your employees to bona fide commitment. And the only way to successfully realize this is by vigilantly piecing together the many personal benefits that accrue to employees when they do their jobs and do them well. You've got to make your employees understand that these benefits are very real and immediate, and not some pie-in-the-sky-when-you-die mumbo jumbo. By shaping a work environment that fully taps into this natural human desire called self-interest, you've completed the very important first step. People want to better themselves. It's in their self-interest to do so. And remember that self-interest is not the same thing as selfishness. Instead, it's a vital part of humanity, and it's what drives all of us to some extent (albeit some of us more than others).

You can inspire commitment to the job at hand by empathizing with your employees' self-interest. By closely working with them—as coaches do—you can effectively make the case that their personal goals (present and future) are in complete sync with the company's current goals and needs. As you might imagine, this is not always an easy case to make. Most people are justifiably skeptical of the notion that laboring in the salt mines to sweeten the profits of a big company is somehow essential to their personal and professional growth and development. Naturally then, this makes going all out for the company difficult and sometimes near impossible.

FACTS

Coaches do not motivate their employees; they inspire them to motivate themselves. This is best accomplished by allowing employees to see clearly where they stand in the organization versus where they want to be in their careers. That is, what are their self-interests versus what the company can offer them.

If, however, you paint a clear picture, you can illustrate just how and why your employees personally benefit by self-motivating themselves to produce results for the company. And when you as a coach succeed here, and inspire your employees to a commitment to give it their all, you've accomplished something that you can take great pride in. You've moved people to move themselves—and that's the most intricate and difficult task of any style of managing. But, remember, it's a task that coaching welcomes.

Inspiring commitment takes into account creating a work climate that's employee friendly. This isn't a Knute Rockne "win one for the Gipper" pep talk. You're not promoting a "don't worry, be happy" climate, either. Instead, you are advocating a workplace that makes employees feel part of a team effort, while simultaneously making them feel that what they're doing right now is an integral part of all their respective futures.

Understanding What Motivates Employees

This section takes a look at some of the motivational tools you can use to encourage your employees to self-motivate themselves. As a coach and a manager, you are afforded many ways to reward your employees for a job well done and spur them on to further productivity. Here are just some of the possibilities at your disposal:

- Pay raises
- Bonuses
- Stock options
- Promotions
- Positive performance reviews
- Positive feedback
- Paid holiday or added vacation time
- Opportunities to travel (for the company)
- Increases in job responsibilities and challenges
- Equipment upgrade (laptop computer, cell phone, and so on)
- Gifts (for personal pleasure ranging from dinner to a timepiece)
- Educational training (advanced degree)
- Mentoring
- Telecommuting option (work from home)
- Public acclaim (via company newsletter, award, and so on)

ALERT

Know the difference between being assertive and being aggressive. As a coach, you've got to be assertive in dealing with your staff. This means confronting problems at the source and continually communicating with your employees. Aggressive, in-your-face managing, on the other hand, is highly counterproductive.

Performance Planning

Coaches work with performance plans or work plans to keep employees motivated. They work with these kinds of plans for each and every one of their employees. Performance planning is often what separates successful coaches from their less fortunate brethren, the dinosaur managers living in the corporate equivalents of Jurassic Park.

QUESTIONS?

Can performance plans span longer than a year?
Technically, yes, a performance plan can span one, two, even ten years. But realistically it's best to keep such plans under six months. Longer periods of time tend to make such plans lose their precision and focus.

Goals

The first phase of a performance plan consists of goals, sometimes referred to as objectives. You work closely with your employees in getting their input into the various performance-related goals that inaugurate performance plans. Then, in concert with your employees, you fix target dates for reaching these goals and establish the time parameters of the plans. Throughout the entire developmental process of performance plans, your employees must be fully in the loop. Under your careful supervision, employees should largely author their own performance plans and, of course, be responsible for seeing them through.

FACTS

The goals or objectives in a performance plan are very simply what you—the coach—expect your employees to accomplish. As a coach, you arrive at these goals in one-on-one consultations with your employees.

Each employee should simultaneously work with several performance plans (no more than six), covering the full range of his or her jobs and responsibilities. And each individual performance plan, inaugurated with a realistic goal, should span a time period limited to six months or less. Planning beyond that amount of time often results in fuzziness and a loss of clarity, something all coaches want to avoid like the plague.

Standards of Performance

The standards of performance—the quality bars that you set—are your next consideration to insert in performance plans. Standards, for short, are essentially the meat on the bone of the goals, establishing expectations for the quality of the results and overall performance in achieving each goal. Depending on the nature of the job or project, this could mean upgrading customer service to a certain level, meeting specified sales targets, product upgrades, and so on. This brand of thorough planning stands in unmistakable contrast to the management methods that operate one day at a time without an eye on tomorrow, let alone thirty, ninety, or 180 days down the road. "One day at a time" may work well in self-help programs, but it's poor business planning, especially where foresight is an essential ingredient, and particularly in this fast-paced, technologically advanced world that you now live and work in.

ESSENTIALS

Performance plans are part of the arsenal of every good coach. You work with these plans, which are comprehensive road maps designed for each one of your employees, specifically detailing what they are expected to do. Performance plans are collaborative efforts made by you in concert with your employees.

Plan Your Work, Work Your Plan

Setting goals and standards are merely the first pieces of the performance plan puzzle. Once you've fixed the goals and a standard of performance that you expect each and every one of your employees to execute in reaching the goals, it's time for you to get down to the specifics of how exactly all of this is going to happen.

Action Plans

Action plans are the next hurdle that you, along with your employees, must leap over. Think of action plans as akin to gasoline in a car. Let's say, for example, that you've built a snappy-looking, powerful automobile with all the necessities and extras to not only "burn rubber," but to do so in stylish comfort. Even the best-quality and fanciest cars in existence are useless (other than as museum pieces) without the fuel to put them in motion. And so it is with both goals and standards in reaching them. As a coach, you could have the most laudable and far-reaching goals in place for your employees. You could couple them with the most rigorous of standards. But that and a ten-dollar bill will get you into a movie nowadays. So, what you need to do next, in close concert with your employees, is develop action plans to grease the skids of each goal and standard in each performance plan. These are the plans within each plan—the fuel of performance plans.

FACTS

Action plans are the meat and potatoes of performance plans, and contain the specific ways that tasks and jobs get done. If a goal in a performance plan is to cut costs in a particular area, action plans provide step-by-step methods on just how and when this is going to be accomplished.

Action plans are crisp and clearly defined directions—A to Z—detailing precisely how the desired goals are going to be reached, and what physical efforts (actions) are expected from the employees in the process of getting there. Action plans essentially summarize why employees were hired in the first place. It's what they do. Nobody is left in the dark with action plans. Everybody knows what they are expected to accomplish, in what time parameter, and how they are going to execute their plans. There's no guesswork.

Measures

Lastly, in a thorough performance plan replete with clear goals, standards, and precise action plans (there could be several for each goal), there must be measures to check the quality of the results. It's one thing to cast your fate to the wind. It's quite another thing to cast your employees' performance plans to the wind and hope that everything in the end comes out exactly as planned. Plans without regular checkups are like English muffins without toasting. They just don't happen. Appropriate measures must be in place from the beginning to the end of all performance plans. While affording your staff great autonomy, you must nevertheless periodically monitor the progress of each one of your employees' performance plans.

In the 1980s, when President Ronald Reagan signed historic arms control accords with Russian President Mikhail Gorbachev, he was asked how he—a staunch anti-Communist—could sign on to a deal of such breathtaking proportions and importance with an undemocratic nation and totalitarian form of government. Reagan quoted the Russian proverb, "Trust but verify." Translation: Show good faith and accept at face value that a former foe (in this instance) can be trusted. But continually verify that the agreed-upon arms control reductions are actually taking place when they are scheduled to take place. Measure! Measure! Measure!

You must likewise show trust in your employees, but you must also verify on a recurring basis that they are doing exactly what was mutually agreed upon at the onset of their performance plans. You must verify that all concerned are in fact reaching their targets—in terms of time and quality—on the way to achieving their final goals.

Measures inserted in performance plans as checkpoints are not the equivalent of showing a lack of faith in your employees. On the contrary. As professionals in the private sector, men and women must come to expect continual measurement of their performances and be held strictly accountable for their work efforts.

Measuring Performance

What are some of the performance plan measuring tools available to you? There are many, so feel free to use any and all of these measures as appropriate. Here are some of the popular ones.

Show Me the Money

There are no better measures than raw numbers. Sales figures, cost reductions, and the like are prime examples of data that can be easily measured at any point in a maturing performance plan to assist you in getting a fix on how things are going and whether or not targets are being met, and so on.

Time Bomb

Another measure utilized in many performance plans revolves around timelines. Because these types of plans are generally conceived within defined time parameters and specific performance goals, it is imperative to regularly measure results at agreed-upon junctures to see whether or not the plan is meeting expectations or coming up short.

The Five Senses

In some performance plans, depending on the industry or particular department in the company, there are physical by-products, i.e., samples, that can be regularly measured. For instance, a product developmental performance plan will showcase something that you can see and maybe even hear, smell, touch, and taste. An ice cream flavor under development would be something worthy of a taste or two along the way.

Reports

Old reliable paperwork on the status of the performance plan is always a plus. Written records—even though they are mostly on disks today—haven't lost their importance. A coach needs to be fully apprised of what's happening every step of the way, and written records of all that's going on provide a beneficial paper trail as the plan unfolds.

Audits

In particular areas of business operation, such as finance, audits are practical measures. Audits are also used to perform quality checks in other areas.

Feedback

What are people saying? Many performance plans involve directly servicing customers. So who better than the customers to talk to in these instances! They are the ultimate fonts of information on the success or failure of plans involving their satisfaction.

The Eyes Have It

Just as with old reliable reports and written notes, there's another measure that can't be beat—observation. Depending on the exact nature of the performance plans, there may be an opportunity to watch employees in action (selling, communicating, and so on) and see with your own eyes and hear with your own ears whether they are meeting their goals and living up to the agreed-upon quality standards.

By the Employee, for the Employee

A successful performance plan is a thing of beauty. In order for a plan to reach this awe-inspiring level, however, it has to be a blueprint in large part drafted by the employee for the employee, with your wise and overseeing counsel and final imprimatur, of course. The traditional manager-employee doctrine more or less says that the manager is the boss—period. And that the boss is the one who tells employees what to do—end of story. Employees do what they are told to do, or they are shown the door. Performance planning is the province of the bosses, and the "little people," mere employees, are never "in on" this fundamental decision-making. Coaching torpedoes this anachronistic way of conducting business by fully bringing employees into the important decisions that will most affect their jobs. To a great extent, employees are asked to craft their own performance plans. And courtesy of this forward-thinking approach to managing, employees, in essence, "own" their performance plans. They own their jobs.

After all, who knows better what you can do than you? The dinosaur managers, who dole out orders from their imperious pedestals, and permit little if any employee input into their planning and other decisions, naturally foster more resentment than commitment from their employees. Employees who aren't consulted on their jobs and project assignments often feel that expectations for their performance are unreasonable or even farfetched. And this sometimes means too little work and too few responsibilities. Because commitment is so primary to winning coaching, you cannot bypass your employees in any planning process that involves their participation. A coach understands full well that in order to expect employees to share in a sense of accomplishment on the job, they must be more than mere pawns on a chessboard.

ESSENTIALS

A key tenet in coaching is collaboration between the coach and the employee. Successful coaching includes showing confidence in your employees by delegating responsibilities and challenging them to be self-sufficient. However, this doesn't mean—by any stretch of the imagination—that you make important decisions by consensus.

Keep in mind that performance-plan preparation should always be consummated in one-on-one meetings with your employees. Employees should be given advance notice of when these meetings will occur, and what will be expected of them. This gives them ample opportunity to come ready and armed to author their own performance plans. Performance plans are contracts with clearly defined goals, and so they should be written down and not treated like handshakes. Performance objectives should be verbalized in only a sentence or two because they need to be simply understood. Next, when you and your employees agree upon the various action plans and time schedules of performance plans, you must make certain that they are fully understood. You must feel comfortable that your employees know their jobs, their specific responsibilities, and the deadlines in their performance plans. This meeting of the minds between coaches and employees inevitably leads to more focus by all the players involved. Everybody understands their roles, feels part of the entire process, and works in a genuine team effort. Focus is the forerunner of success.

CHAPTER 4

Mentoring 101

Although people repeatedly pair the words "coaching" and "mentoring" to describe a particular managerial methodology, coaches and mentors are not one and the same. This chapter differentiates between the two and then takes a close look at mentors and the valuable roles they play in countless business environments and situations.

Coaching Versus Mentoring

Some words in our lexicon are overused, misused, and applied to this, that, and the other thing. After a while, the words get so muddled that they lose their original meaning and preciseness. And this has happened to the term "coach," and likewise to the term "mentor," which are often confused in business circles as identical twins. These two descriptive appellations do not mean the same thing, even though they are used interchangeably on many occasions. And to make matters worse, the words "coach" and "coaching" have been bandied about with such frequency of late that the significance of the title "coach," and the practices of "coaching," have gotten twisted beyond recognition, too.

So what is the difference between the words "coach" and "mentor"? This is the gray area where the greatest confusion exists. Discussing the difference is the most appropriate place to get started in sorting out this mess. A coach is a title assumed by many managers these days. These managers are not "managers" anymore but "coaches." There are also many independent "coaching consultants," or external coaches, brought into companies from the outside. Check out Chapter 5 for details of this important auxiliary aspect of coaching.

QUESTIONS?

Is coaching the same as mentoring?
Although there are many similarities, they are not identical. Actually, one of the skill sets within coaching is mentoring. Many coaches are also mentors to their employees. Mentoring is a more informal and open-ended relationship than is coaching.

As Chapter 3 discusses, coaches use coaching applications that revolve around setting goals and thorough performance planning, with employees always an integral part of the process. That is, coaches work in close cooperation with their employees—on an individual basis—to cultivate a healthy and productive work environment. They seek to forge a breeding ground for their employees' expansion of knowledge and the growth of their skills. By so doing, coaches strive to increase employee job satisfaction, overall efficiency in the office, and the company's bottom line. Coaching is nothing if not results-oriented.

A coach can also be a mentor—and often is. This is why the duo of coaching and mentoring often stand side by side in book titles (like this one), in management seminars, and in training video workshops. This is also why there is so much confusion. The terms are inextricably linked and for very good reasons. Both coaches and mentors are bound by a common desire to enlarge human possibilities by carefully guiding people and encouraging them to better themselves in an atmosphere of incessant learning. Both coaches and mentors work with individuals in very intimate ways. Dinosaur managers do no such things.

FACTS

There are many differences between coaches and mentors. The most overt variance is that, in most instances, coaching is a paying job— be it internal or external—whereas mentoring is a voluntary setup.

If, however, you delve a little deeper, you see that mentoring is quite distinct from coaching in some of its practices. And when mentoring stands on its own two legs, as it often does, it is anything but a carbon copy of coaching. The rest of this chapter discusses mentoring—and gives tips on how to mentor well.

Mentors: Show and Tell

What's the first thing you think about when the subject of mentoring is broached? What kinds of images career through your mind? An Ancient Greek pontificating in the Parthenon? A fortunate adult offering hope to an at-risk young person? A wise elder passing on his learned lessons to a wide-eyed understudy, perhaps? Or maybe, a trusted and experienced senior executive in the corporate world, sitting down with a young and ambitious cub manager? These images of mentors and mentees (those who are mentored) are all accurate portrayals and attest to mentoring's long history. It's part of the human condition and always will be. In the corporate realm of today, the mentoring tradition is not only alive but welcomed. Mentoring complements coaching with an informality that works like a charm in the more formal business atmosphere of goals, plans, measures, performance reviews, and the like.

Mentors Are Counselors

A mentor performs the role of prudent counselor, dispensing advice on career paths, and offers helpful problem-solving hints on the more immediate matters of the job at hand. Mentors base their instruction on their real-life experiences. Essentially, the mentor points the mentee, a.k.a. protégé, in the right direction regarding opportunities within the company. Ideally, a mentor is one level (or two or three) above the mentee in the organizational hierarchy.

Encourage brainstorming in all your coaching and mentoring efforts. Brainstorming sessions between coach-employee and mentor-mentee are often quite productive. Nothing should be held back when brainstorming, because there are no bad ideas in these informal settings, only great possibilities.

Mentors Are Helpers Up the Corporate Ladder

Foremost, a mentor must be in a solid position to offer direction on the ways and means of getting ahead in the company and in the corporate world in general. "Movin' on up!" in the fine tradition of sitcom character George Jefferson is often what a mentor means to a mentee. Moving on up not only in job title, or pay and perks, but in personal growth and development as well. Mentors aim to broaden their mentees' job skills, overall worldviews, and understanding of human nature.

Mentors Have Overcome Obstacles

Learning how to overcome obstacles is the most important lesson mentors can pass on to their mentees. Mentors tap into their own experience banks for examples of how they confronted similar obstacles in their career paths. Thus, they show their mentees what worked and what didn't work for them. And these very real situations carry far greater weight than do theoretical textbook accounts of comparable subject matter.

When you succeed in overcoming obstacles in your path, and learn to deal with the predictable bumps in the managerial road, you've learned the most valuable lesson in the workplace—and in life itself for that matter. Successfully attacking the obstacles in your way with ever-increasing self-assurance puts you on the career fast track. For there are few managerial skills more valued than levelheaded problem solving. Getting a handle on tough situations—without flying off the handle—is what separates the men from the boys—and women from the girls—on the managerial scales. By showcasing your ability to overcome obstacles in a professional manner, you reward the faith the company placed in you by giving you a mentor, or making you a mentor, in the first place.

Mentors Have Impeccable Credibility

Needless to say, mentors must be individuals of impeccable credibility and their advice must always ring true. Mentees have to be able to implicitly trust their mentors. Mentors cannot be perceived as hot-air balloons who love the sound of their own voices more than anything else in the world.

Mentors Have Substance

When you're mentoring someone, understand that you'll be looked upon as a vast treasury of knowledge with keen insight on the ways of the business world and maybe even the world in general. A veritable Wizard of Oz. Don't let it go to your head. The best mentors in the business understand their limitations and accept their need to always learn and grow their skills. But if you're always learning, how can you possibly know it all?

Back to the Wizard of Oz for a moment. As a mentor, do you want to be perceived as a person with heart, brains, and courage to spare? Of course you do. But just remember who the Wizard of Oz was. He was something of a fraud, cloaking himself behind a curtain and creating a big-screen illusion of power, fear, and all-knowing wisdom. And that's precisely what you don't want to do. Because, as in *The Wizard of Oz*, your act will eventually be uncovered, just as Dorothy, with the help of little Toto, unmasked the faux wizard, who, it turned out, was a rather pathetic, mousy old man. As a mentor, you must always be grounded in reality and carry yourself with some semblance of humility. An overbearing manner in any mentoring relationship is a surefire ticket to failure.

FACTS

These days you'll find many bestselling books (often anthologies of inspirational stories) that are meant to inspire their readership in some way. Likewise, a mentor's success in the business environs is meant to inspire and teach others.

You have to establish a mutual respect and trust with your mentee. Your tutelage will be welcomed and listened to by your mentee, without any hesitation or dispute whatsoever, if you develop rapport, which is essential in any mentor-mentee alliance, just as it is in any other human relationship.

Mentors Have Achieved

Mentors must back up all their advice and counsel with resumes of past achievement and rich and diverse work experiences. They must be able to recount their stories of, say, having made the move from a claustrophobic mail room to a sprawling office on the forty-first floor with windows overlooking lush Central Park (or maybe a story less dramatic). And you never know—you could well find yourself mentoring someone a peg or two below you, while simultaneously receiving guidance from a higher-up (that senior executive in that dreamy office). After all, many mentors are also mentees.

The Mentee: A Star Is Born

Mentoring is generally offered to the rising stars in a company, not every Joe or Jane who comes down the personnel pike. Senior management trolls the office seas for the senior managers of tomorrow. Middle managers look for the middle managers of tomorrow. And so it goes. For wise managers recognize that nobody lives forever, not even the biggest of big-shot executives in the business world. In fact, part of all good managers' job responsibilities is locating diamonds in the rough. Finding and keeping (for as long as is feasible) good men and women with solid skills and a desire to learn and better themselves is what makes coaching work smoothly and effectively over the long haul. A good coach is always on the lookout for employees willing to take on new responsibilities and bigger challenges; individuals who exhibit a penchant for self-motivation and self-sufficiency. And mentoring fits neatly into this picture of preparing good people for tomorrow's new day on the job. Rising stars in business need an objective ear. Mentors are those objective ears. They are not meant to be obsequious cheerleaders for their mentees, telling them only what they want to hear, and spouting out endless streams of rah-rah platitudes. There's no such thing as a sycophantic mentor.

ESSENTIALS

Use your life story and experiences as a backdrop in your mentoring, but don't ask that your mentee be a carbon copy of you. Your mentee is a unique individual with unique talents and abilities who needs to follow a unique course in life.

Mentors fully grasp the fundamentals of the company and the overall business picture because they've "been there and done that." They assist their mentees in wading through difficult situations and transforming all of those job-related lemons into opportunity lemonade. Mentors enrich their mentees' knowledge base by always answering their questions and giving them feedback on their job performance. Mentors are readily available to their mentees, to help them solve the inevitable problems encountered while working with real people with real personalities in a real work environment. Mentoring is the real thing and not a detached textbook lesson or listless lecture.

Moving from Mentee to Mentor

If you've been among the select few who've been assigned a mentor at some point in your career development, that means that you've been groomed for bigger and better things. You then may have been asked—or will be asked—to mentor an employee below you in the organizational hierarchy. Mentoring at various levels in an organization is a forward-thinking approach to managing and increasingly commonplace in the corporate world. Companies that have embraced coaching and mentoring and all that their practice entails know that the benefits of providing tutors throughout the organization—from top to bottom—are demonstrably positive. Because of the knowledge transfer and perpetual sharing of ideas and observations, mentees are positioned to adapt more readily to the fast-paced changes in the organization and the overall business environment. The mentor-mentee relationship is one that is alive and fluid at all times.

Mentoring Do's and Don'ts

Whether you have or haven't had a mentor to assist you in your rise to your present position is not the decisive factor in determining whether you can mentor another person effectively. Obviously, having had a trusted mentor who helped you grow and develop as manager material and as a human being is a big plus. You have a role model to pattern your style of mentoring after. But, regardless, there are certain approaches to mentoring that all successful mentors practice and, equally important, don't practice. Let's check out several of them.

A Mentor Is Not a Greyhound Bus

The longstanding Greyhound Bus advertising slogan is "Leave the Driving to Us." A mentor's slogan must never be "Leave the Decision-Making to Me." You should never make decisions for your mentee. Your counsel to the mentee is designed to fill in the blanks—to provide the mentee with options and more options—but the mentee must always make his or her own decisions. Mentors endeavor to make their mentees' ultimate decisions as informed and reasoned as possible. One of the overriding themes in all coaching and mentoring applications is the intent to help people help themselves.

ESSENTIALS A mentor always exercises the power of suggestion. That is, wise mentors offer up plenty of suggestions to their mentees. They pose alternatives. But they refrain, as much as possible, from telling their mentees what to do.

Know When to Say When

As a mentor, you must recognize that your guidance is most appreciated when it's specifically asked for. This is not to suggest that you, as mentor, sit idly by like Marcel Marceau or Mini-Me, mostly silent or grunting every now and then. However, specific advice to the particulars of your mentee's job responsibilities should be held back until your mentee asks you for that advice. Refrain from "let me tell you what to do" kinds of instructions. People are funny that way. In many self-help programs, for instance, it is practically written in stone that continually imploring—nagging—an abuser to shed an addiction is counterproductive. Overcoming an addiction is a very personal journey. The decision to try to get back on the straight and narrow stems from recognition by the individual that his or her life is spiraling out of control. The same reasoning applies to the mentor-mentee relationship. Unsolicited advice on an unremitting basis will inevitably clog the ear of the mentee, who will eventually come to automatically disregard everything that you've got to say.

The Dialogue

In every successful mentor-mentee relationship, there is a dialogue. Leave the monologues to Leno and Letterman. This dialogue should be the rule and always relaxed and candid. As a mentor, you are not a college professor delivering a lecture in an auditorium-sized classroom, with your mentee sitting around taking notes that he or she will have to memorize for a final exam. No, this is a one-on-one relationship with a robust give-and-take.

Mentoring is all about sharing experiences. It is about mentors imparting the multiple lessons that they've learned to their mentees and helping them better navigate through their own careers. By absorbing these lessons—of mentors' mistakes and successes—mentees are better prepared to move forward with knowledge and confidence.

Timesharing

To further expand on the importance of real dialogue in a mentor-mentee relationship, let's touch upon the notion of intimacy. It's been said that the mentor-mentee relationship is an "intimate" one. And it is. Get your mind out of the gutter—not that degree of intimacy. A firm handshake should be the extent of physical contact between the mentor and mentee. More to the point, an intimate mentor-mentee relationship necessitates genuine sharing of insights, observations, and suggestions. This give-and-take dialogue should be entirely uninhibited.

The Mentoring Model

If you fancy yourself a gourmet chef and know your way around the kitchen, then you know that cooking is an art form—not too far removed from coaching and mentoring. Okay, that's a bit of a stretch. You guessed it, though: An analogy (yes, another one!) is on its way. An analogy between preparing a tasty repast and laying the groundwork for a scrumptious model of successful mentoring.

Unless you use cult inventor Ron Popeil's "Set it and forget it" Showtime Rotisserie Oven, cooking is more involved and demands that you pay close attention to what you are doing at all times. It matters what kinds of ingredients you use, how much of them you use, and when you use them. It matters what you cook in and what you cook on. It matters how high a heat you use, when you choose to stir, flip things over, and so on. Get the picture? True gourmets, just like mentors, have a lot more in their pots than mere ingredients. Figuratively speaking, they put themselves in their pots. Give the same recipe to two people and look at the final product. Oftentimes the differences are startling. And the same applies to mentoring basics. This book, and others on the subject, can provide all sorts of direction on the do's and don'ts of proper mentoring, but it all boils down to the individual players and what they do with the materials.

ALERT

A solid mentor-mentee relationship is rooted in trust. A mentor is aware of this important bond and is constantly on guard to maintain this trust. A mentor knows that the foundation of trust can take months to build, but only a moment to destroy. Ditto for coaches.

That said, this section gives you a simple recipe for mentoring—a model. And as with all recipes, it's what you do with these ingredients that will determine the results. Your character and approach to mentoring will determine whether you get a moist and mouthwatering pineapple upside-down cake (a mentee who is better for having had your tutoring), or a gooey pool of flour, milk, and eggs (a mentee who is no better off than when he or she first met you).

The four chief mentor-mentee ingredients are:

- **TRUST**   - **TIME**   - **DIALOGUE**   - **SHARING**

Trust has to be established from the beginning of the relationship. Once this firm bond is secured, the mentor must be freely available to the mentee. None of this "Don't call us, we'll call you" kind of stuff. The relationship must then be rooted in a rich dialogue between the mentor and the mentee. The overall atmosphere should be one of sharing—and caring, too. Information should be freely and regularly exchanged. When these four elements are put in the mix and properly executed, both parties reap the benefits of a lively, insightful relationship. Most important, mentees are stimulated to grow and develop their knowledge and skills so they can overcome obstacles, make deliberate and more informed decisions, and improve their understanding of and empathy for coworkers and people in general.

CHAPTER 5
Using External Coaches

This chapter takes a look at coaches hired from the outside world. You have a wide range of external coaching options, from trainers who hold seminars or sell videos, to hands-on consultants who resolve specific problems, improve certain skills, adapt a manager to a new position, or deal with an employee's communication deficiencies.

Understanding Why Companies Seek Outside Assistance

Do you need any outside help? Here are a few reasons why companies go outside for help in securing coaching and mentoring services.

QUESTIONS?

Can anybody be a coaching consultant?
Today, anybody can place an ad in the yellow pages advertising his or her services as a "coach." No special education or accrediting is necessary. However, calling oneself a coach and being a competent one are two different things.

Skills

The technology of today demands different skills from the skills of yesterday's technology. And tomorrow's technology will demand different skills from today's. This means companies are sometimes compelled to find external coaches who can acclimate employees to some of the new skills essential in getting the immediate job done and staying competitive.

Professionalism

External coaches play important roles in tutoring managers and employees alike on proper behavior in the workplace. Knowing how to behave is indispensable for career advancement. This may sound like third-grade stuff, but it's a serious problem. The educational system has graduated a lot of students who, besides not being able to read and write up to snuff, do not know how to deport themselves as professionals in the work environment. (For a full discussion on what constitutes professionalism, see Chapter 10.) The retail and service sectors of the economy reveal this truism for all to see. You walk into some of these stores and you're treated as the Invisible Man or the Invisible Woman. You're ignored and looked upon as an intruder. Where are the managers in these poisonous work environments? Oh . . . the managers are right there, actively participating in the inappropriate behaviors. Coaching and mentoring's next conquest is the retail and service businesses. (More on this important subject in Chapter 18.)

FACTS

External coaches are often brought into companies to deal with complex relationship problems. An example of one such multilayered people problem involves the challenges facing newly promoted employees, now in managerial slots, who are confronted with subordinates who were, only a short time ago, their peers and pals.

Mentoring

External coaches sometimes serve as sounding boards and advisers for career development, providing help to the manager or employee preparing for a new job. An example of this is a coach hired to counsel and train a promoted employee who finds himself or herself in the role of boss over former coworkers. Not always an easy adjustment to make.

Lack of Trust

"What's the cause of all that laughter emanating from the lunchroom of Company XYZ?"

"Oh, the employees have just been handed the company's Mission Statement, which says, 'Our people are our greatest asset.'" Along the way in your career path, how many times have you encountered this rather cloying sentiment in an annual report or company newsletter? It has become something of a corporate cliché. And, because it's not intended to get laughs, it's not very funny. A company that makes use of this "our people are our greatest asset" motto and doesn't really mean it has a serious problem on its hands.

The best and brightest in the labor pool gravitate to the companies that genuinely believe in providing their employees with more on-the-job responsibilities, challenges, and opportunities for real advancement— companies that truly view employees as their "greatest assets." On the other hand, companies that spout empty platitudes and offer vague promises will be revealed for what they are, and won't get the best people to work for them. There's nothing more depressing than a work environment where employees know beyond a shadow of a doubt that they're being used. And used for one purpose only—to get the most work out of them for the least compensation. These sorry folks know, too, based on what they've observed on a regular basis, that they are as expendable as yesterday's news.

Coaching and mentoring embody the antithesis of this dog-eat-dog management philosophy. This managerial methodology aims to build a commitment in employees. It seeks to enhance employees' skills by providing them an atmosphere of perpetual learning with responsibilities and challenges worthy of their talents and abilities. But companies in this situation may need outside help to let employees know they're serious about making people their greatest assets.

Managerial Sea Change

Many external coaches find themselves brought into companies that are in dire need of a sea change in managerial attitudes and approaches in dealing with their employees. Often these outside coaches work with line managers, team leaders, supervisors, and fledgling managerial talents, to tutor them in the ways of coaching and mentoring—ways that are both satisfying to employees and pleasing to the company, and get the most out of their staffs.

If you, in any managerial position, need assistance in making the transition from directive-style managing to coaching, an external coach is something worth considering. Keep your eyes and ears open at seminars and conferences for these outside coaching specialists. Look for the right fit. Not all external consultants are alike. They have different specialties and methods, and get dissimilar results. Some are the real thing, the Coca-Cola of coaches, while others are more like a generic supermarket brand cola—cheaper in price, sugary sweet, but rather pedestrian. The average manager of today, and the manager of tomorrow, does not possess coaching and mentoring skills by birth. A one-on-one coaching education can perform miracles in schooling self-motivated managers and others on the procedures of coaching and mentoring. And it's on-the-job training—not in a sterile classroom—where real results can be observed, commented on, and fine-tuned.

There are plenty of conferences, seminars, and workshops that teach coaching and mentoring tools and techniques, and the "secrets" to managing as a coach and behaving as a mentor. In addition, there are comprehensive training videos offering hours upon hours of training, which you can watch at your leisure in the comfort of your home, if that's what you desire.

No matter how you slice it, though, coaching and mentoring, whether internal or external, desire to uplift employee performance. In any guise it's about overhauling the structure and culture of the workplace. It focuses on communication between managers and employees. As a matter of fact—and you've probably seen plenty of examples of this in performance planning—coaching and mentoring bring employees into the heart of the business operation by making them feel an important part of it. Employees are coached not to be mere clock punchers, but, instead, to be on a mission. A mission to improve their lives by making their jobs both a meaningful and satisfying part of it. Tying together today's job with tomorrow's job, and the job after that, is what good coaching and mentoring accomplish.

FACTS

External coaches charge their corporate clients $150 to $200 per hour for their services. Some charge as much as $400 per hour! There are some coaches earning more than psychologists and psychiatrists.

Dialogue is a thread that winds its way through all coaching and mentoring efforts. Employees must feel comfortable with their managers. They must always feel free to speak their minds and let it all out from time to time. Employees want to feel in control of their own futures. Chapter 6 addresses in some detail the importance of a coach's listening skills in the comprehensive coaching process. There is nothing more disheartening for employees than to be left twisting in the wind. Employees who are put in these awkward positions eventually blow away. Good coaching doesn't let this happen. It strives valiantly to keep top-notch employees in the fold and away from that wayward wind.

Determining Whether You're Ready

Are you ready to bring a coach in from the outside? External coaches brought into companies to rectify particular shortcomings, or teach new skills, are increasingly working alongside internal coaches these days. That is, coaches themselves are going outside their own companies and looking for specialist help. Even the best coaches sometimes find themselves confronted with particular problems that are beyond their expertise, or, perhaps, they don't have the time to address. There are only so many hours in a day and so many days in a week. And depending on the size of the staff and the results that are expected, even a coach may need a helping hand from time to time. On these occasions, a supplementary coach from the outside world—an expert at a task desperately needed— might be just what the doctor ordered.

ALERT

If you need an external coach to supplement your own coaching efforts, check out the human resources department in your own company for possible leads. Look into seminars, professional organizations that are dedicated to training coaches, and the various publications in the field of coaching and mentoring.

As a manager and coach, you may be hesitant in bringing in help from an outside source. This is understandable. It's human nature for managers to desire control of their staffs and their job responsibilities. Managers—even those wearing the coveted "coaching" label—are, after all, judged by the results their employees deliver, just as all other managers. Well, fear not, coaches! There are a few things that you can do to make this arrangement work like a charm. First, the more self-assured you become in your managerial odyssey, the less trepidation you'll feel about bringing in an outsider to assist you in getting the most out of your employees' talents and abilities.

Our discussion that follows focuses on the coach who is looking for additional coaching help from an external consultant, not on a company that's using an external consultant to set up the coaching model for the first time.

Using External Coaches Effectively

When you bring in a coach from the outside to assist your own coaching efforts, you must first make absolutely certain that you have a very specific, clearly defined reason for doing so. The objectives that you want the external coach to achieve must be clearly spelled out to him or her and also to the employee or employees who will be working with this adjunct coach.

Preparing Your Employees

You should never dump an external coach on your employees without explaining to them what you have in mind. These kinds of surprises are not appreciated by employees and violate a basic tenet of coaching and mentoring—open communication, employee involvement, and so on. Such a unilateral path reduces the chances of a fruitful relationship ever developing between an outside coach and your employees. On the other hand, fully apprising employees of just what these ancillary relationships will entail increases the possibility that any added coaching they receive will succeed.

Getting Your Employees on Board

Listen, too, to what your employees have to say about a prospective relationship with an external coach. If your employees are dead set against the setup, you might want to reconsider going through with it. External coaches, remember, aren't philanthropists working free of charge. So, if you feel that your employees' resistance to this tutorship is as hard as a diamond, then you are confronted with three choices:

- No external coaching.
- Convince your employees to give the relationship the "old college try."
- Tell your employees that they are getting the extra coaching—end of story (not a coach thing to do, by the way).

Setting Parameters for the External Coach

Let's suppose for argument's sake that after deliberating with your employees, you settle this matter in the affirmative. The next step is to bring the external coach into the fold and lay down—clearly—the parameters of the job you want done. The time frame is essential here. Never give external coaches a blank check and an open-ended invitation to linger until they feel the job is done. This often leads to the Unwanted Relative Syndrome making its way into the office. You know, the cousin who came for a weekend visit, liked your hospitality (or more likely, the free room and board), and hung around for two months.

You must have unambiguous objectives you want the external coaching to accomplish. And you must also have a precisely defined time frame in mind for this external coaching to realize those objectives.

ESSENTIALS
When you bring in an external coach to work with an employee, be sure to keep tabs on the relationship by regularly meeting with both the coach and the employee. But also recognize and respect the importance of confidentiality in such a relationship, if it is to work as planned.

Staying Fully Apprised

Just as with the performance plans of your employees, you must stay fully apprised of the external coach-employee relationship from beginning to end. You are still the head cheese, and you are responsible for your employees' performances in all areas. You can't step away from this sidebar relationship just because it will be over in short order. You've got to know what gains (if any) your employees are making, and how those gains will impact your relationship with them, and on all future projects in which you will be working together.

Throughout this entire process, it's imperative that you consult frequently with the external coach and share your thoughts on the progress of the tutelage and whether it's getting the results that are desired. And likewise, you need to talk to your employees about how they feel the special instruction is going. That said, this doesn't mean that you impose yourself on the relationship. As a coach yourself, you know that the coaching process is about giving employees latitude and as much freedom as is possible and sensible. This same latitude has got to be extended to an external coach. Outsiders, in particular, need to feel comfortable right from the start. They need to work in an environment of relative independence, performing their specialty without interference and unnecessary roadblocks. Coaches-for-hire are usually specialists at what they do, with track records of accomplishment, and shouldn't be treated as upstart employees. They are working for you, yes, but they are also independent.

ESSENTIALS

Seek and ye shall find help. Liberally use outside resources to supplement your coaching and the special training efforts that come with the territory. Potential sources of help include professional associations, books and periodicals, public workshops, college courses, technical seminars, and so on.

So you've got another fine line to walk. That's part of the life of being a coach. You need to be fully aware of what's going on within the confines of your office space, taking measure of everything from time to time, but you also need to respect others' abilities in doing their jobs with minimal amounts of interference and nit-picking on your part. This certainly extends to external coaches, who need to maintain a certain level of autonomy in working with employees, while simultaneously being on the same page as you, the coach who brought them in to fix a problem or teach a skill.

Using Internal Sources as Mini-Mentors

As a coach, have you thought about calling on help from the inside? Yes, the inside! That is, have you considered asking a member of your staff to work with another one of your employees? Think about it. You have a wealth of resources at your fingertips—the people who work for you. As already seen in the examination of the ways and means of coaching and mentoring, people and their unique personalities, talents, and abilities are what make this birdie fly.

So, because you're on the subject of individuals and their special talents and abilities, it stands to reason that your employee Pam may well possess certain competencies that are eluding her colleague, and also your employee, Matt. If this is indeed the case, why not permit Pam to tutor Matt on his shortcomings? You can, in effect, allow Pam to take Matt under her wing in an informal setup within the perimeters of the workplace. By implementing such a relationship within your team or department, you're exercising a very prominent coaching and mentoring technique. You are maximizing your talent base by filling in the gaps of knowledge and skills that invariably exist in one employee with the expertise of another one of your employees. It's no different than high school or college tutors who help their classmates.

FACTS

Advancing employees' skill levels and abilities to take on greater responsibilities and challenges is the surest way to keep employees in your fold. Employees whose job interest remains high are more likely to want to stay put than are bored or disgruntled employees.

We'll call these in-house "taking under the wing" efforts mini-mentoring. The passing on, from one person to another, of know-how is the main feature of mentoring. Tutoring and upgrading the knowledge base and skills of another is mentoring at its finest.

Understand What You Want to Accomplish

Now, just how do you make this setup work? Aren't there a lot of egos just waiting to get bruised? Again, just as with bringing in external coaches, you have to know precisely what you want accomplished. Before you apprise your employees of your mini-mentoring idea, make sure you yourself can clearly verbalize just what you have in mind, and just what you want to achieve by initiating a mini-mentoring relationship.

Establish Time Parameters

Next, you've got to establish a time parameter for this mini-mentoring, too. Open-ended relationships of this kind often set in motion the Law of Diminishing Returns. You've seen it happen time and again in so many teacher-student learning relationships, and in comparable learning environments. They start out fresh and with a sense of grand purpose. The bright-eyed and bushy-tailed students are, at the onset, sponges for learning. Real sponges eventually become waterlogged and require a squeeze or two, or the absorption ceases. Ditto for the students absorbing their lessons.

Monitor Progress

So, carefully consider your objectives and time frame, and, of course, monitor the progress of the relationship from both sides of the employee aisle. That is, periodically talk to the employee recruited to assist her coworker—Pam, in this example. Ask how things are going, and if she feels she is making headway in the education of Matt. And then reverse the process and query Matt about how he feels the relationship is working.

CHAPTER 6

Developing Coaching Skills

Understand the key skills that go into making good coaches, including all-important listening skills, which make or break so many coaching efforts. This chapter also touches upon questioning techniques and the significance of dispensing consistent feedback to employees.

Developing Empathy

Coaching and mentoring demand a multilayered knowledge that dinosaur managers don't need to call their own. They ask of those who coach and mentor to get to know the people they work with as individuals. And so, a coach is required to be empathetic. That is, you've got to grasp fundamental human psychology and recognize the importance of elevating both body and soul to get the job done, and done right. And showing empathy for a fellow human being is not something that can be readily gleaned by reading a book or attending a seminar. Empathy is rooted in life experiences. "I can understand how he's feeling right now." "I can see she needs a word of encouragement, because I've been there." "That happened to me once."

A solid analogy can be drawn between parenting and the art of coaching and mentoring. Can anybody be a father? A mother? Well, most adults at some point in their lives have the biological tools to answer in the affirmative. But, as you can plainly see all around you, some people do a better job of parenting than others do. Some mothers and fathers totally abrogate their parental responsibilities and lack even the most rudimentary of skills—and yes, the empathy—to undertake what parenting entails.

The Coaching Blueprint

If you want to become a good coach and mentor, consider the following points and make them part of your day-to-day interactions with your employees. Here's a simple blueprint for success.

FACTS

A lot is expected of coaches. They are expected to raise employees' self-awareness, self-confidence, and self-development. And when these three come together synergistically, the results are stronger employee performances and a more healthy work environment.

Embrace the philosophy. The purpose of coaching and mentoring is to unlock human potential on the job by fashioning a work environment that is most conducive to helping employees reach their personal best.

Understand the individual. Understand that each and every employee is a unique person who needs to be recognized as such, if the philosophy is to be lived and realized.

Encourage self-motivation. Bridge the gap between an employee's self-interests and the organization's self-interests and make them one and the same.

FACTS

For two seasons (1961 and 1962), the Chicago Cubs employed the first—and last—of its kind: a college of coaches. Different coaches rotated in managing the team. It was a short-lived, failed experiment. Consistency is a key to successful coaching—anywhere—with one person setting the tone and making the decisions.

Establish goals. Assist in establishing on-the-job goals for employees on an individual basis based on each person's level of skills and desire to advance and grow, and on the organization's needs.

Commitment. Forge a firm commitment from employees to simultaneously work for the organization, for the coach, and for themselves.

Communicate. Keep open lines of communication between the coach and the employee at all times. Give regular and copious feedback on job performance, using your ability to listen, hear, and understand employees.

Resolve conflict. Practice immediate and assertive on-the-spot problem solving. Solve today's problems today, not tomorrow, and not next week.

Be solution-oriented. Always seek positive solutions for positive outcomes. Every obstacle and problem is seen as an opportunity to redress and move forward.

Delegate responsibilities. Recognize your obligation to provide employees with added job responsibilities, challenging tasks, and opportunities for career advancement. Understand that this is the best way to keep productive employees in the organization and to attract the best employees from the outside.

Show appreciation. Reward progress and positive results on an individual basis. Recognizing a job well done today increases the chances of a job well done tomorrow.

ALERT

Coaching and mentoring travel a two-way street. You are expected to delegate important responsibilities on a consistent basis. In return for the confidence that you show in your employees, just remember this: Freely impart responsibilities as a coach, yes, but insist on responsibility in return.

Never stop learning. Create a work atmosphere of continuous learning, where augmentation of knowledge and growth in skills are always encouraged and never capped. Offer workshops or lectures to help employees stay up-to-date with their respective jobs and industry sectors. Solicit topic suggestions from everyone in the company.

Listening Skills: The Ears Have It

You may think it's incredibly obvious to suggest that you be a good listener to successfully coach people. But it is too often taken for granted. Coaching and mentoring require dialogue between coaches and employees, mentors and mentees. Some people, however, consider a dialogue anything that permits another person to utter a word or two edgewise. That is, 98 percent of the conversation comes out of their mouths versus 2 percent everybody else's. That's not a dialogue! That's more like a David Letterman monologue with a question or two posed to an audience member.

Coaches and mentors must finely hone their listening skills, because employees should be listened to and heard on a regular basis. This entire managerial methodology revolves around raising the level of employee participation in defining their own jobs, so it stands to reason that employees should have some say in what's going on. And by say, that means that they need to say a few words on occasion, and be heard. This isn't to suggest you must always like what your employees are saying. It doesn't mean you have to implement their suggestions or grant their requests. Not at all. Coaches are still managers and are the final arbiters in all decisions, unless the responsibilities for the decisions have been specifically delegated to others.

The listening tool of coaching is highly beneficial in dealing with your employees in matters ranging from performance planning to behavioral problems. It's similar to brainstorming in the sense that it can't hurt to listen. Listening opens up new doors. You can discover so much by merely hearing what your employees have to say and connecting with them in a confidential way.

Employees who are not performing up to speed have to be listened to all the more. What's causing their slumps in performance or hostile attitudes? What do they consider their roles on your team? Where do they see themselves in a year's time in the company? Do they think they've got a future in the company? Ask—and listen very carefully and respectfully—and ye shall find out. Don't ask and don't listen and you'll never know. The decisions that you ultimately make after these listening tours will be fairer and sounder than they would be if you managed with cotton in your ears.

ESSENTIALS You must be an active listener, which means that you must make certain at all times that you are both hearing and understanding your employees. You do this by clarifying points along the way by paraphrasing and asking probing, open-ended questions that can't be answered with just one word.

Okay, you've got it. You listen to your staff. You talk to them on a one-on-one basis and let them all speak their pieces. That's the first step. But now it's time you learn the precise skills of being a good listener. Yes, there are genuine skills involved in listening, and it is important for a coach to possess them. Listening to your employees without hearing what they're saying is not listening at all. Some managers fancy themselves employee-friendly with an "open door policy." And, yes, they'll let you come in and sound off when something's on your mind. But in the end, nothing ever seems to come out of all this "listening." That is, you lodge a complaint, ask for a new job, request a raise in pay, a time extension on a project, and so on—and nothing is ever done about it. Eventually, you come to realize that talking to your manager is about as fruitful as talking to the makeshift wall in your office cubicle.

As a coach, you can't be this kind of "open door policy" manager. You must both listen and hear. This is one of many important aspects that distinguish coaching from the more traditional management styles. Employees should know that when they are talking with their coach, they are being heard. They should feel confident that what they ask of their coach will be acted upon in some way—either affirmatively or negatively. The employees must, in turn, accept the reality that maybe they won't get what they want. But at least they know their manager—their coach—will always take what they have to say under careful consideration and not completely disregard it. That's really all employees can ask for: a fair hearing.

Paraphrasing Skills

You've got to be able to paraphrase what's being said to you to show your employees that you're indeed listening to and hearing them. During any parleys with your employees, periodically paraphrase what they're revealing in the conversations. "So what you're saying is, you'd like more challenging tasks in your next assignment." Punctuating your listening with such paraphrasing reassures your employees that you're not a brass monkey—not a department store mannequin—but a real person listening, hearing, and understanding what they're saying.

If your employee feels that you are truly doing these three things (listening, hearing, and understanding), you've passed the coach's listening test. Remember, though, that you aren't the judge on whether you are an accomplished listener. You may sincerely feel you fully understand your employees when they come to you with their various concerns. But what's key here is not what you think, it's what your employees think. It's whether or not they believe you understand that counts. That's the true test you must pass.

Checkup

Sometimes our perceptions of ourselves are not quite the perceptions that others have of us. This is precisely why you need to find out how you are perceived and whether you are in fact connecting with your employees in the way that you would like. After each and every coaching encounter and "listening time" with your employees, you need to do a checkup—on yourself. You do this by requesting feedback from your employees on whether they feel that you are listening to and hearing what they have to say. You ask them directly whether they feel that you are understanding their concerns and responding to them appropriately or completely off the mark. If you think that you know the feelings, hopes, and desires of your employees, and consider yourself in perfect tune with one and all—that's peachy keen, if in fact it matches the true feelings, hopes, and desires of your staff members.

Consider this checkup your reality check. And you owe it to yourself, your employees, and the organization to positively understand where your people are coming from. You are, after all, seeking to bring about a choice work environment for getting the best results possible. And you know that this path to positive outcomes cannot be traveled alone or with a deaf ear.

Open-Ended Questions

To travel still further in enhancing your listening skills, there's another very important verbal device that should be added to your coaching toolbox. To fully connect with your employees, you must make certain that you are in sync with their points of view and perspectives. The use of questions in addition to paraphrasing will enable you to keep all your listening encounters in line. You will not lose your way in a talk with employees, if you intermittently question them throughout a discussion. Pepper your employees with questions. Not in an aggressive manner designed to put them on the spot, but to clarify points along the way and aid you in that key thing called "understanding" that we've been talking so much about.

Our *Declaration of Independence* assures us all that we are created equal. It says nothing, however, about all questions being equal. And they aren't. Questions can be classified as either close-ended (requiring an answer of just a word or two) or open-ended (requiring an explanation). Which do you think should be a considerable part of a coach's querying arsenal? (Open-ended questions, of course.)

Close-ended questions are posed for definitive and short responses:

"Where is the lunchroom?"
"How long has Michelle been supervisor?"
"What time does the meeting begin?"
"Is that Mr. Roach's real hair?"

You can clearly see that these questions are not designed for elaborate answers. A couple of words in response will do. Close-ended questions have their necessary place for closed answers. But they are not the driving forces in a dialogue.

Open-ended questions, on the other hand, are very powerful coach weapons. These style questions are calculated to produce thoughtful rejoinders. They are posed with an "open end" and have no right or wrong answers attached to them. Open-ended questions complement genuine listening. For they provide you a great opportunity to draw more out of your employees. You can question them on any cloudy points that they make, or ask them to flesh out some of their opinions, suggestions, or requests. Here are some examples of open-ended questions:

"How do you feel about your coworker John leaving in the middle of the project?"
"Can you further explain this idea of yours?"
"Is your performance plan unfolding as originally anticipated?"
"What's your opinion on the change in bonus policy?"
"Do you have any thoughts on why sales are down in your department from last year?"

All of these questions are meant to elicit honest and thinking responses, answers that transcend a mere "yes" or "no."

Coaching and mentoring methods use open-ended questions frequently because they in effect "open up" the workplace environment. Employees are afforded opportunities to more freely express themselves in response to them. They are given a chance to discuss the progress of their work assignments, their feelings about their status in the organization, their relationships with their coach and coworkers, and just about anything else.

Of course, not all open-ended questions are positive in nature. Questions leading with "Why," for instance, are in fact open-ended, but often put the employee on the defensive. "Why did you make that decision?" "Why did you choose this new approach instead of the one that worked so well last time?" These open-ended questions are somewhat loaded and accusatory in nature. How about using instead: "What was the thinking process that went into your decision?" or "Please explain the reasons you chose this new approach to solving the problem instead of the previous one."

Mirroring Feelings

A final listening skill, and the one that really gets to the heart of understanding employees, revolves around their "feelings." Yes, coaches need to be sensitive in ascertaining the emotional states of their employees during day-to-day encounters with them. Granted, this isn't always easy. Some people are poker faces by nature and carefully rein in their emotions. On any given day, they could just as easily have won $50 million in a Powerball lottery or been diagnosed with a terminal illness, and you couldn't tell the difference. Most of us, however, are not so accomplished at completely concealing our true feelings. And so our emotions—in varying ways and degrees—are visible at all times, with the office environs being no exception. Thus, you can unearth so much just by gleaning the moods of your employees when you speak with them. How your employees are feeling when they are in your presence cannot be discounted as immaterial and unrelated to the job at hand.

If an employee is visibly upset when he or she speaks with you, it's important that you listen and respond with this reality in mind because feelings run deep. And just because they're shown in the workplace, feelings cannot be cast aside as irrelevant. An individual's feelings directly translate into job performance. Coaches and mentors know this and don't shy away from it. Dinosaur managers, on the other hand, don't invest too much in understanding their staffs' feelings. It's not part of their managerial curriculums to tap into such human emotion, such personal stuff, and tailor their decisions to them. Contrarily, coaching and mentoring—rooted so deeply in people, performance, and positive outcomes—equate feelings and mind-set with productivity. Coaches never ignore employees' feelings because they recognize and appreciate that these feelings are not separate from the productive individuals behind them.

So, what you've got to do is incorporate into your listening skills, and overall coaching approach, the ability to mirror the feelings of your employees in your responses to them. Use open-ended questions to more fully comprehend why your employees are feeling this way or that way. Get to the heart of unhappiness if you have to. Understand where anger is coming from. You can't treat an employee who's overtly upset in the same way that you would deal with an employee who's as happy as a squirrel with a peanut. The one-size-fits-all managing approach doesn't work here. Receptivity to others' feelings adds a powerfully empathetic dimension to the art of listening. It enables coaches to go beyond the words being expressed by their employees. Feelings properly understood put mere words into a meaningful perspective.

ALERT

When you choose to address your troops as a group, keep your lectures or pep talks to thirty minutes or less. Studies have shown that after a half hour, people's attention spans wane. Most people remember more from short talks. So, get to your point and get through to your employees.

The more traditional managers of the world are apt to equalize the emotions of their employees. Come to work with a tear in your eye and you are advised to go to the bathroom and pull yourself together. Coaches don't pack their employees off to the bathroom in lieu of forthrightly dealing with genuine human emotion and real feelings. They conscientiously tie employees' emotional states into their job performances, and are right to take this approach.

Giving Feedback, Not Criticism

Soliciting feedback from your employees, querying them on their perceptions of you, is very important. It enables you to make adjustments in your coaching and helps cement rapport between you and your employees. But you also have to dispense constructive feedback quite liberally in all your coaching endeavors. It's a valuable communication technique that you should wield wisely because it is the greatest information dispenser in town. Feedback focuses its lenses on employee performance problems and other workplace concerns. Feedback is your observations and is not based on personal feelings and subjective judgments.

Employees clamor all the time for information concerning their work performances and what they need to know to improve themselves on the job. Feedback from their coach provides them with just that.

Keeping Feedback Objective

The feedback that you offer your employees, however, needs to be as objective as is humanly possible. It needs to be honest, succinct, and lucid. "Beating around the bush" feedback is bad coaching. That is, don't start an important meeting with your employee with a discussion about the weather, football, or your preference for boxers over briefs. Be up-front and get to the point. If the feedback is negative in nature, don't leave your employee squirming in his or her seat for what seems like an eternity. Explain very precisely where you see the problem and what you believe is the root cause or causes of it. Discuss openly possible solutions to correcting the problem, and, of course, solicit return feedback from the employee and an assessment of your feedback.

Separating Feedback from Criticism

Remember that feedback and its objective nature differs from outright praise or criticism. When feedback is offered in a manner like, "You really screwed up on this project," it is subjective and critical. Overt criticism is not a self-motivating tool. It immediately puts the employee on the defensive. It often leads to anger, humiliation, or both, and thus warps any helpful, give-and-take dialogue and makes finding proper and positive solutions that much more difficult.

Yes, there are many managers who use praise and criticism like a policeman's billy club. They attempt to build up or bash their employees into greater productivity. Fear of getting hit over the head with the boss's cudgel is sometimes a temporary impetus for an employee to perform at a higher level. Fear of losing one's job also works on occasion—that cannot be denied. But these are short-term solutions at best and unprincipled on top of that. Dinosaur managers who use these heavy-handed approaches don't create an optimum work atmosphere—that's for sure. Anything but!

ALERT

Test your trust quotient by asking yourself these four questions: Am I consistent? Do my employees believe what I say? Do they perceive me as competent to carry out what I say? Do they perceive me as looking out for them? Answer all four in the affirmative and you pass.

What, then, is the difference between negative feedback and criticism? Negative feedback is open-ended; it is not condemnatory. It is dispensed with good intentions, in hope that the bad performance or behavior can be corrected. It seeks a solution to a positive outcome. Negative feedback is intended to point out just where and why mistakes were made and how logically they can be corrected in the future. Criticism is close-ended and usually personal in nature. It is not solution-oriented. Solutions and suggestions intermingled with criticism are often ignored because they tend to get buried beneath the vitriol or harshness of tone. "Ed, you've been dragging your feet on this project for weeks now. Your group is near mutiny. You'd better fix this problem, or you are in serious trouble, my friend." "My friend" suffixes are often giveaways of criticism, by the way. Let's try it this way. "Ed, you're running behind schedule on your project. You're going to have to come up with solutions—and fast—because your group is very unhappy with the progress and your leadership. This is unacceptable. Do you have any ideas how you can right this situation?"

Negative feedback. You've made it very plain that you are dissatisfied with Ed's performance. He's been told that his group is displeased with him, and that he needs to make changes in the way he is doing his job or suffer the consequences that come with prolonged bad performance. Of course, depending on the severity of the problem, negative feedback comes in many forms. Some of it is light and lean, with subtle references to particular problems that need to be corrected or improved upon. On the other end of the scale, negative feedback could entail placing it all on the line. "Your performance of late has been subpar. You're going to have to make some serious changes in your attitude and work ethic, or we are going to have to let you go. Are you prepared to do what it takes?"

Giving Positive Feedback Versus Praise

Now, you ask, what's the difference between positive feedback and praise? Again, positive feedback focuses on the specifics of job performance. You bolster your employees with a critique of all the things that they are doing that please you. "Sandra, your communication skills have dramatically improved over the last couple of months. The report that you just prepared for me on your project status was thorough and concise. I appreciate all the work you've put into it, as do your team members, who have informed me that you are always there for them in answering their questions." Praise on the same subject might go something like this, "Full speed ahead. Keep up the good work!" Obviously, the positive feedback received by the employee carries greater weight. It's more uplifting to her because it goes to the heart of her job performance and what she actually does.

You may have worked for a boss who offered praise in lieu of substantive positive feedback. And the workplace atmosphere was probably a distant one. Managers who dispense one- or two-sentence praiseworthy comments to their employees, and never any positive feedback, inevitably leave their staffs with empty feelings in their guts. In these kinds of situations, employees feel that they are there for one reason and one reason only—to work for the bottom line. They feel no sense that they are appreciated as individual talents with specific desires to learn and grow on the job and in their careers.

Constructive feedback—positive or negative—is a coach's way of letting employees know where they stand. Feedback is forward looking and not intended to either launch or sink any boats. Rather, it promotes dialogue and is solution-oriented without personal judgments and opinions getting in the way.

Giving Feedback Only When You're Calm

As a coach, you may be justifiably enraged at certain employees from time to time and feel like dressing them down. Take a deep breath on these occasions. It's best to avoid such turbulent encounters. This may entail that you put off a meeting until you can temper your temper and look at things less emotionally and more objectively. So avoid, "Ed, get in my office right now!" Instead, tell Ed in a controlled tone of voice, "I'd like to have a discussion with you on the progress of Project Mindshift. In my office at ten o'clock tomorrow morning, okay?" This will give you time to cool off and think through the feedback that you'll be imparting to Ed about his project performance and overall behavior on the job.

ESSENTIALS   In all verbal encounters with your employees, you should be cognizant of your tone of voice and bearing. That is, avoid sarcasm, haughtiness, and the attack mode. Be objective and consistent in your demeanor at all times. This will maximize your employee-employer relationship and performance results.

Where Predictability Is Trust

"Oh, he's so predictable." How often have you heard this sentiment expressed about somebody? And when it is applied to a person, it's usually not meant as a compliment, but is said pejoratively. In other words, being "predictable" is a put-down. Ironically, predictability is a trait that employees value very dearly in their managers. Not predictability in innovation and delegation, which is really a contradiction in terms. But predictability in managerial style and temperament.

We've talked at length in this chapter about listening, hearing, and understanding, i.e., communicating with your employees and connecting with them. And it all comes back to that little matter of trust. Trust and predictability go hand in glove. You need to be predictable in so many ways, so that your staff will know what to expect from you at all times and on any given day. There are no big surprises in predictability. Employees feel more secure in workplaces that are stable and run by coaches who are predictable in their methods and routines (i.e., what meetings are like, consistency in follow-ups, overall competency, dependability, and so on).

Trust blossoms from this general predictability. The worst thing that you can do is say one thing and do another. Because the next time that you say that you are going to do something, your employee will be less inclined to believe you. And then comes the negative snowball effect. The employee will say, "Why should I do X, based on the coach's saying that he's going to do Y, when I don't believe that he's going to do Y?" Yes, there's much to be said for predictability in coaching. It's not separate from trust—it's an essential part of a workplace atmosphere that is both stable and serene.

CHAPTER 7

Overcoming Workplace Obstacles

Workplace problems are a part of all coaches' lives, whether it's hiring new employees or dealing with lackluster performances, bad attitudes, and skill deficiencies. Learn how to discover telltale signs that cry out for special training. You will also find out how to teach skills to your employees to overcome workplace obstacles.

High-Octane Coaching

There are unique situations in the workplace that demand extra special attention. It's during these crucial times when you need to pull out your metaphorical whistle, briskly blow into it, and concentrate on the considerable coaching work to be done. Let's examine some of the workplace circumstances that are ripe for this kind of high-octane coaching.

The New Kid on the Block

The most unmistakable moment that requires special training is the introduction of new employees onto your team. Fledgling employees are wont to feel ill at ease in their new surroundings. And that goes double for your existing team being asked to absorb new members into their fraternity. People who work together are often clannish, particularly after an extended period of time, and they reflexively view outsiders with unease and as a threat to their way of doing things. More times than not, the new employees gain the confidence of the group. Sometimes this acceptance is immediate; on other occasions, it takes a while, depending on the personalities involved. High-octane coaching asks that you pay special heed to your new hires. It is your cleanest opportunity to instruct and orient them. You fill them in on the ways of the organization as a whole and the peculiar customs of your office. This is the right and proper time to let your new employees know exactly what is expected of them and the procedures that they must follow if they are to work for you and on your team. By taking this early and upfront approach, you avoid the on-the-job training method comparable to a father teaching his son to swim by hurling him headfirst into a six-foot pool of water.

Improving Skills

As a manager, major league baseball Hall of Famer Frankie Frisch famously lamented, "Oh, those bases on balls." Frisch was referring to the damage done when a pitcher awards a free base to an opposing player by not throwing strikes. A common coach's lament is "Oh, those missing skills." If you've been paying attention—and of course you have—you know that the coaching and mentoring methodology is firmly committed to growing employee skills. And the reason for this is quite simple. Skills, self-motivation, and professional work habits are what translate into productive workers. And new skills are needed all the time to keep pace with rapid technological advances.

FACTS

Coaching and mentoring are dedicated to upgrading employee skills, every day and always. Skills are categorized as either hard skills or soft skills. Soft skills refer to communication abilities, interpersonal relations, and so on. Hard skills cover the more technical, hands-on skills required to do a job.

So, part of your coaching responsibilities involve training, or setting the training in motion (via external coaching, employee mini-mentoring, mentoring, and so on) to raise your employees' skill levels, or perhaps teach them completely new skills. Technology and the razor sharp competitiveness in today's business world make retraining of employees more often a necessity than a luxury. Thus, your job as a coach requires that you be keenly aware of what's happening all around you. You've got to know what's going on in your own office, of course, but also in the organization as a whole, and indeed in the entire industry that you work in. It is also imperative that you keep one eye on the overall health of the economy and understand how the business cycle impacts on your industry, company, and the employee skills needed to compete and survive.

Repeat Mistakes

The philosopher George Santayana once remarked, "Those who ignore history are condemned to repeat it." And, of course, he was referring to the mistakes made time and again by societies that lead to wars, oppression, appeasement, and just about everything else that's deleterious to humankind. As a coach, you need to take special heed of Santayana's advice. When your employees err, you need to be right there to correct their missteps and offer them instruction on what exactly went wrong and why. By working closely with your employees on a personal basis from day one of your relationship, you are more apt to spot performance slip-ups and other problems, and catch them early, too. When you give them on-the-spot tutorials, you are disciplining members of your staff not to travel down those same roads again. In doing so, repetitions of the same mistakes, errors in judgment, and interpersonal conflicts leading to poor performance are less likely to occur a second time. Learning from one's mistakes is a time-honored cliché, but it is also very true. A good coach is conscious of this fact of human nature from dawn until dusk.

Grooming

No, this is not something that you ask your employees to do each morning when they look into their bathroom mirrors. (You hope that they know enough to brush their teeth and use mouthwash without you having to tell them.) This is what you do when you find employees who stand out above the rest; who show that they are clearly ahead of the pack in skills, professionalism, and self-motivation. Grooming these bright lights for bigger and better things is what allows coaching and mentoring managerial practices to not only keep pace with swift technological advances, unavoidable employee turnover, and intense competition, but also to thrive and come out on top

Corrective Coaching

Corrective coaching needs to spring into action when certain attitudes and behaviors point to serious problems down the road. Performance problems and dissension inevitably arise in workplaces and must be dealt with promptly and intelligently. These kinds of workplace issues are a given. What you essentially want to accomplish via corrective coaching, then, is problem solving at the source. You want to tackle problems in their infancy and dispatch them in short order. Your grand aim, with corrective coaching actions, is to reduce the quantity of problems that come your way. The fewer the problems the better. But you also want to lessen the severity and disruptiveness of those that do surface.

But what about friction in the workplace and all of those predictable problems that come with it? In every work environment with two or more employees, there are eventually going to be squabbles; there are going to be performances adversely affected by interpersonal relationships not being what they should be. In Chapter 12, we'll look closely at troublesome employee relationships and attitude problems and how coaching handles them. Meanwhile, as we get increasingly enmeshed in the fast-paced, fluid corporate world of today—where the stakes are higher and the salaries are, too—the obstacles and variable pitfalls loom larger and more complex. It stands to reason, then, that these more layered problems need to be more thoroughly understood. And nobody is better qualified to manage in this new-fashioned age than an insightful coach.

FACTS

Corrective coaching specifically refers to coaching applications that address explicit problems ranging from incompetence in jobs, to performance dips caused by declining interest in the job, personal problems affecting job performance, or other behavior-related problems.

Okay, now that we've established beyond a scintilla of doubt that an office led by a coach is a better managed place than one run by a traditional manager, we can set the stage for the specific problems and obstacles that invariably roam workplaces everywhere and anywhere. Foremost, coaching and mentoring don't claim to be problem-solving panaceas—there are no such things; however, they comprise a managerial approach that attends to root causes of problems and gets at them fast and furiously. It's an active style of managing that attempts to cut problems of any kind off at the pass and stop their onerous spread. How exactly is this done? In consultation with your employees, you set high but attainable expectations for them. In addition, you expect each and every one of them to be responsible and accountable for their ultimate performances. It is with this solid foundation that you address and dispense with the problems that arise on your watch.

Recognizing the Symptoms of Common Workplace Problems

Coaches one and all, listen up: We are going to address some of the common workplace problems that you will be asked to untangle during your coaching career. First, it's important to identify the symptoms of problems in the making, because a full-blown problem is often so far along that finding a positive solution is very difficult at best. For example, if terminating an employee is your first resort in ridding yourself of a problem, then you've more than likely let the problem fester for far too long, or didn't detect it early enough. Your job is to find solutions leading to positive outcomes, and that means you're going to have to tackle problems in stage one of their development and not in stage two, six, or fourteen. This highly aware and very aggressive posture affords you more options in your decision-making. The more room you have to maneuver in problem areas, the more circumspect and productive your ultimate decisions will be.

Employee Incompetence

Let's start with the most obvious workplace problems—obvious, but not always easy to solve. These are performance problems directly related to employee competence or motivation. The question you've got to ask yourself in these situations is whether or not you've made a mistake in evaluating the skill level of an underperforming employee or, perhaps, whether the performance deficit is rooted in a lack of motivation and commitment to the job.

If the performance problem rests in competence, then you are presented with two unmistakable choices. The first is further training of the employee, to raise his or her skill level to what is required to do the job. The second, if you determine that the employee is the wrong fit for what you need and not likely to pick up the necessary skills, is to bite the bullet and let the employee go. Teamwork in the workplace today is dependent on each and every employee understanding his or her individual job responsibilities and being highly competent in fulfilling them.

It is your assessment of the precise reasons for the poor performance that matters most. If you feel that this employee can be brought up to the productivity level that you need, then you've got to act fast and impart the necessary job-related skills to this underachiever. You could personally offer the employee a little extra of your own time and expertise. Or you could have a coworker take this underachieving employee under his or her wing for mini-mentoring. You could even find someone from another department in the organization to help out, or go outside for external coaching if need be.

Letting employees go (firing them, we might as well just say it) is the single most difficult act of a manager, and it's even more so for you, a coach, who keeps people and their unique talents and abilities foremost in your thoughts. But the productivity of employees cannot ever be glossed over if it is below the established bar. That's the bottom line. Hopefully your empathetic tendencies will make the parting of the ways as painless as possible under the unfortunate circumstances. A person's lack of key skills in one work environment doesn't preclude another environment proving a better fit, where the skills more appropriately complement the job that needs to be done.

Performance Dips

From bad performance we go to those mystifying performance dips. No, these aren't the things you plunge your potato chips into. They're what you see when employees show a noticeable slip in productivity. Your corrective coaching skills must spring into action when you discern that a formerly productive employee is no longer as productive as in the past, and it's your job to find out exactly why. Is there a personal problem behind the performance turnaround? Is it boredom with the job itself? Is the employee overworked and burned out? Having difficulty working with a new teammate, perhaps? Whatever the cause of the problem, it's your responsibility to uncover it and address it in a very timely fashion. Coaching, in stark contrast to the more traditional managerial approaches, is tailor-made for comprehending the reasons behind performance dips. By establishing and building relationships with employees on a one-on-one basis, you're in the unique position of genuinely knowing and understanding the people behind the performance problems. You have rounded profiles of all of your employees and substantive work histories to refer to and gather clues from.

Poor performance based on a lack of skills is one thing. And, as we've indicated, this problem can be dealt with in a straightforward manner, i.e., upgrade the skill level or not. Employees, however, who have proven that they can do the job, and do it well, present a much more complex dilemma for a coach when their performances regress. Dinosaur managers who encounter performance drops in their employees are inclined to address these problems in rather simplistic ways. Basically, the age-old ultimatum: Raise that productivity level or suffer the consequences. You know the score: demotion or termination. There's no serious attempt in this approach to understand why there are the performance problems in the first place; no serious attempt to get at the causes of these turnarounds. Meanwhile, back in Coachville, you reach into your skills' arsenal and pull out your always sharp communication tools. It's precisely in situations like performance dips that your listening skills (open-ended questioning, paraphrasing, mirroring feelings, and so on) play key parts in getting to the crux of what's wrong.

ESSENTIALS

A continuous and dynamic learning atmosphere in the workplace—which includes opportunity for advancement—is the key to staving off employee boredom. Boredom on the job inevitably leads to drop-offs in performance and the desire to look elsewhere for employment.

As a matter of fact, there are no better circumstances to employ open-ended questioning than when confronting slumping employees. There are no better times to mirror their feelings. These are not moments to come on strong and to bully. Common sense tells us that performance slips are not camouflaging happy times—on the job or off—except, perhaps, if an employee won $50 million in the lottery and is sticking around until the first check arrives. Proceeding on the assumption that the performance reversals of your employees are not lottery-induced, you must then attempt to unearth the reasons for the problems without leaving scars in the process. You don't want to put your employees on the defensive. Instead, you want to carefully engage them in dialogue, while bringing to the surface what's bothering them, and if it is connected with the performance decline.

Here are some examples of open-ended and probing questions that are appropriate in delicate situations like these:

- "Your performance has dropped off of late; you're missing your deadlines and coming up short in reaching your goals. Do you see where there's a problem? Are there any reasons that you can think of for this decline in your productivity?"
- "Do you feel comfortable working with your team? Are there any problems with any of your coworkers that you feel are impeding your own job in any way?"
- "Any ideas as to why your performance has been slipping these past couple of months? Are you unhappy with your work assignments or role?"

Again, you must be persistent but understanding. You also must be candid and encourage your employees to behave similarly by looking into themselves for the reasons why their performances are heading in the wrong directions.

In many instances, oversimplified as this may sound, coaches find that a thorough airing out of a problem puts things right again.

The Boredom Bomb

A dip in employee performance is sometimes the result of sheer boredom. Work that's all too familiar—not challenging anymore, intellectually unfulfilling, or not the least bit interesting—is a boredom bomb waiting to detonate. To ensure that your employees don't get bored, you must create a work environment that is conducive to learning. If it's anything else, employees will rightly feel that they are treading water by working for you. And it's then that boredom sets in. Boredom and declining productivity, the most dastardly of dance partners. What can you do to make certain that you coach in a continuous learning environment? For one, keep a watchful eye on your employees. Periodically evaluate whether or not each one of them is being sufficiently challenged in his or her individual job, and whether or not the employee is genuinely afforded opportunities to advance and grow in the organization.

Alas, because we don't live and work in a heaven on earth, we have to concede that even a coach's world doesn't always run strictly as planned. And employees feeling that they've been rendered immobile and stuck in inhibiting jobs are not quite so rare. Boredom on the job requires healthy doses of corrective coaching. If you believe you've got a bored employee on your hands who has shown potential and sports a solid knowledge and skill base, plus an insatiable desire to learn, then you need to act, and act fast. You've got to alter the circumstances of this employee's job responsibilities and role in a positive way before it's too late. A bored employee is an employee poised to fly away from your nest.

Failing to Delegate Responsibilities

Delegating important responsibilities is a big part of what coaches do. But it has got to mean more than delegating trivial tasks. Let's see, Janice made the coffee for the month of January. Dennis, I am confident that you can handle the month of February. Remember, though, that it's going to be a cold, snowy month, and coffee consumption's going to go up. So you've got to keep an eye on that pot all day long. But I think you are the right man for the job and I have every confidence in you.

This isn't what delegating is all about. True delegating requires showing confidence in your employees' real talents and abilities. It means giving them important jobs and increasing their overall roles. By doing this, you are entrusting your employees to perform not only for you, but for their teammates as well, not to mention the company's bottom line. Real delegating is a yawn buster. You can jumpstart your sagging employees by offering them significant job responsibilities. You can show confidence in your listless employees by putting them in roles that matter, not only to them but to so many other people as well. So, sit down with your deflated employees and pull out your finely attuned listening skills—again. Initiate a dialogue with probing, open-ended questions that get to the heart of exactly why your employees are bored and not performing as in the past.

It's important to keep in mind that "Bored with the job" is not a one-size-fits-all description with a one-size-fits-all solution. One employee's lackluster performance and discontent with the job may be quite different in nature from another's. And you should fully grasp these differences. It boils down to personalities and self-motivation again.

FACTS

Opinion polls suggest that more than 50 percent of workers name a "sense of accomplishment" as the chief ingredient they desire in a job, over and above even compensation. Coaching and mentoring aim to furnish employees with freedom, challenges, and opportunity for advancement, affording them—yes—a genuine sense of accomplishment.

You might assume, with all of our talk about coaching and mentoring as the people-approach to managing, that coaches, by nature, have to be sentimental softies who bow to their employees' every wish. Not true at all. The art of coaching and mentoring is not about being nice, per se. It's certainly not about being nasty. Instead, it's about getting the best results possible and understanding how best to get there. Major Frank Burns of the TV classic *M*A*S*H* once eloquently uttered how "it's nice to be nice to the nice." And it is. But "niceness" is not a business mantra. Business decisions are rooted in the dollars and cents reality of what's best for the company. So if your employees are out of bounds with their requests, you've got to set them straight and offer objective feedback on your honest assessment of their performances, overall talents and abilities, and immediate futures in the company. You must strive to be fair above all else, and that even includes being nice.

Coach Certification: Teaching Skills

If you're a coach, you're a teacher—you have to be. Okay, so you didn't necessarily get a degree in education or get certified by the state, but you are a teacher nonetheless. You've been entrusted with the job of managing people who produce results for you—or you're out of a job. So let's explore some of the specific skills that you might be asked to teach at some in time in your coaching tenure.

Technical Skills

This is the most intricate and diverse area of teaching that you'll be responsible for. Technical, job-related skills run the gamut from engineering to human resources, whatever the job requires. If you work in a financial area, the skills, obviously, will revolve around interpreting and processing numbers. If customer relations are what the job entails, then people skills are the most important skills required for the job. Whatever the necessary job skills, you've got to know your stuff inside and out and be eminently prepared to lead and to teach others.

ESSENTIALS Technical skills refer to the indispensable knowledge and very precise skills that are required to perform a particular job. You've got to make certain that these skills remain sharp and current, if you sincerely hope to maximize employee performance in today's ultracompetitive business environment.

Computer Skills

This is tied in with technical skills. Today's job reality is that there are very few white-collar jobs that don't use computers in some capacity. Computers are not luxuries anymore, but a necessity in conducting business. And regardless of what position an employee holds, use of computers, even if it's merely inputting data, is necessary more likely than not. As a coach, you're responsible for making certain that all your employees are not only computer literate, but also competent in exactly the computer applications you need. This could mean lessons in word processing, data entry, graphics, and so on.

Reading and Writing Skills

Bet you never thought that you'd have to concern yourself with teaching reading and writing in a corporate setting. Well, surprise, you do. Courtesy of a sometimes wanting educational system, many students wind their way through higher education without mastering some of the most rudimentary reading and writing skills. If you have any doubt about this, check out some of the financial discussion boards on the Web. Presumably, most of these investors are college graduates. Just read some of their posts. It's downright frightening.

Teaching new skills to your employees should always be done incrementally. Crash courses usually don't work. It's like cramming for an exam the night before. Retention is limited. Paced learning is required to master a skill. Step A must be fully absorbed before moving on to Step B.

In the business world, written communication is a must. There are constant memos bandied back and forth and lots of reports that have to be written. Because communication is one of the pillars of coaching and mentoring, you cannot ignore this aspect of the job. An employee of yours who cannot read and write at the level of an adult in the business world will be unable to communicate with the clarity necessary to perform at a peak level. And—we've said it before—so much of business today is teamwork. And this makes each individual's performance, or lack thereof, all the more important to so many others.

Behavior Skills

You've no doubt heard the tales of infants being raised by wolves and growing up to behave like wolves and not human beings. And so it is with many people in today's workforce who were, in effect, raised by MTV, Jerry Springer, and crude sitcoms. Couple all that with minimum educational standards and you've got men and women in the workplace who, in some instances, do not know how to behave. They lack even the most basic skills to deal with coworkers and customers in a professional manner. (Check out Chapter 10 for a full discussion on what constitutes professionalism in the workplace.)

ALERT

Teaching soft skills is often more difficult than imparting hard skills, such as computer applications and the like. Teaching employees utterly lacking in people skills how to behave in a professional manner on the job is one of a coach's greatest challenges.

Setting the Tone

You garner respect and acquire the trust of your staff, not by flaunting an authoritative title and throwing your weight around, but by earning it with your words and deeds. You must always be approachable and frank, delegate responsibilities to the responsible, and listen to and hear your employees' concerns. You've got to be consistent in your methods and—above all else—competent at your own job. All of this amounts to positive tone setting by you at the managerial level, which filters on down to all of your staff members and makes coaching—high-octane, corrective, and so on—successful.

QUESTIONS?

Why is tone setting so important in the office?
All managers set the tone of their office and lead by example. If the example is a poor and unprofessional one, the workplace reflects that. Coaches must set a positive tone with respect and trust at the forefront of a continuous learning environment.

CHAPTER 8

The Power of Positive Thinking

I n 1952, Norman Vincent Peale wrote a best-selling book, entitled *The Power of Positive Thinking*. A half-century has passed, but the message is the same. As a result, this chapter looks at coaching and mentoring and their accent on positive outcomes: welcoming greater challenges, solving problems, and maximizing employee productivity.

Judgment: Good and Bad

It's par for the course nowadays to be rebuked with such sweeping assertions as, "You're too judgmental" or "You have no right to judge people." Is that so? Well, actually, you have every right to judge people based on their attitudes and behaviors. Civil society rests on just those kinds of judgments, and so does the business world. Like so many things in today's society, this rigid nonjudgmental chorus has been taken to a ridiculous extreme. It is sophistry at its pinnacle. That is, nonjudgment often acts as cover for low standards and corruption. And that's a shame, because there is great merit in a nonjudgmental tone and nonjudgmental posture in managing people. Judgment, really, is like cholesterol. There is a good brand of judgment and there is a bad brand of judgment.

Good Judgment

The good brand of judgment is a a vital part of our everyday living. We make judgments all the time—we have to. Judgment and rules are society. Judgment and rules are business. We choose our friends, whom our kids should play with, where to send them to school, whether or not to give money to a particular charity, whose phone calls to ignore, whom to leave our money to when we shuffle off this mortal coil, and the list goes on and on. And there are all sorts of reasons for making these kinds of decisions that require—dare we say it—judgments on all of our parts. And some of them are quite personal.

ESSENTIALS

As a coach, you need to be judgmental in situations that call for it. You must, however, know the differences between the good brand of judgment and the bad brand of judgment.

As a coach, you cannot be stripped of your ability to judge. When you preside over a staff of diverse people and personalities, decisions are made all the time that demand real judgment on your part. This is, in essence, the glue that binds the office together and makes the managerial support arrangement work effectively. Of course, it's wise judgment that you must demonstrate—and that's the good brand of judgment. We'll differentiate between the good brand and the bad brand in a moment. For now, you can heave a sigh of relief. You can freely welcome the fact that you not only can judge, but also must judge on many occasions. It may initially surprise some of your friends, but they'll understand it all when you explain the differences between the good and the bad brands of judgment.

Bad Judgment

Why don't we tackle the bad news—that is, the bad brand of judgment—first, while looking at the coach's critical role in sometimes playing both judge and jury. As a solutions-driven, results-oriented coach, you must aim to find solutions and achieve positive outcomes to any and all problems that come your way. We've made that abundantly clear.

Searching for negative outcomes to problems would certainly make you unique in the annals of coaching and mentoring, but you'd soon be savoring that singular distinction on an unemployment line. You are in place to solve problems and overcome obstacles, from performance problems to interpersonal conflicts to, yes, even poor employee hygiene. And the reality is that you don't achieve positive outcomes by managing with the disposition and manner of Judge Judy. You don't say to an underperforming employee: "Boy, you are really stinking up this office! What the heck is wrong with you? Do you have half a brain?"

Now that's rather judgmental and a stark example of the bad brand of judgment in action. If you go down this route in your problem-solving efforts, you aren't about to realize positive outcomes. You don't solve the problem of underperforming employees by branding them as "nincompoops." If your goal is to chase employees away (by hurling invective at them until they quit), then you are not worthy of being a coach. Turn in your credentials this instant!

Using Judgment in Your Coaching

Because you are a coach in good standing, you must utilize the tools and techniques (listening, probing with open-ended questions, constructive feedback, and so on) outlined in Chapter 6. You must establish healthy dialogues with your underperforming employees that sharply focus on finding solutions (positive outcomes) to poor performances. Instead of delivering judgmental broadsides (such as "Boy, you are really stinking up the place"), you lay the groundwork for civil, productive dialogues with your employees. You make it clear to them that you're seeking to correct their performance problems, and that you're not there to pass judgment in any way on their personalities, but to make things right on the job, which is, of course, your job. "Can you think of any ways to get your project back on track? Are there any changes that you feel can be implemented to put you back on schedule?"

Your job as a coach is to effect positive outcomes in all areas of your managing. You accomplish this by looking at every problem in the office—big or small—as having an optimum solution. Thus, you address every problem from the angle of its best possible solution.

Remember, also, in your positive outcome posture, never to allow discussions with employees to turn into debates. Leave the debating for the forensic club in high school, or aspiring politicians promising their way into office. Coaches don't debate their employees. And, really, there's no quicker way to snuff out positive outcomes to problems than by engaging employees in contentious disputes. Civilized dialogues are the best breeding grounds for real solutions to tough, even seemingly intractable problems. And very often, this give-and-take, free-flowing exchange of ideas leads to employees owning up to their mistakes or performance slips. And not only that, but finding their very own solutions to correcting their work-related problems.

The coaching and mentoring methodology seeks to mold employees who can think for themselves and take initiative, and this encompasses an ability to solve problems on their own, even righting their own wrongs and seeing where they've messed up, or why they are not performing as in the past. Positive outcomes are more often the result of employees figuring out how to rectify their own problems, than of a coach dictating solutions to them. Dictated solutions to problems are often received with resentment. And resentment doesn't inspire self-motivation, nor enhance job satisfaction.

Keeping Negative Feedback Positive

Has it fully sunk in yet? You have to walk on the positive side of the street when coaching your employees. But wait just a minute, what about this thing known as negative feedback? It's discussed in Chapter 6, and it's an important part of a coach's job to dispense it when appropriate. You are no doubt thinking, how does negative feedback jibe with all of this power of positive thinking stuff we are championing?

First, let's refresh our memories a bit and recall that negative feedback lies under the beach-sized umbrella of constructive feedback, which means its aim is just that—to be constructive and advance a positive outcome. It's not meant as criticism. It's not personal in nature. It's not intended to be judgmental in the negative sense.

ESSENTIALS

Part of your job as a coach is to offer constructive feedback—positive or negative—as warranted. You must also make it clear to your employees that negative feedback is dispensed with the purpose of achieving positive results, i.e., helping them correct their negative behaviors, and not as personal attacks.

Negative feedback has to be parceled out to an employee if he or she exhibits a performance or behavioral problem. When things go wrong at the office, you're not expected to ignore this reality in the interest of somehow being positive. There's nothing positive about ignoring problems and hoping they go away. Things don't work out like that in real life. Dealing with problems fast and firmly—even if it means dispensing negative feedback—is positive, because the end game is to uncover the best possible solutions in solving them.

Yeah, right! Tell that to employees who are the recipients of negative feedback! Not everybody takes negative feedback in the spirit in which it is intended. Some employees feel that the negative feedback given to them is—well—negative. And they don't see it as delivered with their best interests at heart. So, guess what your job is in these circumstances? Convincing your skeptical employees that you're not being critical of them, but merely seeking solutions to problems (yours and theirs), of course.

Working with Employees Who Have a Tough Time with Feedback

A coach's life is never dull. Employees now and then are going to take things personally, even if your feedback is calculated to help them in the Abraham Lincoln tradition of "with malice toward none—with charity for all." Accept this as part of the reality of dealing with so many temperamentally unique employees. Some people are very sensitive souls and are prone to be defensive. Hence, they may have a tough time with any kind of negative feedback. But you have no choice but to work with these personalities. They can't be avoided, nor can they be treated just like everybody else. That said, you've got to treat sensitive and defensive employees with extra special care. We're not talking about TLC or anything so syrupy. We're talking about you understanding that individual personalities react to your coaching methods in distinctive ways. The advantage of being a coach, in contrast to the more traditional manager, is your adaptability to a variety of situations and a variety of temperaments.

With employees who are hypersensitive and apt to be on the defensive, it's imperative you practice sensitivity plus with them when problems arise. That is, make a very concerted effort to modulate your tone and overall presentation, and make them anger and personal judgment free.

The important first step in this adaptability mode requires that you accept that not everybody in your employ will fully appreciate what you're trying to accomplish in your role as a coach. It's just the nature of the beast—insecurity lives on Main Street and on Wall Street. Okay, you accept that negative feedback given to Ellen impacts her in a positive way, which is what you want. But the same negative feedback given to Chuck impacts him in a decidedly negative way, which is what you don't want. When your employees accept your feedback, run with it, and make the necessary adjustments in performance or behavior to improve themselves, you've achieved your objective. On the other hand, if your employees receive the feedback and react defensively and angrily, this is liable to lead to negative outcomes to an already negative situation. And this compounding of the negative with a negative is unacceptable to a coach.

Tweaking Your Negative Feedback

Is there an alternative to giving negative feedback? The answer is yes and no. No, negative feedback is an important part of coaching. But yes, there's a way to tweak negative feedback a bit to make it more palatable to the sensitive sorts in your employ. Get out your communication tool kit and add sensitivity plus to your already sensitive managerial methods.

Sensitivity Plus

Sensitivity and mirroring your employees' feelings is something we've previously touched upon. You employ this perceptive approach in all your coaching encounters with your employees. It is an important technique that cements a bond between you and the members of your team. Courtesy of your sensitivity antennae, you learn to decipher who among your employees require this extra special treatment—this sensitivity plus. You learn to separate the thin skins from the thick skins who work for you. Sensitivity plus, for the thin-skinned, entails you being thoroughly cognizant of your tone and overall manner of presentation when you sit down with a sensitive employee to discuss a problem. For starters, always keep in mind that you are functioning in a business environment— sensitivity plus or not. Negative feedback, when justified, must be passed on to its deserving recipients—or undeserving, as the case may be. But even negative feedback can be expressed in a variety of ways.

Keep Anger Out of the Picture

Foremost, anger must never be permitted to rule the roost in a dialogue between you and a member of your staff. Even when you're trying to keep it at bay, sometimes anger works its way in there. Okay, it happens.

Stay Matter-of-Fact

However, with the ultrasensitive types on your team, you've got to be on special guard to stay even-tempered and matter-of-fact in your presentation at all times. This exacting control is an important personality technique of coaching. That is, coaches must maintain complete control of themselves (from their choice of words to tone of voice) when dealing with certain personalities, or they risk negative reactions to their negative feedback, which inevitably leads to negative outcomes. (Negative plus negative equals a negative.) Exacting control also asks that you be on guard to leave the bad brand of judgment (personality-related opinions) out of your feedback. Defensive personalities often react to perceived negative judgments—even if strictly related to their job performances—as personal attacks. It is essential that you deal straightforwardly with these personalities.

FACTS

Coaching and mentoring, from top to bottom, asks both managers and employees alike to be solution-oriented at all times. Concentrating on finding solutions to problems, instead of affixing blame on people, fosters collaborative efforts that lead to creativity and positive outcomes.

Don't Butter Up

Conversely, avoid the buttering-up, soft pose in dealing with these same employees. This is a common mistake managers make all the time. Employees who are hypersensitive to any kind of negative feedback are also highly sensitive to diversionary tactics. So any hesitancy in delivering your punch only compounds an already awkward situation with more apprehension as the result. Needless to say, a sensitive and defensive employee does not thrive in an extremely apprehensive environment! Who does?

Yes, you need to mollycoddle these touchy employees and accept their quirks of temperament. If you hope to find lasting positive solutions to their problems on the job, you've got to impart negative feedback in a manner they can easily digest. So serve your feedback to them as if it were pabulum. You don't want any of your employees becoming angry, pulling back, and ultimately shutting down completely, when you need them most to do just the opposite.

Don't Avoid the Inevitable

All that said, you must never avoid dispensing negative feedback to employees who have earned it. Some managers love traveling down the path of least resistance. That is, they avoid confronting particular employees with negative feedback for fear of their predictably hostile reactions. All employees, regardless of their personalities, have to produce results and be held solely accountable for their performances, attitudes, and behaviors. And when employees are not performing up to speed, they have to be informed of it. When the appraisal is negative, employees have to be able to accept it and make every effort to turn the negative around into a positive.

It's your responsibility as a coach to communicate with all of your employees, and this entails dispensing with good as well as bad tidings. Thus, you've got to work your magic in delivering your message—be it positive feedback or negative feedback—to each individual, sensitive and defensive personality or not. Adaptability in your methods—yes. Capitulation—never!

Giving Regular Feedback

You want all your employees to fully understand that feedback is a technique you will wield, and wield very frequently at that. You want your employees to be comfortable receiving it, and to expect it as a matter of course. When your employees anticipate feedback as the rule, and not the exception, they are less likely to be intimidated by it, and more apt to see it as a beneficial summary of exactly how they are performing at their jobs.

Nobody likes operating in the dark. Even when things are running smoothly, employees should be acknowledged. Positive feedback is a recognition tool that is just as important to dispense when things are going well, as is negative feedback when things aren't running as planned. Don't overlook the most productive people on your staff. There's a tendency sometimes to take for granted the biggest achievers on your team, simply because they do their jobs and do them well. Sure, it is tempting to say to yourself: "Why should I worry about Lisa? She runs ahead of schedule on all her projects, and the quality checks always check out. She never utters a negative word or a complaint. If she's got a problem, she'll find her own solution. So I'll concentrate my time and efforts on Fred, who doesn't always seem to be too sure of himself and rarely meets his goals."

ESSENTIALS

When you must deliver negative feedback to employees, look at the overall picture of their performances and readily acknowledge the positive aspects as well as the negative aspects of them. This enables your employees to view the negative feedback as opportunities for improvement.

Yes, Fred does indeed need to be watched more closely and consulted with more frequently than Lisa (high-octane coaching in action). But this doesn't mean you cut Lisa out of the feedback loop just because she's doing her job with such alacrity and aplomb. Positive performances need to be recognized and rewarded. There are a lot of Lisa types who move on in jobs, not only to greener pastures, but also to pastures where the feedback is more generous and enriching. These are the people, remember, who are the coaches of tomorrow, the ones being groomed for greater responsibilities and bigger challenges. These are the people whom you want to keep in the organization.

A Positive-Thinking Case Study

Here's a real case study from the coaching files. It deals with an employee who exhibited a serious behavioral problem that negatively impacted an entire team.

His name was Larry, a highly competent computer systems analyst, as good as they come. Whenever a technical problem arose in programming or working with the newest software, Larry was the man who had the answers. And he was willing to help anyone at any time, even if his bluff manner was sometimes supercilious. Chuck, the manager and coach, appreciated Larry for his abilities and didn't much think about Larry's personality excesses. Specifically, Larry's problem was that he liked his female coworkers. Maybe "like" isn't the right word. Rather, he occasionally made inappropriate comments and leered their way.

QUESTIONS?

What will foster employee participation in problem-solving? Encourage your employees to do it for you. That is, allow your employees to determine corrective actions for their own behavioral problems or poor performances. By creating an atmosphere of healthy dialogues and regular feedback, you nourish self-sufficiency in your people.

Melissa, a coworker, found working closely with Larry very uncomfortable. And there was no avoiding him, because her job required that she be in constant contact with him. She actually admired Larry's skills at tackling difficult problems and squashing all those awful job-related bugs. But even though she learned a lot about the job from Larry, which she knew would benefit her immensely down the road, she could not ignore the fact that he crossed the line with his unprofessional behavior.

Fed up one day, Melissa decided to go to her coach, Chuck, and tell him all about Larry's unbefitting side. She was hesitant at first, knowing that Chuck was a big booster of Larry and his technical expertise. Nevertheless, it had to be done. She remembered Chuck's initial orientation to her about the importance of communication between the employee and the coach. Chuck had advised her on day one to come to him with any problems or concerns that she might have, and that he would do his best to help her find the proper solutions to improve the situation. So she told Chuck all, not holding back the fact that other female members of the staff didn't appreciate these same aspects of Larry's personality, either. She told Chuck that while she admired Larry's competence in doing his job and his willingness to help others, she nevertheless couldn't tolerate any more of his shenanigans.

ESSENTIALS

A coach should maintain a policy of dispensing regular and consistent constructive feedback, so that employees come to expect it as a rule. This above-board approach to managing, of keeping employees apprised of their performances, makes for a healthier workplace with fewer misunderstandings.

Chuck listened like a good coach should, asked questions, and promised immediate action. And true to coaching methods, Chuck called Larry into his office the following day. He gave great thought to what he was going to say to him and how he was going to say it. When Larry sat down before him, Chuck informed him that a serious problem had been brought to his attention. He proceeded to tell Larry of the complaint lodged against him. He intermingled his negative feedback—about the unacceptability of Larry's behavior—with positive feedback on his consistently solid performance in his job. Chuck told Larry, "Your knowledge and skills are an asset to the company. You wouldn't want to see your future impeded by behavior unbecoming a man of your talents." Larry was quite surprised at what he was told. Like so many people with such behavioral excesses, they often don't get it. They don't see their antics as in any way a problem, and they can't understand why anybody would be offended. So Chuck had the additional burden of communicating to his employee not only the problem itself, but also why it was a problem in the first place.

Finally, with persistence and tact, Chuck got his point across with the help of the sensitivity-plus approach. He allowed Larry his ample say in response, and ultimately the two reached solutions to a positive outcome. Larry agreed to be strictly business from that moment forward. He also set out to apologize to all the injured parties. His ideas, too! He told Chuck that his job was extremely important to him, and that he didn't want to hinder, in any way, his rising up in the organization. Chuck then offered to give Larry follow-up feedback in the ensuing weeks. Melissa also agreed to wipe the slate clean, and graciously accepted Larry's apology and promise to rectify his behavior.

This was a positive outcome to a very difficult, negative situation. Performance-related problems are usually clearer cut than are these dicey interpersonal situations. Now, if Larry's apology subsequently proved insincere, Chuck would have another problem to confront, and his search for a positive outcome would inevitably lead him to very different solutions the second time around.

CHAPTER 9

Communicating Vision and Goals

The most successful business enterprises know exactly where they want to go and how they're going to get there. In other words, they visualize their futures. This chapter highlights the importance of visions and goals set for the companies themselves, their coaches, and the many people who work for them, showing how coaching and mentoring in management smoothly facilitate projecting into the future.

The Role of Coaches in Vision and Goals

The coaching and mentoring managerial philosophy is the ideal fit for forward-looking companies with a vision. All the tools and techniques described in the first eight chapters of this book are future-oriented. From performance planning to problem solving to trust building, the emphasis of coaching and mentoring is on doing the job today with an eye on tomorrow. Simply put, coaching and mentoring in management aim to make today's workplace a better place. But part of making a better today requires thinking about tomorrow's productivity, too. Coaching and mentoring comprise a results-oriented managerial methodology that views every business situation and every personality through a prism of positive light and forward movement. This is why it's the right style of leadership for the unique demands of running a business in the twenty-first century. Demands, by the way, that require wisdom and keen foresight for businesses to thrive and indeed survive over the long haul.

FACTS

Your mini-vision of the future of the company as it pertains to both you and your employees is more important than the company's mission statement. This is because you, as coach and mentor, translate your company's broad, long-range goals into meaningful individual goals your employees can achieve today.

The duty of senior leaders in any company is, among other things, to articulate a vision for the entire organization. But it's your job as a coach and manager of a particular niche in a company, to take that grander vision and transpose it into a mini-vision of your own to guide all of your coaching decisions. A big company can espouse a lofty vision with noble, aggressive goals for its future. But, realistically, to the average employee in such an organization, a vision from up high doesn't amount to a hill of beans. The lower-echelon employees in a company are far too removed from the big picture to get overly excited about it. This is precisely why the vision you articulate and apply as a coach has a whole lot more influence on your employees than the company's glowing, but rather general, goals for tomorrow and the tomorrow after that.

Vision Quest

An organization's vision often stretches out over years—ten and twenty years in the future are not unusual, and sometimes even longer than that. And that's fine and dandy for a company's long-range hopes and aspirations, but it's far too futuristic for the job you have to do. Neither you nor your employees are thinking much about the company in the year 2020. All of you, however, are thinking about what you've got to accomplish in your current jobs today. What this amounts to is that you—as a coach and leader—have to worry, first and foremost, about the immediate future. You need to persuade your employees that what they do right now, and over the next six months to a year, is material to both their present job situations and their long-term job futures, too. The coaching and mentoring mind-set always links today's job with tomorrow's job.

You're actually charting many futures in your role as a coach—your own, your employees', and the company's to some extent. This is why you must keep your coaching objectives sharp and measurable. What do you have to accomplish? What would you like to accomplish? What kinds of employees do you have on your team to get the job done? How will you utilize them to maximize their talents and abilities? How will you deal with their different personalities on an individual basis?

ESSENTIALS

Goal setting is an important tenet of coaching methods. Not only do employees need to work with goals, but you, as a coach, also need to be guided by them. Goals must always be realistic and reachable. Aggressive and bold, yes, but always attainable.

Spread out your objectives over a six-month to a year time frame—and no longer than that. After that period of time, start the process over again with new objectives, equally sharp and equally measurable. Throughout this vision process, make sure your employees understand that the building blocks for their long-term careers are formed in their present jobs, working for you.

Goals Provide Direction

In order for any company's vision to unfold as planned over a period of years and decades, people like you—in coaching positions throughout organizations—have to see your own mini-visions through. Your vision is, of course, derivative of the company's way of doing things. It has to be. You can't entertain a competing vision with the company that employs you. You need to connect with your company's vision by establishing goals for yourself. You then set out with your employees to mutually establish their various goals on a person-to-person basis.

ALERT

Constant innovation is indispensable for companies that want to succeed. And that includes employee innovation at all levels of the company. Coaching and mentoring invite employee innovation by both respecting employees and challenging them to find ways to do their jobs better and more efficiently.

This notion of goal setting sounds a lot simpler than it actually is. You don't just sit around and, off the top of your head, blurt out a goal. Goals are serious business if you want them to be taken seriously. The office isn't like the third grade, when Mrs. Victory asked you what you wanted to be when you grew up. Your goal may be to fly around the world in a hot air balloon. That's nice. But the reality is that most people won't likely take your flighty goal very seriously.

Goals Are Realistic

Your goals—and the goals of your employees—should be realistic and attainable. If you espouse goals that are out of touch with reality, you'll promptly destroy your capacity to lead, and will probably be standing on an unemployment line in short order. In our discussion of employee performance plans in Chapter 3, we mentioned the job-specific goals that are the key starting points of all the plans. These goals essentially summarize what each employee is expected to achieve (via action plans) within an agreed-upon time frame.

Individual Goals Tie In to Company Goals

But goal setting in the workplace transcends employee performance plans. Setting goals in all areas of a company is indispensable in today's business climate. Goals are direction, and when realized, make the whole organization better in some fundamental and measurable way, not to mention the individuals who reached them.

Goals Come in All Shapes and Sizes

We've talked at length about performance goals and monetary goals, the quintessence of business. But there are goals that revolve around attitudes and behaviors on the job; goals that focus on overall job satisfaction; goals that center on the growth of new skills. And the list of goal possibilities is endless.

Career Development: Tomorrow Takes Shape Today

As a coach, you care about your employees. This personal touch is what most distinguishes you from your dinosaur manager counterparts. You care about your employees' futures. In fact, this is one area where you have no choice.

Caring about Your Employees' Career Development

You must concern yourself with your employees' career development because of the very nature of today's job market. That is, you must preside over an enriching job environment, where your employees can grow their skills and not fall behind the times, or you're going to lose them to competitors. If you box in your employees, and cut off all learning opportunities, many of them will leave your employ. It's that simple! This is another reason why goal setting is so important. Employees' goals are in essence their growth and development potentials verbalized.

Expect Bold Goals

When you set goals for yourself, you anticipate being more adept at something when the goals are achieved. Think it through. If, for example, one of your goals is to see your entire department increase total sales by twenty percent in a six-month period—over and above the previous year's same time period—and you achieve that goal, you are a highly prized managerial commodity. By reaching your bold—but obtainable—goal, you've positively altered your future. You've immediately afforded yourself more choices in where you can venture next in your career.

FACTS

Remember that career development is a personal journey, unique to individuals. It's not your job to make career decisions for others. A coach's job is to cultivate and maintain a learning environment.

As for goal setting with your staff, the same sound reasoning applies. Your employees are thinking about their careers—their futures—and not yours. Don't feel too bad about this! Just work closely in assisting them in setting their uniquely personal goals. Be cognizant at all times of how their present on-the-job goals impact their futures. By making this important long-range connection with your employees, you bond with them like crazy glue, and they in turn work their arms and legs off for you.

Let Your Employees Structure Their Goals

Both you and your employees should always view goals in the larger context of what all of you will have gained when they're met. This is precisely why your employees' job-related goals must be made with your employees and not for your employees. When your staff members are largely responsible for setting their own goals, they more fully understand what the goals mean for them now and for their individual futures. You know what's best for your own career development. But it would be presumptuous of you to assume that you know what's best for any one of your employees' careers. Remember that coaching is a support system first and foremost. Support doesn't mean dictating jobs, goals, or career moves.

Career development is a very personal thing. And your job as a coach is to assist your people by providing them with all that we've talked about in this chapter and in previous chapters—a vibrant work atmosphere with opportunities for growth and development in jobs. If you do all that, you've done your job, and nobody could ask for anything more.

Advising Employees in Their Careers

Here is some key career-development advice you should drive home to your employees. It's based on the experiences of successful men and women in business, their many lessons learned, and an overall understanding of the way things work.

Establish Credentials

No matter what kind of work you do, keep on doing it, and doing it well. A successful track record of accomplishments gives you the vaunted credentials that so many jobs demand. Whether you want to write a book on botany, or hope to manage an office staff of sixty people, you're going to be asked, "What are your credentials?" If you've majored in accounting in college, and worked as an investment banker, and have nothing else on your resume, you're probably not the best-qualified person to write a book on botany. Similarly, if your job history is that of a night watchman at a milk bottling plant, you're not the best candidate for managing an office full of people in the light of day. So always give it your best in Job A, for it will help you get Job B. And Job C will be largely based on Jobs A and B. That's the way it usually works. A solid job track record means solid job credentials. And with solid job credentials, you can write your own career ticket.

Strengthen Strengths

Coaching and mentoring deem individuals to be unique beings with special talents and abilities all their own. They labor valiantly to maximize individual performance by carefully tending to people, and understanding them, on a one-on-one basis. And as one of those unique individuals, it is important in your own career development to attend to your particular interests and strengths, and maximize yourself as a complete person and prized worker commodity. You know best what you excel in and what you most enjoy doing. These are the areas you should concentrate on and rely on to fulfill your career ambitions. There's nothing more deflating than individuals in careers that bring them little joy, even when the money fields are green. Develop your special talents to the fullest. Strengthen your strengths and know your weaknesses. Don't end up a square peg in a round hole job.

FACTS

Career development is something coaching and mentoring management practices are cognizant of at all times. Both you, as the coach, and your employees are in an environment where achieving on-the-job goals places you all on higher planes as worker commodities with more positive options in your career paths.

Grow

Look for a variety of tasks and projects in which to showcase your aptitudes. View a host of experiences as career enhancers, adding versatility and adaptability to whatever are your job-specific talents and skills.

Be a People Person

Don't ever look upon your coworkers as if they are invisible, or worse, as obstacles in your career path. The most successful businesspersons are the ones who work alongside people and produce results in harmonious team settings. These successful men and women view their peers as extraordinary individuals—each with something to teach them. And they know that someday, one of these people may be in a position to help— perhaps in getting a job or supplying the name of somebody who can provide an important lead. The bottom line is: Establish amicable, professional relationships throughout your whole working career. Do this and you'll have plenty of useful contacts to tap into as your career unfolds and takes those inevitable twists and turns. It helps to know people. People, that is, who both know you and respect you.

Instilling a Sense of Destiny

A crucial role of a coach is to instill in workers a sense of destiny. If you manage with the realistic goals we've talked about, for both you and your employees, and you all achieve them, you are on to something very special. If you set realistic goals and your employees achieve them, the success your employees enjoy will convince them, like nothing else, that they're the prime movers in charting their career courses. By seeing goals through, employees are better for having set out to do big things, succeeded in doing them, and emerged from the whole goal-setting process more valuable worker commodities and better human beings, with greater knowledge, skills, and self-esteem.

Conduct a Reality Check

All of this focus on the importance of goals in the workplace sometimes confuses people unfamiliar with the purposes of coaching and mentoring in business. They think that coaching gives rise to a workplace more on the entertainment side of things than the work side. These misguided souls envision the work climate under the leadership of a coach as something akin to visiting a theme park with cotton candy melting in their mouths and big red balloons in their hands. It's time to burst those balloons.

ALERT

Please your staff and the company that pays your salary, and you've accomplished what you were hired to do.

Coaching and mentoring have nothing to do with employees having a grand old time, nor are they about satisfying workers' illusions of grandeur. They're nothing if not firmly planted in reality—the reality of what people can do, and what makes them want to do it and do it well.

It's absolutely necessary that you always keep your employees rooted in the possible, because impractical goals are more than just pointless; they are disruptive in a business setting and harmful to job satisfaction and the overall bottom line of the company. On a one-by-one basis, you've got to assess what each member of your team is capable of, and in what time parameters he or she can produce the results you need.

Know Your Employees

The key tenet of coaching and mentoring is the importance of getting to know your employees. The reason for this is not to become best friends with them, but to correctly identify their real talents and abilities—their job skills, be they technical, interpersonal, leadership qualities, and so on.

> **ALERT**
>
> When you know your people inside and out, know exactly what their specific jobs are and how they are performing in them, you are best prepared to stave off debilitating disruptions in performance and maximize positive results.

It's one thing to know that your employee Albert just became a father for the first time, but it's far more important to know what Albert can do as an employee of the company.

Help Employees Become Self-Aware

Some people, let's face facts, are not self-aware, and very often they have perceptions of their talents and abilities that don't jibe with reality. It's often the case that these folks believe they can do things that they plainly cannot. And vice versa. Some men and women are capable of doing many things that they don't think they can do.

We know all too well from our experiences with people that perceptions and reality are not always one and the same. An important part of your job is to make perceptions equal reality in the office. You can't have it any other way in a business setting. You can't allow employees to lead important projects just because they want to do it. There must be compelling evidence that they are qualified and up to the jobs. If you, and/or members of your team, don't feel that these ambitious employees are ready for such key jobs, then you know what you have to do. Just say "no." Yes, a coach has got to say "no" on occasion. When perceptions do not measure up to reality, this is one such time. This doesn't ever mean that you condemn employees to their current level of skills or jobs. Not at all. Among your many roles as a coach, you are a matchmaker, too. But it's compatible jobs, not soul mates, that you are finding for your employees. Come to think of it, the right job is a soul mate of sorts.

FACTS

Often you will be confronted with employees who have perceptions of their talents and abilities that don't agree with reality. An important part of your coaching job is to put people in jobs they can do, not just think they can do.

Match Employees' Goals with Their Skills

So much of coaching involves evaluating employee abilities and matching those abilities with specific jobs and roles. Mismatching employees' abilities with their jobs—not uncommon in the business realm, sad to say—leads to lackluster performance, overall disarray, and widespread dissension. You're not in a coaching position to perform as the blue fairy granting your employees' every wish and satisfying their every desire. You're expected to put the right people in the right jobs and to inspire them to a commitment to perform at their highest levels. If your employees are overrating or underrating themselves, it's your job to set them straight. People with strong people skills should be in jobs where people skills count most. People with top-notch skills in financial management should be showcasing their skills in this area. And so on and so forth.

A Coach's Performance Plan

Now is the time to organize all of your coaching efforts. Chapter 3 laid out the key elements of performance planning and discussed how each employee works closely within such plans. However, we bypassed mention of a coach's own performance plans. Yes, you heard it right. A coach's performance plans! These are not formal contracts, as are employees' performance plans. It is, nevertheless, essential for your own edification to work with several performance plans of your own.

ESSENTIALS

The coach sits atop a coaching triangle with communication and coordination at its two bottom angles. Regular and consistent communication leads to solid coordination of jobs, which in turn ensures positive outcomes.

Your acute supervisory role in the office makes it imperative that you be a model of probity and consistency throughout all of your coaching actions. That is, design your own performance plans based on the coaching standard known as principled coherence. Principled coherence merely asks that you do exactly what you tell your employees you are going to do, and when you tell them you are going to do it. For example, the safety checks inserted into your employees' performance plans are put there for sound business reasons. If you neglect follow-up evaluations on the progression of these plans, you will fast lose your credibility as a coach. Similarly, when your employees set goals of any kind, you've got to always be aware of what they are, and whether or not they're on course to meet them. Your own performance plans must thus record when any employee evaluations are to take place and what measures you'll be using in doing the evaluating. Don't expect your employees to come to you and say, "It's time for my evaluation!" It doesn't work that way.

CHAPTER 10

Measuring Your Coaching Effectiveness

There comes a time in your life as a coach when you need to take a thorough inventory of all your coaching and mentoring efforts. To do that, determine whether your distinctive coaching and mentoring style is consistent and coherent in getting the positive outcomes that you need as a manager in a highly competitive, results-oriented business setting.

Evaluating Your Coaching Success

Coaching, unlike the more traditional managerial methods, anticipates and welcomes adjustments in managerial thinking. It's a very resilient style of managing. Coaching is prepared to make changes at a moment's notice. This is precisely why thorough, but not smothering, supervision of your employees' overall performances is so vital. Coaching facilitates smooth changes and shifts in planning, based on these regular evaluations, without upsetting the office apple cart. You know that goals, performance planning, and checkpoint measures play critical roles in coaching. Regularly taking stock of your successes and failures as a coach is equally essential. Ascertaining whether your coaching efforts are at the level they should be will help you maximize your performance, which in turn maximizes your employees' performances.

ESSENTIALS

You want to regularly evaluate not only your employees' performances, but also your own. Taking stock of the effectiveness of your coaching is something you should do on a frequent basis if you desire keeping your managerial tools and techniques sharp and employee performances maximized.

Examining Your Coaching Style

Coaching manages and works with employees on an individual and very intimate basis. It stands to reason, then, that your coaching style will be quite distinct from the style of another coach working in a completely different setting, with a totally unique bunch of personalities. Coaches are people, too. You are a peerless individual who will interpret the many tools and techniques of coaching in a way distinct to your personality. Coaching formulas are pliable and open to some interpretation, because coaching is always a work in progress.

Chapter 9 considers the problem of perceptions versus reality and how you must recognize the differences between the two with regard to your employees' talents and abilities. But before you can make any of these critical judgments about your employees, you have to first make absolutely certain that you're on solid ground yourself. That is, you have to know how your coaching style is playing with your employees. You have to know how your staff perceives your leadership. You have to know if you really are getting the most out of their performances, while simultaneously crafting a satisfying and healthy work environment conducive to maximum productivity.

Looking for Clues

But how exactly do you know whether you're maximizing your own job performance? There are many signs that will tell you whether or not your decision-making is leading to maximum employee performance and the positive outcomes that are the foundations of successful coaching. Let's say, for example, that you go out on a limb and tap high-performing employee Kelly as an ideal candidate for mentoring. You see her as ripe for advancement because of her growth in skills, her insatiable appetite for learning, and strong self-motivation. In your estimation, she's done everything you've asked of her and more. You've in effect taken her under your wing, and you believe now would be the appropriate time to give her a mentor—a higher-up in the organization to groom her for advancement into the managerial hierarchy.

In taking stock of your performance as a coach, pay close attention to your enthusiasm and passion for the job. It has been proven that leaders who exhibit passion for their jobs create the trickle-down effect, with their staffs following their committed lead.

So you talk with Kelly about the idea. She's excited about it and expresses her gratitude for the confidence that you're showing in her abilities and potential. Soon after your discussion, however, with the wheels set in motion, you notice that Kelly is neglecting her immediate job responsibilities, with a noticeable drop-off in her performance. And as if that's not bad enough, you hear she's been telling a few coworkers that she's interviewing for jobs with competitors. Hey, you've got a big problem here. You've also got an early warning signal that your overall coaching decision-making and evaluation apparatus has a few bugs in it.

Identifying Your Mistakes

Your employees are going to make a lot of mistakes and behave unprofessionally on occasion. And even you, a noble coach, are going to make your fair share of misjudgments, too. You've always got to manage with this unmistakable reality in mind. You've got to learn from your mistakes and move forward, not wallow in them and backtrack. Our previous example of your mentee Kelly tells you that you made an evaluation error. It's incumbent upon you to fully grasp what ingredients go into your decision-making process. What were the variables that went into your tapping of Kelly as a rising star in the organization? Why did you place your complete trust in her? Why did she rebuff the loyalty that you showered on her in this instance? Was it something in your coaching approach that caused this apparent breach in faith? Was there something in your coaching that caused you to misread Kelly's intentions? You've got to uncover whatever are the causes of a predicament like this and every problem in the office that involves decisions and judgment calls made by you.

QUESTIONS?

Is "work ethic" another term for "hard work"?
The work ethic encompasses more than mere hard work. It carries with it an overall meaning of conscientiousness in doing a job. There are some very hard workers who are unprofessional to the core in their attitudes and behaviors.

Measuring Professional Behaviors

This book presumes that you know, without a lengthy explanation, the difference between professional and unprofessional behavior on the job. Supreme Court Justice William Brennan, in trying to define pornography and what constituted it in a legal sense, once said, "I know it when I see it." Most coaches say the same thing about professional and unprofessional behavior; they know it when they see it. Nevertheless, in this epoch of the general coarsening of our lives, the line between professional and unprofessional behavior in business has been blurred, just as it has everywhere else.

FACTS

The professionalism that you insist on as a coach, and as a leader of men and women, defines the overall work habits that reign in the office, and hence, the results. When your employees function in their jobs as true professionals, a positive work environment is the inevitable by-product.

Understanding What Is and Isn't Professional

Basically, professionalism gets to the heart of right and wrong; what's ethical and what's unethical. It can't be easily measured because it often involves attitude and certain behaviors, and not hard, quantifiable results. For example, monetary objectives produce quantifiable results—they're either met or they're not. But how one achieves these monetary results—and all other results in business—is just as important as the results themselves. This statement might come as a big shock to some businesspersons. However, the ends do not justify the means in any organization that puts a premium on fairness and on the integrity of its personnel. For instance, Ed, in sales, may be a wizard in finding new customers and pumping up orders. But if his selling tactics involve deceit, or browbeating his coworkers to generate more of this business, then his inflated results are not something to laud or reward.

Professionalism on the job encompasses how the job is done. It's about the methods that employees use to go from point A to point Z and work their jobs. It's about their interactions with others, be they on the inside (coworkers) or the outside (customers). The corporate world is awash in overambitious men and women, some of them seemingly successful if measured by their 401(k) plans. But this measurement of their success is meaningless if the road to their ever-increasing riches is littered with unprofessional actions.

Seeing How Your Team Mirrors Your Professionalism

You need to measure the professionalism of your team because it is the ultimate reflection on your leadership. Problems, and the importance of striking at them early, often mean confronting the unprofessional attitudes and behaviors of some of your employees. And although unprofessionalism covers a wide array of these attitudes and behaviors, it is nevertheless important to stress that no manifestations of them should be permitted to take root. Negative outlooks, actions, and work habits disseminate more easily and freely than do positive outlooks, actions, and work habits—another unfortunate but important fact of life that coaches need always remember.

There are the people who think, "John uses a lot of people for his own ends and cuts a lot of corners—and nobody notices or seems to care. So why am I being conscientious in my work and doing all these little extra things, when it doesn't seem to matter?"

ESSENTIALS

You may have the most knowledgeable and skilled employees in town, but if they don't exhibit the professional work habits to match their know-how, you might not get the results you expect and desire from them. Solid work habits fuel talent and expertise.

This kind of chain reaction mentality is common. Bad attitudes and bad behavior spread like a cancer if the unprofessionalism of one employee is ignored, or in any way tolerated. This is why the ethical boundaries and work ethic that you establish at the core of your coaching must be defended as well as declared. You must insist that the proper ethical attitudes and behavior be adhered to faithfully on the job. By requiring anything less, you render such behavior standards frivolous.

Your employees must never be permitted to regard professional behavior as vague or some nebulous textbook stuff. They've got to see ethics on the job as something living and real, as something that matters, and as something that is faithfully guarded by you, the coach, without exception. (See Chapter 2 for a more thorough discussion of the critical importance of setting ethical boundaries as the centerpiece of your coaching.)

Professionalism: The ABCs

The movie classic *Love Story* gave us a haunting melancholic theme and the oft-repeated platitude, "Love means never having to say you're sorry." Well, coaching means never taking anything for granted—anything at all. So don't fall into the trap of taking professionalism for granted. Don't assume that all the men and women who work for you fully grasp the ABCs of professionalism. This is a roundabout way of saying that you are going to have to teach some of your employees these essential ABCs. Some of them will need more help in this area than others. A few unrefined employees may even fall into the Ernest T. Bass (boorish to the core) category, but most will be reachable and teachable.

In your initial orientation and training of new employees—high-octane coaching—your job is to make known the basic ways the office functions, including the specific expectations you have for each one of your staff members. Don't neglect to mention here that a professional demeanor is something that every employee of yours, regardless of job description or role, is expected to maintain at all times—no exceptions. Some managers inculcate their employees with performance expectations ad infinitum, and focus on bold goals and growth opportunities, while giving short shrift, or ignoring completely, the professional attitudes and behavior behind performances that are equally, if not more essential.

Can you teach professionalism to the uncouth employee? In *The Andy Griffith Show*, Sheriff Taylor failed to impart refinement to Ernest T. Bass, but Bass was as crass as they come. As with so many lessons, learning is entirely up to the student. A receptive student can readily absorb the important tenets that characterize professionalism. But just as in our past discourse on motivation, it all boils down to the particular individual's willingness to move forward and better him- or herself. Nevertheless, you've still got to unequivocally define for all of your employees what professional behavior means in the workplace. And you've got to hold them to the standards of this exacting definition. And if any of your employees repudiate professional behavior, and refuse to make the necessary adjustments in their work habits, then you don't want them on your team. Period. End of story.

Here are five points of professionalism that you must insist your employees both understand and abide by at all times while working for you:

Honesty and Integrity

If you can't trust your employees to be truthful—open and up-front with you and their coworkers—you won't maximize their performances, nor will you preside over a robust, positive work environment. In addition, the other points of professionalism to follow will be rendered meaningless if honesty and integrity are not firmly entrenched, because they are the bedrock of professionalism.

What happens when honesty and integrity aren't King and Queen in the office? You get workplaces that are rife with backstabbing, deceit, and slothful performances—unprofessional environments in which to conduct any kind of business. So it is incumbent upon you to closely monitor whether you are always getting the straight facts from your employees, variations of the truth, or—in the worst case scenarios—bald-faced lies.

You've got to be eternally vigilant in this area and fully appreciate that in today's business world the sharing of information is essential. This means that one person's veracity or lack thereof has a negative impact on so many other people and their jobs.

 **SSENTIALS**

An employee attribute that you always want on your team is reliability. You need the men and women who work for you to deliver both timely and quality results on a consistent basis.

No workplace, or any other place for that matter, exists in a state of chastity. But this is one of the reasons why coaching in corporate management was born. Its tools and techniques confront and correct imperfections far and wide. Unprofessional behaviors (imperfections) need to be nipped in the bud in the workplace before they become the predominant behaviors and win the day. When they win, you lose.

There is a societal paradox that powerfully impacts business. And that's the conflict between what we know is right and just, and our embracing and even endorsing proven liars in our culture. Nevertheless, we need to not only expect and demand professionalism in the workplace—where again, honesty and integrity are at the apex—but to insist upon it, too, in our families, friendships, and political leaders. It has been said that we live in an increasingly smaller world—and that's become distressingly obvious based on what's happened of late. And because of this reality, we can't isolate things like professionalism and reasonably expect that one can behave rudely, crudely, and duplicitously at home, and then come to the job and be a paragon of professionalism.

Learning and Initiative

The second point of professionalism is learning and initiative. A professional employee exhibits a perpetual openness to learning and displays initiative and creativity. In the fast-changing world of business, nobody can sit back and allow these changes to pass by. Professional behavior involves a desire to acquire knowledge and new skills, coupled with a willingness to take this new knowledge and these skills to a higher level. As a coach, you are a teacher and trainer in a continuous learning environment. Your aim is to be the proverbial magnet for talent. You want to attract people to join your team and your organization—men and women who exhibit a hearty appetite for learning and forward movement.

Resilience

The third point of professionalism is resilience. Professional people can take a few punches and not fall down. Professionals bounce back and acclimate to new circumstances. They aren't averse to change, but instead welcome it as an inevitable part of working in the modern business world. Resiliency, in fact, is more than ever necessary in these technologically driven times. If you aren't resilient in today's workplace, you are doomed to dead-end jobs in low-skilled occupations.

Positive Attitude

The fourth point of professionalism is a positive attitude. Employees with negative attitudes, sad to say, are roaming the business landscape like Bigfoot. One of the greatest challenges in all of coaching is sorting out exactly why a particular employee is so negative, so unprofessional. In these cases, you've got to determine if the poor attitude stems from the job itself, a personality quirk, a personal problem, or a combination of all three (which is often the case). The truth is, even one employee's negative attitude in a workplace is a very toxic thing in the close confines of an office. There are always employees harboring negative attitudes who spread discontent to their coworkers, and plant the seeds of additional problems with an incessant instigation of others to see things their way. Keep a watchful eye out for these kinds of people.

Teamwork

The fifth and final point of professionalism is teamwork. Much of corporate life today involves working in teams or groups. And, because of this strong reliance on others, you've got to get all of your people to harmoniously work together. You've got to make sure your staff gets along with one another as professional men and women pulling toward the same positive result. That everybody must be "on the same page" is truer now more than ever in business. The need to share information to get the job done makes it imperative that you have team players working for you. If you permit a lone wolf to run around howling to the office ceilings, when coordination of efforts is an absolute necessity, you're going to face disruptions and other serious problems in the workplace. Professional behavior and the ability to work well with others are tightly linked.

The Work Ethic

Can we all agree that smoking is a bad habit? Even if you're a smoker, you will probably concede that point. We probably could forge a consensus that a Twinkie and six cups of coffee is not a healthy breakfast, too. But these kinds of bad habits can be tolerated in the work environment provided they don't adversely impact on job performance. The bad habits of particular interest to coaches are work-specific and need to be weeded out and corrected.

The work habits, i.e., the work ethic, of your employees are what will make or break you as a coach. This chapter talks about taking stock—

making self-evaluations—of how you are doing. And many of these evaluations are not so easily measured because they are abstract in nature. That is, they are subject to a great deal of interpretation on your part. Interpretations, often, on your own conduct, decision-making, and overall leadership abilities. The work ethic in your office, and on your team, runs the entire gamut of what we've spelled out in this chapter. Professional behavior on the job means that work habits are strong and consistent. If you don't see to it that both you and your people maintain a work ethic that is solution- and positive-results-oriented, you will not thrive in the role of coach.

FACTS

The five points of professionalism that you should regularly take measure of in your inventory are: honesty and integrity, learning and initiative, resilience, positive attitude, and teamwork. If your staff measures up to these professionalism points, you're doing a solid job.

There are many human treasuries of knowledge who sport exceptional technical skills. These are people you want on your team provided they marry their impressive credentials with a professional demeanor. Those who lack the professionalism to get the most out of their know-how and skills do more harm than good in the workplace. We don't elect a resume as president. Nor do we hire a resume as an employee. The person most qualified to do the job may not be the one with the best credentials on paper. Education, experience, and technical skills are obviously important, and that's where your employee search begins. But it's people with the best work ethics and desires to improve themselves who often emerge victorious when the final hiring decisions are made.

In Chapter 11, you begin at the beginning—the interview process and selecting employees to work with you. Your coaching methods sink or swim based on the people who ultimately do your bidding—your employees. So make the right decisions right from the start of your coach-employee relationships. Then, guaranteed, taking stock of your coaching inventory down the road will be more satisfying to you.

First Impressions: Interviewing Prospective Employees

The coach's role in hiring people, is a key, though often-ignored, aspect of coaching. Not only can you use an interview as a time to begin regular and effective communication with a future employee, you can also evaluate some of the job applicants before they worm their way into your employ and cause you countless headaches down the road.

Going Back to the Drawing Board

In Chapter 10, you begin to take stock of your coaching aptitude. Well, you might as well begin at the beginning. That is, examine thoroughly your hiring methods.

Wise Hiring Decisions Lead to Better Employees

American patriot John Adams once said, "Facts are stubborn things." The fact is, if you're encountering more workplace problems than you had anticipated; if you're confronted with less than stellar employee performances; if you're surprised to see a lack of skills in certain employees—if, if, if— perhaps you didn't do a good enough job at the start of your coach-employee pilgrimage. Specifically, you didn't make the wisest decisions in hiring the right individuals in the first place.

FACTS

Billionaire Donald Trump asks prospective job applicants the unusual question, "How brilliant are you?" He hopes to catch them off guard, he says. When applicants answer that they're not very brilliant at all, Trump says he's inclined to take them at their word and doesn't hire them.

The job interview process is as essential to coaching and mentoring as it is to every other managerial approach. But because so much of coaching focuses on individuals and their talents and abilities, a coach's hiring procedures are expected to be more enlightened and more meticulous in not letting all of those important little things slip through the cracks.

Not Any Tom, Dick, or Harriet Will Do

The philosophy of coaching and mentoring is misinterpreted in many ways. (See Chapters 4 and 20 for more on this subject and the many myths surrounding it.) It's not a managerial methodology that turns water into wine and multiplies fish and loaves of bread. It's not about partying-on in the office. Nor is it a benign business boot camp capable of turning "anybody who wants a job" into a veritable Bill Gates or Warren Buffett.

Nevertheless, coaching and mentoring, and what they personify, offer much more than traditional management methods because they are dedicated to equipping employees with a work environment replete with learning, challenges, and career development opportunities. That said, it's nevertheless up to individuals to display a willingness to work and grow as workers and human beings. Self-motivation makes the difference here. The point is, not any Tom, Dick, or Harriet will do as an employee, even in an enlightened coaching and mentoring environment.

ESSENTIALS   Among the most important traits you need to look for in an employee is creativity. You want people working for you with ideas of their own on how to more efficiently do their jobs.

Going on a Treasure Hunt

In your capable hands, the job interview process is an opportunity to go on a treasure hunt and find things out about your future employees. Things those less aware managers would never in a million years uncover because they wouldn't even be looking for them in the first place! Your tenacious communication skills start the ball rolling, as you pepper the individuals who want to become part of your team with a stream of open-ended questions. You listen carefully to their answers and followup again and again if necessary.

Asking Open-Ended Questions

What's the first thing that you want to know about prospective employees? What their credentials are, of course! Obviously, you want somebody to fill a job who can do certain things and display certain skills. If you're in need of an employee to work intensively and extensively with computer programming, you can't ignore solid computer skills. But, as we've made abundantly clear throughout this book, useful skills are by no means limited to the mere technical skills.

SSENTIALS Among the areas you should explore in the interview process of prospective employees is their salary requirements. The open-ended question, "Explain why you feel you deserve what you're asking for" allows job applicants to make a case and justify their monetary pleas.

Asking the Questions

So you commence the interview process by finding out the overall talents and abilities of a wannabe employee. You find out what exactly this individual has to offer in both hard and soft skills across the spectrum. Here are some examples of open-ended questions you can pose to job applicants in the initial interview:

- Can you describe your greatest strengths? Your greatest weaknesses?
- What skills do you have that you'd like to improve?
- What hard decisions have you made in your work career?
- When confronted with problems and conflicts in the workplace, how do you address them?
- If you've been in work situations where you've had to persuade people to follow your lead, how did you accomplish this?
- How well do you work with people? What do you believe are the requirements of a team player?
- How do you handle pressure situations?
- How do you adapt to change?
- How do you deal with performance plans and their deadlines?
- What knowledge and skills have you acquired in your current job?

Questions like these reveal a potential employee's work ethic, which we mentioned in Chapter 10. The hard technical skills come first, but they need to be complemented with strong work habits, and many important soft skills, or they are useless to you.

ESSENTIALS

In the interview process, don't avoid prospective employees' educational backgrounds. This is an area worth exploring with open-ended questions like, "How did your college experience change your life?" and "What extracurricular activities did you participate in?" Don't forget, "How does your education prepare you for the job you're seeking?"

Examining the Answers—and More!

Most people—you can count on it ninety-nine out of 100 times—will give all the anticipated "right" answers. Scripted answers, remember, are scripted only up to a point. And sooner or later, interviewees go off script, and you've got to be especially attuned to their words when this happens. In fact, it's your job to get interviewees off their scripts. Consider the interview process an engagement at the Improv. "When confronted with problems and conflicts in the workplace, how do you address them?" This question is broad and loaded with opportunity—for you, looking to hire a capable employee, and for a job seeker, wanting to exhibit some depth of thought and reasoning.

Hunting for Experience: Good Versus Bad

In your hunt for skilled personnel, you need to aim your bow and arrow at the experience that potential employees bring to you. When the right experience matches the right job, great things can and often do happen. So, when you're conducting an interview, you want to know all about not only potential employees' work experiences, but also their life experiences and what they say about them.

Keep in mind, however, that experience cuts two ways. A person who works with a lousy manager often picks up many bad work habits. Experience gained. Another person works with a wise manager and acquires knowledge and new skills. Experience gained, too! Which kind of experience do you prefer working for you?

In the interview process, and indeed in all coaching communications, the anticipated first response of a prospective employee to a question is assigned less weight than the more meaningful exposition response. That is, answers that are expanded upon are ordinarily worth more than predictable first replies to questions.

Paying Attention to Experience Details

So, naturally, you must pay particular attention to the kinds of experiences that those looking to work for you have had. If an applicant is used to doing things one way—because that's his or her experience—and you do things a decidedly different way, then that's not the kind of experience you want in a new employee. When you traverse beyond the resume and deal with an interviewee in the flesh, the questions you ask should take you well beyond the words on that piece of paper. Experiences chronicled in an impressive list, or grand-sounding words about skills and abilities, must be put in their proper perspective.

Asking Questions about Experience

Here are some questions that draw out the substantive experiences of your prospective employees:

- What are some of the work experiences you're most proud of?
- How have your work experiences prepared you for the job you're seeking with us?
- What do you consider some of your biggest achievements? Your biggest failures?
- Do you have any ideas on how to avoid such failures in the future?
- Why do you want to leave your present position? Why did you leave your last job?
- Who was the manager you most enjoyed working for and why? Least enjoyed working for and why?

- Of all your work experiences, what are some of the things that you've learned that make you qualified for the job you're interviewing for?
- What are some of the specific things that you'd like to see in this job that you didn't have in past jobs?

Of course, don't forget to ask, "May I check your references?" Quite often the most you get out of checking references these days is confirmation that the person in question did in fact work where he or she claimed to have worked. Don't expect too much information beyond that.

Looking for Lies

Outright lies on resumes—about employment history, for instance—are bad signs, to put it mildly. It's one thing to inflate job skills and abilities (you know, to overcome obstacles and the like) with all the flowery adjectives in a thesaurus. It's quite another thing to create a phantom job history. This degree of prevarication brands anyone an unfit candidate for a new job. However, once you confirm the validity of a prospective employee's job history, the open-ended questions just cataloged afford you the opportunity to determine whether you believe the job experiences of the interviewee are more positive than negative; more in sync with your present needs than way out in left field.

The Right Fit

Okay, you've gathered all the information that you want about a potential employee's skills and experiences. Is that enough? No, of course that's not enough. Now's the time to build on what you've carefully culled so far and complete the picture. The next line of open-ended questioning to add to your interview repertoire revolves around the open position itself, and specifically what the company's appeal is to the job seeker.

Focusing on the Job You're Hiring For

This is the prime opportunity for you to get down into the trenches and shift the focus from the interviewee talking about the interviewee, to the interviewee talking about the open position and the company at large. The job you're seeking to fill, depending on its skill requirements, will attract a diverse group of applicants. And information elicited from this hungry group about why they want to work for you will be very enlightening indeed. If you're truly concerned about workplace problems down the pike—and you've got to be as a forward-thinking coach—opportunity knocks. The interview process is the time to ask those who want to join your team, and work with you, just why they want to do that.

Asking Questions about the Job and Your Company

Here are some interview questions zeroing in on the open job itself:

- What brought you to this company, seeking this position?
- What special attributes do you offer that make you suitable for the open job?
- What specifically do you look for in an employer?
- Describe your short-term goals? Long-term goals?
- What challenges do you seek in a job?
- What makes you the best-qualified person for the job?
- Is money more important to you than responsibilities and challenges?
- How do you think the company would benefit if you were hired to fill this position?

FACTS

The interview moment is your golden opportunity to strike a blow at future workplace problems by thoughtfully questioning job applicants and determining—in addition to the requisite technical skills—whether these prospective employees displayed the right temperaments and character to join your team.

As you can see in these various queries, the thrust of the questioning shifts to the job at hand and what the would-be employee could do for you and the company. There is, of course, some overlap in questions about skills, experience, and position, but it's in this particular line of questioning where you can get very specific in your follow-ups, and hone in on what you know the job requires.

Your insider information on the various job-related skills needed to perform the everyday tasks and roles, and in what time frame, allows you to probe and poke around and determine whether or not an applicant has what it takes—beyond skills and experience—to do the job and do it well. You can get a very clear idea whether or not a person interviewing for the job fits into your vision and can work well with your team.

Don't Go There: The Wrong Questions

In a coach's world, which seeks to get to the heart of what makes people perform, the interview moment is rife with so much possibility. You want to kick off your relationship with an employee the right way. And, for starters, the right way is with the right employee.

Books, magazine articles, and seminars on the subject of interviews abound, from both the employees' and employers' perspectives. These resources have been around for some time now detailing the necessary preparation for both asking the right questions and giving the right answers to those very same questions. Job seekers prepare themselves for interviews, and so do coaches. Coaches are prepared for the prepared, including the overprepared and the underprepared.

When you fully prepare yourself for an interview with a potential employee, you approach the get-together with a full agenda. You view the hiring of a new worker as impacting both your immediate future and indeed your long-term effectiveness as a coach. You accept that a vigilant interview process is essential to your daily managing efforts tomorrow and six months into the future, and that decisions made in hiring are basically office snowballs in the making. They gather size and strength over time, and can bowl you over if you're not eternally vigilant. A coach's job is to avoid getting buried by these snowballs.

Before we part on this important subject of the coach-employee interview process, there are certain questions that should never be asked of job applicants. There are questions that are inappropriate, some simply because they have no place in a business setting, and some because they're against the law. You're a coach, and a human being, and so you may be curious about a whole host of things about a person who wants to work for you. Prurient matters may titillate you. But you must always remember that you aren't the host of a trashy TV talk show interviewing a human curiosity; you are a coach interviewing somebody who wants a job. You are managing in a business environment and don't need to know what is none of your business. Here are some questions that you have no business asking during an interview:

- What is your age?
- What is your marital status?
- What is your sexual preference?
- Do you have any physical or mental disabilities?
- Have you ever been convicted of a crime? Arrested for any reason?
- Do you have any serious health problems?
- Are you religious? Do you attend a church? A synagogue?
- Do you drink alcohol?
- Are you a Republican? A Democrat? A Green?

And this list could go on and on. In your questioning, just stick with skills, experience, and why the job applicant wants to work for you, and you won't get into any trouble.

And as for your curious nature, you'll find out the answers to many of those personal questions in due time, if and when the interviewee makes the cut and joins your team. Most people don't hide their marital status, religion, politics, drinking habits (that's for sure!), and the many other things that have no place in interviews, but are general knowledge in the office.

CHAPTER 12

Tackling Conflicts

I nevitably, conflicts will occur in the office environment between your employees, and between you and your employees. And don't forget the ubiquitous bad attitude. Discover how proper coaching can make these seemingly negative circumstances wholly positive by extracting important lessons from them and moving forward.

Meeting Conflicts Head On

Because your ultimate job responsibility as a coach is to advance a productive workplace, personnel skirmishes and attitude problems can never be brushed aside.

ALERT

Don't ever ignore a bad attitude in an employee. Such an attitude is often the first act in an overall bad performance. It is therefore imperative that you address any attitude problems on your staff before they become full-blown performance problems.

You must not only establish, but also maintain, solid relationships with all of your employees. And, aside from making sure that employees get along with you, you need to make certain they get along with one another. You're the leader of a team effort. Most of the work that needs to get done in your office setting requires close interaction between and among employees. And that means that employees who have personality clashes with their coworkers or with you, or flaunt bad attitudes, cannot be ignored.

In This Corner . . .

There will come a time when you'll be compelled to confront dissension of some kind in your ranks. Even the best coaching efforts can't altogether avoid such workplace problems. In fact, it's not whether you're going to see conflict (you will) as a coach; it's how you deal with it that will determine your success or lack thereof. You'll have to address the less seemly sides of the human condition from time to time in your coaching.

Some people take their squabbling and disagreements to an even higher level, and fight with one another. In an office setting, fighting doesn't mean fisticuffs, or tearing at one another's clothing, although this kind of behavior's been documented. It's verbal hostility, leading to harsh words and protracted arguments, with the results being performance breakdowns, that should most concern you as a coach. It's the malcontent with a poisonous attitude who should fully engage your attention and light a fire under your corrective coaching side.

Beware the Bad Attitude

It is every manager's worst nightmare to have a treacherous attitude problem in his or her midst. Unfortunately, though, it comes with the territory. Bad attitude problems are commonplace in today's work environs.

FACTS

An employee's attitude refers to his or her overall thinking process, views, and opinions on all things great and small. An employee's behavior refers to his or her physical actions. You've got to prevent negative attitudes from becoming negative behaviors.

The Way the Workplace Used to Be

The Depression and World War II generation of workers looked upon work and responsibility in a different light than do the majority of people in today's labor force. Most members of that past generation were grateful for just having a job—or jobs, in so many instances. They did what they had to do to support themselves and their families, and it wasn't always easy or pretty work.

The Way the Workplace Is Now

As we became a more and more affluent nation and society—with yesterday's luxuries becoming today's necessities—the expectations of those in the labor market changed. In essence, today people want more and more, and so do companies, which have become more demanding and less forgiving because of the extremely competitive realm that most businesses find themselves in. And some companies do mishandle their workers by not respecting them as human beings. But the reality is that increasing numbers of companies are employing the coaching and mentoring methodology and laboring valiantly to meld individual needs with business needs.

The Bad-Attitude Crowd

But, alas, lurking in the bushes of every business is the bad-attitude crowd. Working with an employee with a poor attitude is something that you will go up against at some point in your coaching career (and probably at many points!). Fear not, though. You are armed and ready to deal with these personality-related obstructions because you are—let's all say it together—solution-oriented. Dinosaur managers are less adequately equipped to deal with these disconcerting employee attitudes. In stark contrast to coaches, they react to behavior only—physical actions—and oftentimes this is too late. In other words, the dinosaur managers allow attitude problems to grow into disruptive performance problems.

SSENTIALS

If you determine that it's not humanly possible for you, a coach, to change a troublesome employee attitude from bad to good, you've got to insist that the employee concentrate solely on doing his or her job, and leave the bad attitude outside the work environs.

Attitude Versus Behavior

Attitude is the precursor of behavior, which is the forerunner of performance. That is, a negative attitude engenders mirror actions, which lead to poor performance. There is an important distinction between attitude and behavior. Attitude embodies an individual's overall thought process, how he or she relates to things. Behavior, on the other hand, is attitude in action.

Attitude covers a person's viewpoints and outlook on the world at large. You've heard the expression that some people see the glass as "half full" and others as "half empty." Well, you've got to insist as a prerequisite for working for you that your employees see things as half full, or you'll drown in a sea of discontent for sure. Ignoring employees' negative attitudes, in many instances, means preordaining unacceptably low performance levels. You can easily differentiate negative attitudes from positive ones. Sometimes just a sigh or two emanating from an employee while you are talking to your team clues you in as to who is not with you and what you want to accomplish as a coach. Sometimes it's something said in response to your ideas or something trivial and unrelated to the job.

Attitude calls home the mind and manifests itself in body language and the ubiquitous tongue. Behavior, in the confines of the workplace, defines specific actions—both visible and assessable—that go far beyond the wagging tongue. And this is, ultimately, what counts regarding your employees. However, you cannot isolate attitude from behavior. Attitude may reside in the cozy confines of the mind. But the mind is one powerful instrument. And while you can't be 100 percent certain that a bad attitude will translate into a bad performance, you can be sure that it's an unhealthy thing. You can go to the bank on the fact that negativity is the Black Plague of the office world—contagious and ugly.

The Bad Attitude Spectrum

Is trying to overhaul an employee's attitude from bad to good in your powers as a coach? Is it in your bag of tricks? Of course it is.

FACTS

There are lessons to be learned, even in conflict. Be it an attitude adjustment or reshaping an on-the-job relationship, opportunities abound in improving oneself as both a valued employee and human being. A coach is a catalyst who aims to forge productive confrontation, i.e., converting dissension into positive solutions.

Locating the Source of the Bad Attitude

If it's job-related, it's certainly within your power to turn chicken feathers into chicken soup. Sitting down with employees and talking with them is a coach's modus operandi. Employees with attitudes that negatively impact either their own job performances or others' job performances have to be called into your office for a candid, no-holds-barred discussion. This much is a given. The first item on your agenda is to locate the source of the bad attitude.

Let's say, for example, that your employee Paul, who is highly competent in his job, gets passed over for a promotion that he thought he richly deserved based on merit. This perception (and maybe even a reality) is enough to turn a formerly positive attitude into a negative one. Now, allowing Paul to roam around the office in a bitter, angry frame of mind is an open invitation to increased restlessness in your ranks. If Paul is permitted to convince others that the meritocracy, which ideally should be at the center of all coaching promotions, is not in fact practiced, you've got a major credibility problem on your hands. And credibility is a coach's underpinning. Thus, you've got to make the case to Paul that he was bypassed for reasons that were fair and sound, and based solely on qualifications. You've got to convince him with whatever evidence you have at your disposal. You've also got to recharge Paul's batteries by giving him positive feedback on his overall job performance and offering words of encouragement about his future.

By the same token, you must also rebuke him in no uncertain terms for going negative and for not coming to you first to talk about his perceptions and feelings. If you are in fact on solid ground, Paul will have no choice but to accept the fact that he was not the most qualified person for the promotion, or he will have to look elsewhere for a job. A stark but absolutely necessary choice in a positive work environment.

Employing Straightforward Communication

Here's another employee bad-attitude conundrum to consider. Let's say that Meg from Company A comes to work for you in Company B, and immediately starts grumbling about how much better it was working at A than it is working in B. This kind of griping is not unusual but is totally unacceptable in any workplace.

What do you do? That's easy. You call this motormouth, Meg, into your office and immediately lay it on the line. "Look, Meg, you applied for this job; we were impressed with your credentials and your interview; we offered you the job; and you accepted the terms of employment. So, can you explain what your problem is with us?" Straightforward communication here often turns a problem attitude like this on its head, because many of these purveyors of negativism, like Meg, are unaccustomed to open and frank dialogues with their bosses. And when confronted as such, they're often impressed and regret what they've done in spreading bad cheer. Sometimes they're chagrined and even intimidated by the fact that their unprofessionalism has been discovered and taken to task.

FACTS

The most intractable of employee attitude problems often represent the employee's attitude toward life in general and not to the job per se. Employees who are attitudinally disabled showcase bad attitudes from dawn to dusk, anywhere and everywhere. You've got to nevertheless insist that any bad attitude remain outside of the workplace.

Curbing Terminally Bad Attitudes

The most difficult of all attitude problems to resolve revolve around the attitudinally disabled. These are the people who wake up and don't smell the coffee. And if by some chance they do, it's burning. Of course, in a business utopia, you would prefer to have weeded out these negative employees before hiring them in the first place (see Chapter 11). But, as we've said before, this isn't always the way things turn out. Cleverly concealed negative attitudes are a dime a dozen. However, when they finally do rear their ugly heads—and they do—watch out, coaches!

Again, a frank sit-down with any and all violators of this edict is in order. Allow the trespassers of your ethical boundaries to explain themselves. All employees get to speak their pieces under a coach, regardless of the circumstances. Perhaps, through your coaching efforts, you can assist in planting the seeds of a more positive outlook in a thoroughly negative person. Nobody (well, almost nobody) is un-redeemable. If it's personal problems and an altogether tumultuous life that are the cause of an employee's incessant negativity, a little succor and understanding on your part can sometimes go a very long way.

Whatever the cause of the bad attitudes on parade in the office, an attitude adjustment is in order. If you don't feel that a core change of attitude is humanly possible, you've got no choice but to demand that your negative employees keep their unsettling attitudes at bay. That is, ask them to compartmentalize the problems that are being reflected in their poor attitudes. Some individuals have a remarkable knack for doing this kind of thing, and they don't let their mindsets—their worldviews—impact at all their behaviors on the job.

ESSENTIALS

You have to be assertive in all your approaches to managing, but particularly in addressing conflict situations. Assertive communication applied with alacrity is what is required in dealing with the problems of employee discord and bad attitude.

Bad attitudes in the workplace can't be tolerated at any time and for any reason. Utilizing all the communication skills at your disposal, you've got to insist on either a bad-attitude makeover or compartmentalization.

When Employees Don't Get Along

In conflict situations, consider yourself, in effect, a third party—albeit a very interested third party. "In this corner weighing 175 pounds, from Hoboken, New Jersey—Frank, the financial wizard. And in this corner, weighing 115 pounds, from Peoria, Illinois—Dawn, the marketing maven." What do you do when two (or more) of your employees who must work closely with one another, like Frank and Dawn, don't like one another?

First of all, whether or not employees like one another is not what interests us here. The positive, accommodating work environment that we never tire of mentioning is not predicated on individuals liking one another. This isn't Love at AOL. Sure, it helps if your team can give a group hug at the end of a day's work. But it's not a professional requirement—and rather implausible, too. Respecting one another in their jobs is another story. Again, we come back to compartmentalization. It's the job functions that have to get done and done well. If employees can do their jobs, working alongside coworkers whom they dislike personally, then that's peachy keen, and there's nothing you can or should do about it. If, however, the animus felt between employees filters down into less-than-adequate job performance, you've got to act.

But how do you deal with performance problems that very often stem from something outside the business realm? The first thing that you do is own the fact that it is now a business problem, i.e., your problem. You also recognize that the problem has to do with performance breakdown, not solving a Hatfield–McCoy feud between your employees, which may very well be outside your scope.

In the corporate world, when people from all over the country and even the world, from different backgrounds and upbringings, with different values and habits, come together, there are inevitably conflicts, very often stemming from the fact that people just plain don't like one another. Your job as a coach is not to lecture employees on loving one another or celebrating differences, or spouting some other trite bromides. These kinds of lectures invariably do more harm than good. Employees don't like feeling that they're being talked down to. Always talk up to your employees. It's more uplifting.

Let's return to employees Frank and Dawn and their disliking one another. Let's take their mutual disdain one step further with their job performances suffering as a result of it. What do you do? Call Frank in on the carpet and talk to him. Tell him precisely what's expected of him as an employee with a specific job to do and performance goals to be met. Ask him what he thinks the solutions to his performance problems are, and what ideas he has to improve his working relationship with Dawn. Then follow the same course with Dawn.

Once you've spoken your piece, and carefully listened to your two quarrelling staff members on an individual basis, your next move is to call Frank into your office for round two, and tell him some of Dawn's ideas for forging a better working relationship. You need to gauge his reaction to her suggestions. Then, bring Dawn in, and tell her some of Frank's ideas at rectifying their mutually destructive performances.

Round two is indispensable, because round three involves you refereeing Frank and Dawn in the same room, and tying together all that you've learned in your one-on-one discussions with them. You've heard their sides of the story; you've gotten their reactions to what each had to say about the others' suggestions about righting things; and now you,

Frank, and Dawn are all coming together to agree upon solutions to a positive outcome to the problem.

Traditional managers are apt to skip rounds one and two of this process and call in their battling employees right from the start, telling them point-blank, "Work it out between yourselves . . . or else!" This is not the kind of employee self-sufficiency that we've been promoting throughout this book. Sure, in the end, the battling employees themselves will have to resolve to work out their differences, or nothing positive will happen. That much is certain. But you have a much better chance of securing positive outcomes if you talk with each employee individually, gather what information you can as to the causes of the personal or work-related problems leading to the diminished performances, and then proceed from there.

SSENTIALS

You must always be mindful of talking up to your employees and never down to them. You're not their first-grade teacher. You're a manager of adults in an environment where overall performance matters as much to you as to them.

When you simultaneously bring the fighting parties into your office (round three), it is only after you've heard from both sides (round one), and then gotten their reactions to the suggestions and ideas from the other (round two). Round three, then, is as productive as is possible because you did your homework. This fully informed approach stands in stark contrast to what would be a free-for-all, highly emotional one, if you chose to immediately call your combative employees into your office and read them the riot act.

To emphasize an important point: It's not your job to transform Frank and Dawn into the best of buddies (although that would be nice). It's your job and your responsibility to secure positive results in their performances. And if two employees' personal dislike for one another is getting in the way of achieving this, you've got to put a stop to it—or at the very least the outward manifestations of it that are negatively impacting their performances.

The Soda Pop Rule

The old 7-Up advertising slogan said, "You Like It, It Likes You." Did you know that you've got to transform every employee's job into a bottle of that beloved lemon-lime pop? Here's how it works. You focus all eyes on the job itself and its importance to employees. You ask them whether or not they like their jobs. If the answer is "yes," and you are generally pleased with their work—you've got a "you like it, it likes you" scenario. Employees like their jobs; the jobs like the employees.

Back to Frank and Dawn from the preceding section. If both of them like their jobs and are competent in their roles, then it must be made absolutely clear to both of them that they must amend their rancorous interpersonal relationship that is negatively impacting their job performances, or they risk losing their jobs. The soda pop rule in action.

In just about everything that we've said regarding coaching, strong communication has been at the core of it. Employees sitting in your office and talking openly and without fear of saying something that could land them in hot water is a powerful technique that can accomplish remarkable things. Misunderstandings are often cleared up in such give-and-take atmospheres. The better sides of people surface all the time in these aboveboard settings (and, yes, sometimes the ugly sides, too). When you confront the problem and put everything on the table—the good and bad—solutions become clearer, and positive outcomes more likely.

Live and Let Learn

In order to more fully understand and appreciate the subject of productive confrontation, you need only look at situations in your own life, both on and away from the job. Specifically, the confrontational moments that made you a better person in one way or another. You are in the unique position as a coach to show your team how they can benefit from the various workplace obstacles that they encounter. And this means making your employees more adept at rebounding from these inescapable problem moments.

How do you impart to your staff the necessary tools to turn confrontation on the job into productive lessons learned? You do this by communicating from the beginning in a forthright, thorough, and free-flowing manner. You must permit your people to clearly see themselves and the repercussions of their actions. You're the catalyst, not only in detecting problems, but also in taking the guilty party or parties to task, and making them see the error of their ways. Thus, you lead the way in locating the best solutions possible. You effect change and your employees learn valuable lessons in making the necessary changes and moving forward.

ALERT

Remember those lessons learned from bad managers! If you've worked for a manager with bad methods and habits, you're in a position to have witnessed managerial approaches in action that were counterproductive. Naturally, as a coach you don't pattern your style after these men and women.

A happy face has absolutely nothing to do with coaching. Respect and trust are the two features that permit you to effectively deal with disharmony and confrontation within your ranks. Wise intervention is what gives you the leverage to attack bad attitudes and dissension and come out a winner. Firmness of purpose and righteousness make for strong leadership. A happy face getting happy results is the optimum. A happy face getting unhappy results is detrimental and inappropriate in a business environment.

You've absorbed many positive lessons from your experiences. Coaching and mentoring are grounded in passing on these lessons to others. Profiles in success and failure show people the way to the future. It's not really surprising then that many positive lessons learned come out of bad experiences. That's been the thrust of this chapter. Good coaching on your part imparts helpful lessons from all kinds of experiences—even bad ones. And you know what? They're not bad experiences anymore, but good ones, when they are overcome.

CHAPTER 13

Dealing with Employees' Personal Lives

Although you're not expected to concern yourself with the off-hour lives of the many members of your staff, you can't ignore the reality that professional and private lives are bound together in many consequential ways. This chapter helps you deal with the challenges of coaching employees who, inevitably, have challenging personal lives.

Office Sweet Office

Personal problems tend to metastasize into workplace problems. It is a very complicated playing field—a very subtle area and one in which understanding and empathetic coaching can make an enormous and very positive difference. The truth is, you can help your employees to realize their on-the-job potentials, even if they carry a lot of personal baggage. You can help make their jobs into Shangri-las, a respite from what ails them in their personal lives.

ESSENTIALS

> Coaching is not social work, but is keenly aware of the important link that exists between employees' personal lives and their professional lives. Enlightened coaching understands that a satisfying and healthy work environment can make a positive difference in employees' home lives.

The very real personal bond between you and your employees—a proud coaching and mentoring tenet—endeavors to make the work experience a rewarding one. And so, if you create an office climate that taps into people's genuine needs and wants as human beings, you will get what you want—productivity from your team—while simultaneously feeling gratified that you've accomplished this with thoughtful and caring leadership. In other words, you've released human potential like a flock of doves, and not a plague of locusts.

To make the workplace a haven for your employees, there are many things you can do. Things, by the way, that we've talked about at length in the book up to this point. Here are several positive actions you can take that make people want to come to work, make the job personally gratifying, and ease problems at home by building up self-confidence and self-esteem.

Encourage Self-Expression

In all your coaching practices, it's important that you encourage your employees to express themselves in significant ways. In building up your employees' capacities for self-sufficiency, you've got to encourage them to contribute their ideas and opinions. You've got to get them over the hump of fearing rejection. When you listen to employees' suggestions, respect them, and in some cases acclaim and implement them, the positive effects redound to all employees, who see themselves as important pieces of a team puzzle. A sense of accomplishment is a very powerful self-motivating tool. When you afford your employees the opportunity to think for themselves and to make substantial, positive differences in their work, you've set the creative juices in motion. Don't keep your employees on a leash. Unleash them, and you'll be surprised at what they can do.

FACTS

You can make the workplace a haven for your staff, even those with topsy-turvy home lives, by encouraging creativity, problem-solving, and mini-mentoring. Jobs that are dynamic in nature encourage people to tap into their true potential, and this often spills over into all aspects of employees' lives.

Give Greater Challenges

You don't want employees who are as complacent as clams in their beds. Fortunately, most people want more responsibilities and greater challenges in their jobs. It's human nature. Simply put, employees want intricate jobs with problems to solve and obstacles to overcome. This is actually an extension of your promoting creativity in your employees. People look forward to going to jobs that engage their full attention and energy levels. Let your employees loose and allow them to hammer hard at their various job duties. Challenge them all the time. Employees with less than favorable personal lives often seek contentment in the workplace. If they feel appreciated, and are given involved, thinking-intensive jobs, work can partially fulfill what is lacking in their lives away from the job.

Build Skills

Employees prefer working in places where they learn things, so a workplace that grows employee skills simultaneously functions as a career builder. And this coaching double feature is particularly important to those with unrelenting personal problems at home, who feel that their best chance for upgrading their lives is through work and career. When you provide your people with genuine opportunities to better themselves, they respond in a positive way and want more of the same. They want to learn and they also want to teach. Oftentimes employees passionate about their work want to pass on their knowledge to others, and they become mini-mentors and assistants to you in your coaching efforts.

Let Them Help Others

Picking up on this particular theme of knowledgeable persons passing along their know-how and wisdom to others, employees who help their coworkers do their jobs better often feel better about themselves. Humankind is regularly panned for being selfish and greedy above all else—particularly in the business world. This is an unfortunate stereotype because, in business, so many people help others and get a real sense of satisfaction out of doing it, too.

FACTS

When you create a staff of high performers, you preside over a dynamic team. It's much more gratifying for employees to go to work and be part of a team of productive winners than it is to associate with a listless bunch of underachievers and whiners.

Employees with rough home lives often use their jobs to make a difference, and they get a remarkable gratification out of helping their teammates complete their tasks and fulfill their roles. Such team environments allow individuals to make differences in many people's lives. So promote a work atmosphere that puts a premium on everybody helping everybody else. A work environment where the coach looks out for employees, and employees look out for the coach and one another, is a caring and productive place. Again, a place that people want to come to.

Root for Team U.S.A.

The people who want to come to work in the morning are more often than not part of a highly productive, dynamic team. An analogy can be drawn here between a professional baseball team that's on the top of the heap versus a team that's on the bottom—a cellar dweller. The number-one team usually features a group of players who are self-motivated with a desire to win. The last-place team is more apt to be a group of listless losers, who would rather not show up for work, even if the work is play (baseball).

ALERT

In order for you to have and to maintain moral authority, you must exhibit professionalism at all times in the office environs, and this means maintaining a proper personal detachment from your employees and walking a fine line between caring for them and being their boss.

It's no different in the workplace. Playing a role in a strong team effort is uplifting. It goes back to the sense of accomplishment we spoke about earlier. Giving a strong performance in a sea of strong performances is personally fulfilling. A similar top-notch performance on a team of underachievers will not be as sweet. You've got it in your power to put a team together that is both attractive and uplifting to employees, particularly those with personal problems at home.

The Balancing Act: Work Versus Home

This previous section is not meant to imply that the job is as important in any way as home and family. It's not. Yes, there are many people who put work and career at the top of the heap, but they often neglect their spouses and children and their interior lives, and let quality time with their families and themselves slip by, never to be recaptured. Ideally, professional life and personal life should be a part of one another. Unless you've inherited a fortune, work and career are essential for living. But there's no need for work and career to elbow out a rich home life. There's no reason that you have to choose between the two.

It's a popular cliché to say that employees must learn to balance their home and work lives. Your role as a coach is not to do the balancing for them. You've got enough to do in the confines of the workplace itself. However, if you do all the things that elevate your people as worker commodities—encourage creativity, provide challenging jobs, and teach skills—you're helping employees develop passion for their jobs. Passion for work and self-confidence in doing a job often go home with employees. There are no guarantees in life, and you have no magic wand to wave that will make everybody in your employ happy campers. However, you can make them productive campers, and in so doing hope that the right stuff on the job filters down to life at home.

ALERT

Enhance your employees' private lives by making them want to come to work for you. A pleasurable and satisfying day at work can't help but filter down to life at home. An unhappy and disagreeable work experience will filter down, too, and that's something you don't want to make happen.

So, do your best, never get discouraged, and you'll see positive results in employee performances positively impact employees' personal lives as well. It won't be a universal phenomenon, but that's life. Nevertheless, success in this area is one of the noblest achievements of coaching, and where it certainly distinguishes itself from traditional managing.

Friends or Employees?

When discussing the union between career and home life, the question of friendships between coaches and employees surfaces. Should you, a coach, be friends with your employees? It's really a timeless argument in business. But the argument takes on an added dimension when the coaching principles are thrown into the mix. After all, doesn't coaching preach from its bully pulpit that getting to know employees is essential?

Yes, it does. Doesn't coaching mean listening to employees and hearing them out? Yes, it does. Doesn't coaching mean mirroring employees' feelings? Yes, it does. Doesn't coaching mean recognizing employees as individuals with unique personalities? Yes, it does. Doesn't coaching mean being friends with employees? No, it doesn't.

Doesn't Coaching Equal Friendship?

Surprise! The answer is no. This is controversial subject matter for the people who have a difficult time separating the tenets of coaching and mentoring from the buddy system. After all, these folks reason, if coaches really care about their employees, they've got to be their friends and look out for them as only friends can.

Do coaches "look out" for their employees? Of course they do, but in an informal sense. What the "look out for them" principle asks of coaches is that they forge a positive work environment of the kind that we've discussed from the very first page of this book. And that means providing employees with perpetual development opportunities. Coaches want their employees to motivate themselves to do more and be more. That's looking out for them.

Coaches want to be respected, and in turn they want to rely on and respect their employees. Coaches want their employees to trust them, and in turn they want to be able to trust their employees. Coaches want to work in an intimate work environment where open communication and candor are the rule between them and their employees.

Ah, that sounds like friendship, doesn't it? Respect, trust, communication, and candor are the foundations of friendship! But it's not friendship in these instances; it's healthy and productive work environments supervised by wise and caring coaches.

Practicing Detachment

Now comes the hard part for some people: As a coach, you've got to include personal detachment in your technique arsenal. This may sound a little cold and contradictory considering all we've just said. But it's not. In fact, it's essential to maintain a level of personal detachment between you and your employees at all times. Your overriding concern is in getting strong performance results from your employees. Productivity matters most. But if you've established close personal relationships with the same employees, how would maximizing their performances fit into this picture? Would your friendships come first and job performances second?

Nixing Friendships with Your Employees

In life, friendships should come first all the time. That's what friends are for. And that's why friendships should not exist between managers and their employees. Managers can't afford to put personal considerations above the jobs that they were hired to do and the results that they are expected to deliver.

Fair-Weather Friend

Let's take a look at the case of James, a manager of a team consisting of ten men and women. His employees' jobs are varied, but, as in most offices, dependent on one another in a variety of ways. James is a very agreeable fellow and a devotee of coaching and mentoring and all of their myriad tools and techniques. James does much of what's asked of coaches. He tries to run his office in a way that makes each employee feel part of a solid team. He has established open communication and has frequent one-on-one sessions with his employees. So far, so good.

Over time, James developed a strong personal liking for two particular employees named Tom and Sissy. He found that he enjoyed being with them beyond talking about business issues. And this led to the threesome, or sometimes a duo, doing lunch now and then, and then going out after a day's work for a few beers, a movie, and a lot of chitchat.

The very obvious first problem in this scenario is a public relations debacle. The other eight employees in the office are well aware of this relationship. They feel excluded, and, naturally, reason that James prefers Tom and Sissy to them. They firmly believe that James can no longer be fair and impartial in managing the whole team.

One of the excluded employees, Bob, went to James with his opinion that Tom and Sissy are being held to standards different from those of the remaining eight staff members.

Somewhat startled by this perception of things, James said there was no special treatment being accorded either Tom or Sissy. But regardless of what James thinks of his relationship with Tom and Sissy, it doesn't matter nearly as much as what his other employees think of it.

James reacted by abruptly cutting off his lunches and after-hours get-togethers with both employees. Tom and Sissy couldn't understand what the sudden change in their boss's behavior was all about, because they both considered James a friend. As human beings they were deeply hurt and felt that a trust had been violated—the trust of friendship.

Predictably, these events made the work relationship between James and Tom, and James and Sissy, untenable.

Fire Away

You're skeptical? Do you believe you can manage and be personal friends with some of your employees? Do you believe you'll be able to make considered and fair business decisions without taking into account your friendships? Well, you're wrong. What if your employee, also a close personal friend, comes up for a promotion and is competing against another one of your employees, who is not a close friend? You don't believe the friendship factor will play into your decision? Of course it will.

Scenario One: You select your friend based, of course, on the merits. You conclude he was the right man for the job. The runner-up, not your friend, is less likely to accept your decision as being based on the merits only and is apt to see it as favoritism. Right or wrong, that's going to be the perception.

Scenario Two: You tap your employee, not your friend, for the job. You base your decision again on the merits. Your employee and friend is going to feel betrayed, even if he says he accepts your decision. How could a friend not "look out" for a friend and give him the upper hand? And then there's the possible perception that the promotion was given to the nonfriend employee precisely to avoid the perception of favoritism to the friend employee. In other words, this is a no-win situation.

The ultimate and most difficult managerial decision, terminating an employee, would be very problematic for a coach and a friend. Think about that one. Say you have an employee who's your personal friend, but who's not doing his job, what do you do? Keep your friend on board at the expense of performance, positive results, and a strong bottom line? How do you think the rest of your team will feel if they know a deadwood employee is languishing in their midst, simply because he's the boss's pal? They'll be disgruntled. The aura of trust will be shot. The work atmosphere will be negative. And you won't be respected.

For argument's sake, let's say that you went ahead and did the right thing. You terminated an employee who wasn't doing his job, even though he was your friend. You made the right decision, but in the wrong circumstances. That is, you shouldn't be firing your friends, because you shouldn't be friends with your employees in the first place. Plus, you'll probably lose a friend. Friendship is bad for business—and bad for friendship, too.

The Opposite of Sex

There is no quicker way to destroy the coaching bond of trust than for a coach to be fooling around on the sly with an employee. It's commonly accepted wisdom that it's not good for employees to be dating one another, let alone a manager. It brings an element into the workplace that is fraught with outside difficulties that are potentially explosive on the inside. No further explanation should be needed, but this most basic of business social edicts usually falls on deaf ears. But then, it's not the ears that rule here.

Back to you and coaching. Consider this a public service announcement: It is particularly important for you, in a position of authority, to keep personal friendships and romantic relationships out of the managing equation. Managing is complicated enough even when conducted under the best of circumstances. Anything that can be said for the problems with coach-employee friendships goes double for romantic liaisons.

Keeping romance at bay might sometimes requires a little self-control on your part. Self-control is part of virtue, and it's also part of business. If you don't exhibit professionalism yourself, don't expect your employees to show it in their own attitudes and behaviors. And, on top of it all, you won't have the moral authority to exact it from them.

Caring about Your Employees

There are caring behaviors that you can exhibit, however, that appear in the coaching and mentoring handbook. There are behaviors that show you care about your employees in both their personal and professional lives, while simultaneously maintaining that all-important personal detachment we talked about earlier.

QUESTIONS?

What is the "look out for them" principle in coaching and mentoring?
It's a principle that implores coaches to look out for their employees and their careers by fashioning a work environment of continuous learning and opportunity. It does not mean that coaches establish personal friendships with members of their staffs.

Personal detachment doesn't ask that you remain ignorant of your employees' personal lives or that you ignore events in their lives (like birthdays, deaths in the family, and so on). On the contrary, offering congratulations and condolences when appropriate is something you should do. Being detached doesn't mean you function in a different dimension and forget you're managing a close group of people who care for one another. Here are some little things you can do for all of your employees that showcase your caring side as a boss and concerned coach. If these things are meted out on a consistent and fair basis, they won't get misconstrued as signs of personal friendship or favoritism.

Say Thanks

Say thank you for a job well done. On a regular basis, let your employees know that you appreciate what they're doing (and continue to give more thorough feedback, too).

Reward Progress

Reward progress and not just final results. Depending on what's at your disposal (spot bonus, gift, recognition in the company newsletter, and so on), let your forward-moving employees know you notice and appreciate their progress. This is a great self-motivating technique. There's nothing quite like giving deserving employees a day off, or half-day on Friday, as a reward for a job well done. A gift holiday, not taken out of their vacation time, generates good feeling.

ESSENTIALS

In all your coaching efforts, you should reward progress and not only final results. Throughout employee performance plans and their various job tasks, pay special heed to employees making real progress in attaining their goals, and reward them with kind words, a bonus, or a gift of time off.

Do Lunch

Take a deserving employee out to lunch. If you've established a criterion for such events, there's no reason for anybody on your staff to misjudge the lunch as favoritism. However, make certain these lunch moments are special occasions with a purpose (reward for a solid performance, discussion of an important new job or promotion, and so on). Pal-to-pal lunch get-togethers are frowned upon, as you know.

Pass Along Compliments

Pass along any compliments about an employee that come your way. Whether they come from a person within your organization, or a pleased customer on the outside, don't let such positive words rest with you. An employee who is complimented deserves to know about it. It's a two-bagger in one sense. Your employee gets complimented by a third party, and, at the same time, gets complimented by you, the boss.

Keep a Permanent Record of Good Performance

Employees always welcome positive performance reviews. When your employees do their jobs, prepare performance reviews for them. Detailed performance reviews pointing out their solid efforts and achievements are confidence boosters. They tell your employees that you both notice and value their special efforts in overcoming obstacles, solving problems, and other accomplishments. That is, you care about them.

Writing a positive letter for an employee's personnel file is a reward for a deserving member of your staff. Such letters show your employees that you care for them in the here and now, but also that you are thinking about their futures as well.

Write a letter for an employee's personnel file detailing any exemplary achievements on the job. Give the employee a copy of the letter, and let him or her see what you've written. Words on paper are permanent records and more powerful than verbal positive feedback, or even a bonus or raise. Letters are living testaments that'll be forever part of an employee's record.

Make Little Things Count

All of these seemingly little things really aren't little things at all. Little things mean a lot. Some managers rely on the ostentatious Christmas party, or a Memorial Day gathering at a posh resort by the sea, as a substitute for all of these so-called little things. They believe these extravaganzas show they really care about their employees. And there's nothing wrong with pool parties and the like, but they shouldn't be used as substitutes for showing appreciation one-on-one on a routine basis.

Be Warm

Never underestimate the power of kindness to make the workplace better. When employees are happy at their jobs, they are more productive and are more willing to do their best work. Simple gestures and a friendly aura can really make a difference in an employee's job performance and satisfaction.

ESSENTIALS

You can show your employees that you care for them and appreciate their work by doing a host of little things, including saying "thank you" along the way. This lets them know that you are aware of, and grateful for, their efforts.

The business world, in general, has got a reputation for being cold and sometimes even cutthroat. And in some ways, it is a very deserving reputation. Free market capitalism, nevertheless, is still the best system ever devised to improve the lots of the greatest number of people. So if a people-oriented management methodology like coaching and mentoring can ameliorate some of the more harsh aspects of life in the corporate world, it has to be welcomed with open arms. And this is in fact why it's becoming more widespread in management. More and more workers are seeking some direction and indeed some solace in the workplace, and coaching and mentoring are civilizing influences when done right. They don't discount employees' personal lives or their feelings.

CHAPTER 14

Coachable Moments

The greatest challenge facing you as a coach on the business front lines is getting your employees to perform at a consistently high level. This chapter looks closely at various coachable moments that enable you to sustain the level of employee performance that you need in an ultracompetitive business environment.

Using Positive Reinforcement

It's your job to set the right professional behaviors in motion from the start of your relationship with each one of your employees. This requires that you not only verbalize what is expected of each one of them in doing their jobs, but that you identify the right behaviors in the practical reality of the fast-paced workplace. It's your job to teach them and to show them what's right and what's wrong—on the spot and in living color.

Then you need to reward them with positive reinforcement. In doing so, you're teaching your employees to behave the right way as a rule, and after a period of time, their good behaviors will become second nature to them. Your employees won't have to think twice about whether or not they're doing the right thing and behaving as business professionals. Your aware and assertive coaching makes the difference here.

ESSENTIALS

An important coaching technique is positive reinforcement. This entails first identifying the right behaviors in your employees and then rewarding them with positive feedback and other carrots. This positive reinforcement of the right behaviors encourages employees to exhibit those behaviors as a rule—and not the exception—in the workplace.

We've mentioned the many rewards that are used in the business world (bonuses, gifts, and so on), and you can parcel out variations of these to your deserving employees at any time. Most important, however, is that you recognize and note the good behaviors when you see them in action. Positive feedback, or words of thanks and encouragement, is the way to go here in making certain that the positive reinforcement hits its intended target—the particular employee who's performing in a manner that pleases you.

The flip side of the positive reinforcement coin is allowing bad behaviors to go unchallenged. By ignoring any kind of unprofessional behavior in the workplace, you are basically encouraging it to continue. Maybe that's not your intention, but it's nonetheless the result. And to compound your managerial misery, you are, in effect, rewarding the perpetuators of these bad behaviors. Yes, rewarding them! This is, in effect, negative reinforcement, which will lead to more and more similar behaviors. Behaviors, by the way, that will ensure that you won't maximize the performance of your team and get the best possible results out of them.

Bad behaviors on the job can't ever be swept under the office rug. Some managers, who take the path of least resistance, reason that, "What's done is done and I can't do anything about it now." Oh, yeah? When Lenny screws up and you don't say a word about it to him, what do you think is likely to happen next? Lenny's going to screw up again and again. When Sylvia misses her project target date, and you remain mute about it, what do you think is the inevitable outcome? Sylvia will miss her next deadline, and the one after that, and will probably fall way short of her performance targets and goals.

Positive reinforcement can't be overstated, because it's the ball that your employees will run with. True, it is up to your employees to motivate themselves to work hard and reach their full potential. But they've got to be shown the right and proper paths to forward movement, too. And this is where your coaching skills come into play. If you fail to show your employees the right paths to navigate (for growing job skills, job satisfaction, and career advancement), then you've been remiss, and you can't lay all the blame on them for not wanting to improve their lot.

ALERT

As a coach, you must be attuned to what are coachable moments. These are the times in your coaching when the circumstances are ripe for extracting valuable lessons to impart to your employees. It is situational learning at its most effective.

When problem drinkers go to Alcoholics Anonymous (AA), they hear the recurring platitude, "Only you can help you." They see it festooned on clumsily made placards hanging on the walls of meeting rooms, too. But AA is about showing people the ways to quitting drinking, while freely and honestly talking about the right and wrong behaviors that define recovery. Ditto for the workplace and your role as a coach. You can never retreat from your job responsibilities by claiming that your employees have to help themselves and show initiative and a willingness to learn and grow. They do indeed have to do all those things. But you are empowered to help your employees help themselves. That's what you were hired to do. And that's why you're called a coach.

Moments to Remember

Before the term "coaching" was ever applied to managers and consultants for hire in the business realm, it was the province of men and women in sports. There were coaches in other areas, sure, but it was likely a professional sport, or maybe a peewee league, that was being talked about when the word "coach" tumbled off your tongue. When the coach appellation took the business world by storm, it naturally brought with it a powerful connotation—a sports metaphor. That is, the word "coach" was loaded courtesy of its long history on sports playing fields, and in a few other areas where teaching, organizing, and strategizing were par for the course. Do your recall the good old days when you played high school sports (or watched them from the bleachers)? Think about those coaches of yesteryear. What were their roles? What were they expected to accomplish? Did they impart useful lessons and self-motivate you to play hard and play smart?

QUESTIONS?

What are the six categories of "coachable moments"?
They occur when your employees exhibit any one of these: performance results, job-task progression, innovation and creativity, negative performance results, job-task retrogression, mistakes, and lapses.

Fundamentally, your high school coaches looked for coachable moments in which to take charge and improve the performance of the entire team. By dealing with each individual's shortcomings and strengths, and then working on bringing everybody together in a concerted team effort, high school coaches labored to win games—for their own personal satisfaction, for you, and for the esteem of the school.

Coachable moments are what define the nature of coaching—either on the playing field or in the office. The moniker "coach" means something. We've made the case time and again throughout this book that the managers who call themselves "coaches" are operating in a decidedly different way than are traditional managers. When you manage as a coach, you're not quite the football coach (no whistle, remember) or the Lamaze coach, but you're similar in one important sense—you understand the game, you recognize the coachable moments in the office, and you're able to act upon them forthrightly and effectively.

FACTS

The right behaviors of your employees refer to their professionalism and work ethic in the workplace. You are responsible for managing your employees' behaviors and helping them achieve their maximum performance results.

Timing Is Everything

The coachable moments that you should be tuned in to run the gamut, and as you gain more and more experience in your role as coach, you will seize upon these moments with great alacrity. This isn't some New Age twaddle. It's rudimentary human behavior—people learn in circumstances germane to the lesson. That is, not theoretical lessons taught in a staid classroom, but lessons learned on-the-job. Your coaching is most effective when you're playing show and tell, as it were.

Coachable moments await you and will test your mettle time and again. It is during these times when you can upgrade your employees' skills—both hard and soft—and show your people what professionalism means in their daily efforts. But timing is everything, even in coaching.

To put these coachable moments into a coherent context, here's a general overview of the kinds of actions your employee might have demonstrated to produce a coachable moment.

- Positive performance results
- Job-task progression
- Innovation and creativity
- Negative performance results
- Job-task retrogression
- Mistakes and lapses

Ah, the impromptu coachable moments. You never quite know when a golden opportunity will arise for you to really strut your coaching stuff. This isn't, of course, to suggest that coaching is something that you turn on when you wake up in the morning and turn off when you lay your head down at night. You are a coach some of the time in your personal life, but all the time in your work life.

There are prime moments in managing when your coaching can make very measurable and positive differences. You've got to identify these moments, and then vigilantly extract the important lessons to be learned from them. Let's talk about each one individually.

Positive Performance Results

Let's first explore positive performance results and your reaction to them. Getting your employees to produce pleasing results for you (and the company) is precisely what you were hired for. You can call yourself a coach, recite all the bullet points and purposes of coaching and mentoring with the elan of the late Sir Laurence Olivier reciting Shakespeare. But if you don't get your employees to perform in practice, all those recitations will be as empty as a hamburger stand at a vegetarian's convention.

The point is, when you see positive performance, you've got to extract lessons from it. You can't just let out a whoop and a holler and move on. Your coachable moment here involves you meeting with your high-achieving employees and dissecting their successes. You know all about communicating along the way (via constructive feedback, and so on), but the importance of a thorough wrap-up needs to be stressed as well.

When employees' goals are reached or exceeded, you've got to do more than reward them for their achievements. You need to write performance reviews detailing all the things that went right—A to Z. Allow your employees to glean positive lessons from their performances. Don't hold back even the most picayune details of what contributed to their strong performances. Indeed, break down their performances into the various ingredients that contributed to the positive showings. Look at:

Preparation. Just how did the employees' preparations for their jobs and specific tasks lead to their successful performances?

Skills. Just what skills did they utilize in doing their jobs that made a positive difference?

Attitude. Just how did their overall approach to their jobs and work ethic contribute to the final results?

By breaking down the positive performance results into categories, your employees can more fully comprehend their successes, and thus be more capable of moving to the next level, whether it's duplicating successes or perhaps improving on their already strong performances. Recognizing the positive coachable moment is just as essential as dealing with the "negative" coachable moment when you need to catch and correct things that go wrong.

Where there's positive reinforcement, there is also negative reinforcement. Be especially vigilant not to reward the negative behaviors of your employees by ignoring them and permitting them to slip through the workplace cracks. Even if it's not your intention, this is, in effect, negative reinforcement of such behaviors.

Another key area to explore in this wrap-up of your employees' positive performances is outside influences. Did something outside their control contribute to employees' performances that was not considered at the beginning of a performance plan or at the start of a particular project? Sometimes these weigh in on the positive side; other times on the negative side.

These outside conditions range from an economic upturn (or downturn), to a cultural fad, to breakthrough technology, to personnel changes in the company, to a wide variety of other situations. So many things on the outside are, yes, outside both you and your employees' control; things that can seriously impact performances. And it's part of your job to identify them when they happen and find lessons in the experience.

For instance, an economic upswing and shift in consumer confidence can make a huge difference in performance results, depending on your department and the product or services that you offer. The lesson learned could be how to take advantage of these shifting economic winds by recognizing the shift early on and adjusting performance methods and approaches accordingly. Obviously, the same thinking would apply to an economic downswing. Your job is to always impart lasting lessons—where you can and when you can. One of the most important coaching lessons you can impart is learning to adjust plans and approaches at a moment's notice. Resilience is key in many situations.

Job-Task Progression

On to another coachable moment. This one happens when you detect job-task progression in your employees. This is your chance to do what we asked you to do earlier—reward progress and not just results. But part of these reward efforts on your part should involve going beyond mere recognition of progress to the extracting of real and lasting lessons. Lessons, that is, steeped in the many factors behind the progress—behind the forward motion of your employees. You follow the same course as you do with positive performance results, except that you don't wrapup this time. Instead, you dissect, examine, and convey lessons to your employees to keep them doing what works for them; to keep them doing what's the impetus behind their progression in their jobs. At this time, you also make note of the behaviors and attitudes that could be improved upon to take the progress to an even higher level.

Innovation and Creativity

Innovation and creativity on your employees' parts enable them to leap over hurdles by using their smarts and their skills, and by tapping into their talents and abilities. Performance plans and various job projects follow timelines, and there are always key moments in them that will essentially make or break their success—and there are many such moments in the current ultracompetitive business environment. As a coach, you've got to be keenly aware of these moments and reward your employees for their ingenuity, or poke and prod them to be more adaptable and clever at making things happen.

We've said it before that people's potential as workers often remains dormant or is not fully tapped. Coachable moments and bringing out lessons in these special situations are where coaching really earns its kudos. Dinosaur managers are certainly not keeping their eyes open for these moments.

The Flip Side

The flip side of positive coachable moments—positive performance results, job-task progression, and innovation and creativity—are negative performance results, job-task retrogression, and mistakes and lapses. These are also coachable moments. The same approaches are called for. You dissect the performance or the attitude, and identify lessons to be learned. Lessons, this time, should be teaching how to get on the right tracks for your employees who are on the wrong ones.

Coaching for these negative moments can be summed up in a three-part process:

1. Review the moment.
2. Extract a lesson or lessons.
3. Apply the lesson or lessons to another set of circumstances—the next phase of the job, another job, or a career move.

Teaching How to Learn

Teaching your employees how to learn may sound like instructing grade-school kids, but it's not. As you've just read in the previous section on coachable moments, you're called upon time and again to pluck out important lessons from a wide range of work situations. When you identify the consequential lessons to be learned, and scrutinize and discuss them with your employees, you're equipping them to learn on their own. That is, you're giving them the tools to recognize on their own the work moments that are opportunities for learning. You're also showing them how to learn from these moments and move forward in a positive manner.

FACTS

There is truth in the bromide that "Only you can help you." But don't expect your employees to help themselves without a little help from you. Your job as a coach entails showing your employees the paths to learning and career advancement. Walking the paths is up to them.

Learning how to learn essentially means your employees respond to your coachable moments and absorb the lessons therein, and are better prepared to grow their skills, take on more responsibilities, and meet any of the challenges in their jobs. They are more self-sufficient and more capable of seizing opportunities available to them. And employees who are more confident in their jobs and more accomplished at navigating around the many workplace hurdles are the prime candidates for advanced learning.

Red Alert for Opportunities

When your employees reach the advanced learning state, they are keenly aware of what's going on around them. They are mindful of their progression in their jobs and what it means for both their immediate and long-term futures. They are on red alert for opportunities to better themselves. Indeed, when your employees are in this heightened state of awareness in the workplace, they are open to any and all learning situations. They are not only delighted when learning opportunities come their way, but they make things happen by creating their own opportunities.

Looking Outside the Work Environment

As a coach, encourage your staff to look outside the immediate work environs for materials to advance their skills and enhance their performances. Learning opportunities abound in so many places beyond you, your coaching, and the immediate workplace. You should point your employees to good books and magazines on subjects pertinent to their jobs and special skills. Depending on what you and your team need and want, the reading materials could concentrate on subject matter ranging from highly technical skills to professional and leadership skills.

ESSENTIALS

Remember show and tell in grammar school? Well, so much of coaching is a variation of show and tell. That is, you seize on any and all opportunities to teach lessons, on the spot and in real time. These are the most powerful kinds of lessons.

Colleges and universities offer relevant courses on the latest technology, leadership tools and techniques, and just about everything else related to the workings of business. Keep your eyes open for these learning opportunities and match them up with your hungry employees in the advanced learning state. Also consider seminars and workshops, which offer a vast array of business-related subjects pertinent to managing and working in corporate environs and are conducted all the time and all over the place. Again, finding the right employee for the right learning moment is part of your job. And if this means sending an employee from the New York office to a seminar on cutting-edge computer skills in Los Angeles, you might consider committing to it. That is, if you truly believe that attending will make a positive difference for you and for your employee—one that justifies the expense and time away from the office and the job.

Looking Inside the Work Environment

There are learning moments less costly than expensive seminars and the like. It doesn't cost any company dollars for you to instruct your em-ployees to talk to the people whom they encounter in their daily grind on and around the job. Tell them to listen to customers, to coworkers, and to peers in other departments of the company. Convince them of the benefits of hearing what others have to say on business matters ranging far and wide.

The Outer Limits

A lot of men and women are successful businesspersons because, they say, an important and influential person or persons gave them some advice, or showed them some technique, that was instrumental in advancing their careers. Of course, this influential person is often a mentor within the organization, or a good coach like you, but sometimes it's an outsider. That is, somebody who just happened by that made a substantial and positive difference in somebody else's life. Many of us can identify some such influence on our own life.

There are so many people out there with so much to offer others. But they're not going to come to you; you've got to go to them. They need to be drawn out. Translation: It's not going to come to you; you've got to go to it. So, when you tell your employees not to be shy about asking questions of you (a basic tenet of a coach's communication), you should also extend this advice a step further. Tell your employees to network. Encourage them to talk to people within the organization and on the outside, too. Talk, question, understand, and learn.

ESSENTIALS

When you grow your employees' skills to the point where they are self-confident in their jobs and more accomplished at navigating around workplace hurdles, you've got candidates for advanced learning, and should seek to broaden their learning opportunities with books, seminars, mentoring, and more.

Yogi Berra once said, "You can observe a lot by watching." And, as usual, Yogi was right. When you unleash your employees to travel to the ends of the earth—metaphorically speaking—to learn, grow their skills, take on new responsibilities, and welcome challenges with confidence, you've created, not a pack of Frankenstein monsters, but human beings on the way to realizing their work potential.

And doesn't it always come back to that? The purpose of the coaching and mentoring managerial methodology is to take people to their outer limits, not by threats of violence or loss of jobs, but by affording them the knowledge and the opportunities to get there. As a coach, you teach, teach, and teach, and then it's up to your employees to help themselves and achieve. You show the way and your employees determine whether or not to travel beyond their comfortable parameters. If you provide your employees this kind of stimulating work environment, you've done your job and done it well. And, sure, not everybody in your employ will thrive under your tutelage, but most will, and some will do so at extraordinary levels.

CHAPTER 15

Altering the Corporate Culture

When a company adopts the coaching and mentoring approaches in managing its employees, it's getting something more than the maximization of profits. It's altering its corporate culture whether it knows it or not. This chapter shows you exactly what is meant by this culture transformation.

Understanding How Cultural Shifts Occur

Cultural shifts in business don't happen overnight. A revolutionary cultural change in a corporate setting isn't consummated with scattershot applications of coaching tools, techniques, and haphazard mentoring.

How Coaching Can Overhaul the Culture

An absolute cultural makeover entails that companies fully embrace coaching in their management from the top to the bottom of their organizations. That is, companies must employ the coaching and mentoring methodology everywhere and uninterrupted, and not in isolated moments and spots. The companies that fully implement coaching as a managerial art are the ones that are dramatically changing their colors. A cultural overhaul in operations means that the old way of doing things— planning, decision-making, problem solving, rewards, promotions, and so on—is supplanted with a fresh new way of running the whole show. So, if you're managing as a coach in one department of the organization, a coach will likewise run another department. And coaches will manage on the next level in the company, too. And the one after that.

One of the most conspicuous aspects that separates traditional, directive-style management from coaching is that coached employees, unlike those in traditional organizations, are welcomed into the decision-making process, encouraged to be self-sufficient, and made to feel a real part of the company. When the whole corporate culture is grounded in the respect of each individual employee, you know that coaching and mentoring practices have been instituted and are getting results. Results, by the way, beyond the mere bottom line.

Dysfunctional Cultures May Be Tough to Change

Ideally, a corporate family, like any family, should respect all the members within it. Think of a dysfunctional family with a mom, dad, or both, who raise their children in a crude and contemptuous atmosphere. You know how it goes—the kids are always put down and are cruelly mocked. And it invariably starts at the top (just like in business). Mom bad-mouths dad. Dad hits mom. And their kids' hopes and dreams are squashed and deemed unrealistic or foolish. Guess what? The kids will likely grow up and repeat this noxious process with their own kids.

Corporate families that practice this same pestilent pattern of contempt never realize the vast human potential of their many employees. Rather, they hire people to work in specific jobs and do nothing to foster further learning and expansion of their knowledge and skills. These same people then leave their jobs, because there are no challenges and opportunities for advancement, and the process is repeated over and over again.

Coaching is the best managerial method for making the workplace both a productive and a contented place. And the reason is that coaching and mentoring and their tools and techniques are designed to do just that. No other managerial methods marry productivity with contentment in such a consciously coherent way.

Power to the People

Ironically and regrettably, the expression "power to the people" has a disreputable undertone, courtesy of its ironic origins and associations with discredited political ideologies and enemies of the free market and liberty.

QUESTIONS?

What does "power to the people" mean in coaching and mentoring?
It means giving genuine power to the people by respecting their individual initiatives. It means setting individual employees free by tapping into their unique talents and abilities. That's bestowing real power to the people—one person at a time.

Ah, but leave it to coaching and mentoring to clean up the slogan. This managerial art believes in ceding power to the people (employees) by respecting their individuality and initiative. And that's the real thing— genuine power to the people. People are unique individuals with talents and abilities who need to be set free both at home and at work. When these people look for jobs in the corporate world, they want work with high satisfaction levels, and they're most likely to find such jobs in a company committed to giving them power. Power of a kind to chart their own careers without too many restrictions. Roles that unleash their potential as worker commodities and, as we've seen in prior examples, as more thoughtful and wise human beings, too.

An important personal attribute that coaches must always embrace is humility. As a coach, you cannot view your position as the be-all and end-all. In order for coaching to connect with employees, the coach must never be perceived as being imperiously above it all. Coaches don't patronize employees.

If your company is truly committed to coaching in management from the mailroom on up, then you are also more prone to attract employees looking to share in the bounteous opportunities that you offer in both job satisfaction and career growth. That puts you in a position to confer power to the people—your staff.

Company Politics No More

Comprehensive coaching in an organization means that all its company politics are put to bed. Employees can readily see and viscerally feel when politics dominate a company's decision-making process. Indeed, when politics rule in the office, employees feel a sense of powerlessness in performing their jobs in the present tense, with a corresponding sense of hopelessness as far as their futures are concerned. They feel that no matter what they do on the job, company politics will eclipse even their best efforts.

So, yes, we've got another coaching job for you. And that's removing any overt politics from the office, which is your little part of the company—your domain and responsibility. When you work at eradicating this blight, you're handing more power over to your employees. You're raising their levels of satisfaction within their jobs and with the company at large, because the workplace is unfettered with relationships and decision-making clouded by the dreaded, regressive company politics. Just what do we mean by company politics? Looking at problems in unique contexts is important. It broadens your understanding of them and helps you find the right solutions leading to positive outcomes. Here are some examples.

The Blame Game

Deleterious company politics often spawn the blame game, in which the buck never seems to stop on any boss's desk and employees shoulder the lion's share of the blame for what went wrong. As a coach, you must put an end to the blame game if it exists and replace blame with responsibility. That is, put responsibility for doing a job in the forefront of any job assignment or project. Employees then know precisely what they are responsible for doing. They have performance plans to guide them and have settled on goals to strive for. The blame game plays no part in a workplace where there is complete and defined accountability.

SSENTIALS

Don't play the blame game in your office. Make responsibility and accountability the rule, for both you and your employees, and the blame game will cease to exist. Work with individual performance plans and goals, and hold each individual strictly answerable for his or her results on the job.

The Distinctive Relationship

Another area of office politics revolves around the distinctive relationship. Not only the obvious one between manager and employee, but relationships between employees themselves that exclude others. And we're not talking about exclusion in a personal sense, but in a business sense, where employees do not share information or work as a team (both of which are so essential these days in getting a job done right). You've got to be eternally vigilant that these types of distinctive relationships don't take root and cause disharmony and disarray in your office environs. You must foster relationships that you know from experience promote team rapport and competent, concerted efforts.

The Aura of Superiority

Company politics sometimes permit an aura of superiority to prevail in the office. An office caste system, if you will. Yes, you're going to have high-flying employees, the big achievers, whom you will rely on and want to groom for advancement. That's a desirable scenario. But you must be ever mindful not to tolerate your team splitting apart into factions based on skill levels or for any other reasons.

You're responsible for taking any aura of superiority and turning it on its head into an aura of generosity. Those in your employ with more advanced or sharper skills should be encouraged to impart their knowledge and skills to their coworkers (mini-mentoring). And to do so without an attitude of superiority. No employee appreciates feeling like a grade-schooler on the job, patronized and inferior. A team that produces results must share in so many ways, and every member of the team must be made to feel like an important part of it.

ESSENTIALS

Never allow an aura of superiority to hover over your office like a dark rain cloud. Keep your team from splintering apart based on skill levels or any other factors. Foster an aura of generosity instead, encouraging the sharing of knowledge and teaching of skills.

Undue Delegation

When company politics reign supreme, even delegation of authority suffers, and sometimes gets twisted like a pretzel. Undue delegation, also called passing the buck, is in reality no delegation at all. It's an abrogation of somebody's responsibility.

You know by now that coaches regularly delegate important assignments and jobs to their employees. So you are morally obliged to delegate, and as often as you possibly can, or you're not a coach. But you base your delegation of important job responsibilities on what you have to work with in talent and skills. You don't ever pass the buck and call it delegation. That is, you don't get your employees to do your job for you in any way, shape, or form. And you don't allow your employees to get their coworkers to do their jobs for them in any way, shape, or form, either.

ESSENTIALS   Coaches delegate, then delegate some more. It's all part of showing confidence in your employees and offering them added responsibilities and more challenges. But it's not delegation at all if it amounts to passing the buck. When you delegate, you delegate based on merit and achievement.

Undue delegation should be cast adrift like a message in a bottle sent out to sea, with the message being—due delegation only. Due delegation (as opposed to undue delegation) means that delegated jobs and such are conferred on only those who have earned the right by exhibiting the requisite skills, responsibility, and work ethic.

The Exclusive Clique

The last of the company politics issues we'll tackle is the notorious exclusive clique, which is in some ways an extension of distinctive relationships in that it deals with interoffice alliances. The difference is, the exclusive clique sets the rules on how things get done. Everything from soup to nuts. This is the way it's done, period, end of story! And nobody is going to come along and tell us otherwise.

In companies that don't advocate coaching in management, it's not unusual for new managers, let alone new employees, to run headfirst into an exclusive clique and be rejected as unworthy of admission. Managers with new ideas or methods are rebuffed; employees with initiative are shunned. You get the picture. Your job as a coach is to implode the exclusive clique if it's around, and replace it with a team of achievers. Also, you must be circumspect in not allowing any of these cliques to spring to life and grow while on your watch.

Sometimes these cliques can sprout up without you ever realizing it. Hey, you're only human. And when you're working with the same people day in and day out, a certain comfort develops that can lull you into an unsuspecting repose, and yes—a rigid way of doing things. It's when your way of doing things excludes others from contributing their ingenuity and talents that you're in trouble. However, if your way of doing things is coaching in an enduring learning environment, you are, in effect, overseeing a team of achievers, and that's what you want to be doing as a coach. You can't ever be hunkered down with a cozy clique of favored employees if you want to get the best possible results in overall employee satisfaction and performance results.

Hello Support, Good-bye Hierarchy

If you are indeed to work your magic as a coach and manager of people, you're going to have to supplant rigid hierarchy with support.

Removing Barriers Between Managers and Employees

Traditional management methods regularly erect proverbial brick walls between managers and employees. If an organization sees fit to christen you a coach and grant you the leeway to apply the tools and techniques of coaching, it is in effect saying to you, "Make things work." And, as a coach, you know what makes things work. You have to tear down that barrier and implement a support system. When you supersede strict hierarchy with support (and that covers everything that we've discussed relating to fashioning a healthy and productive work environment satisfying to your employees), you've taken a giant step in creating a corporate family in the office.

Employing Coaching and Mentoring Across the Board

There are companies aplenty that don't endorse coaching and mentoring, but nevertheless have wise managers at the helm in various places in the organization applying their sound tools and techniques. In fact, that's a somewhat commonplace scenario. But there are always problems when coaching and mentoring are not practiced by everyone in the company.

For example, Eva works for Heaven on Earth, Inc., and is delighted with her job and thoroughly enjoys working for her manager, John. She is given increasing amounts of responsibilities and challenging job assignments, and her job has evolved nicely over time. Eventually, John recommends her for a new position in the company, a climb up the ladder. Eva is overjoyed at the chance for a promotion, and, of course, the nifty salary increase that goes with it. Her only regret is that she'll be leaving John and her coworkers, whom she thoroughly enjoys working with. But of course, she reasons, she will fast acclimate into her new surroundings. "Don't look back," her boss John tells her. Sound advice as a rule.

FACTS

Coaching and mentoring managerial practices attempt to displace the corporate hierarchy with a support system. They seek to make the customer the center of the office universe and not the manager, the coach. The coach is the leader, but the customer is the king.

Well, unfortunately, Eva does look back, almost immediately as a matter of fact. Even though she has more prestige and more money in her new position, her superior is no John—not even close. Eva's new boss does not employ anything resembling coaching in his managerial conduct. But how could this happen, you ask? Very easily when the whole of the organization is not singing the same tune. When one manager is hitting the high notes like a veritable Pavarotti, and another manager is croaking along like Edith Bunker, you've got an organizational problem. Manager John shouldn't be standing alone in a corporate hierarchy, supporting his employees by lending them his expertise and understanding, only to promote them into a work environment that's the antithesis of the positive and healthy one he presides over. This runs counter to the totality of coaching and mentoring; coaches have to know beyond a shadow of a doubt that their employees have a place to go in the company—a place that will further their growth and not stunt it.

The moral of this story is that the entire company needs to bolster coaching and mentoring, otherwise the company will end up creating even more problems. Coaches have to know beyond a shadow of a doubt that their employees have a place to go in the company—a place that will further their growth and not stunt it.

Satisfying the Customer

The corporate world exists because of customers. And we're all the customers of many organizations. Regardless of what the product or service is, performance results invariably mean pleasing customers in one way or another. Even if the customers are somehow far removed from the workplace, this doesn't mean they're any less important. A powerful thread running through coaching and mentoring is that they seek to shift the emphasis from pleasing the boss to satisfying the customer.

Leading and Setting the Tone

You are the leader and tone setter, of course. As such you must be humble enough to transfer your employees' focus from you to your customers. That is, to the people you, as coach, and all of your employees are laboring in some way to please. Yes, you do the hiring. You communicate. You teach. You work with your employees in devising their performance plans and setting their goals. But this is all about achieving the best possible results. Results for whom? The customers.

Putting the Focus on Results for Customers

You want your employees to deliver results that are pleasing to them, of course, to you, naturally, and to the company, yes indeed. But most of all, you and your employees have to deliver results for the customers, because without customers, there would be no company, no coach, and no employees.

If you've had the good fortune—or misfortune in some instances—of working in a retail or service business, then you know full well that dealing with the walk-in public is not always an easy task. Never mind the physical work required of you, which is often grueling enough. It's the mental drain that's debilitating sometimes, as various customers say and do things to test your patience and very often your sanity. Servicing customers isn't always pretty, but it's a necessity that's got to be done and done right, because satisfying them is what will in the final analysis determine whether a business lives or dies.

Role reversal is an important tool in the coaching and mentoring repertoire. Put it in practice when you want your employees to stand in the shoes of others (such as customers). By utilizing role reversal, you usher your employees into a reality laboratory.

And this truism transcends working behind the counter in a drugstore, or as a waiter or waitress in a restaurant, where customer service is measurable at the point of service. So, while you may not work face-to-face with your company's customers, the company is still in the business of giving its customers what they want and when they want it. And if your company doesn't do these two things, somebody else probably will. For that reason, if you can take the spotlight off yourself and put it where it rightly belongs—on the customers—you'll be making the familial atmosphere of the workplace more cohesive, with everybody working together with the same objective in mind.

Reversing Roles

When you frame a job in the simple terms of pleasing customers, it is an invaluable technique to ask your employees to engage in a little role reversal by putting themselves in the customers' shoes. We're all customers. We patronize countless businesses, utilize so many services, and experience widely varying results in the process. Results that make us want to use, or not use, a particular product or service again. When your employees look at things from a customer's vantage point, they put themselves in the place of the very people they're trying to please. They see things from an unmistakably different perspective. That is, you want each employee working for you to reach into himself and think.

- How do I like to be treated as a customer?
- What can my company do that would please me as a customer?

When you go a step further and ask that your employees answer their own thoughtful, open-ended questions, you're in effect asking them to think as an entrepreneur. And the pièce de résistance as far as you're concerned is putting these answers into action. By using the tried-and-true technique of role reversal, you allow your employees to:

- Think in an entrepreneurial way
- Fashion flexibility
- Empathize with the other side
- Sharpen self-awareness

FACTS

The reality laboratory is a place where employees metaphorically go when they engage in role reversal. It's a place where experimentation leads employees to think as entrepreneurs, empathize with the other side, fashion flexibility, and sharpen self-awareness.

In this role reversal, you are also asking your employees to fashion flexibility by seeing themselves as customers of what the company, yours and theirs, is offering as a product or a service, and how they are offering it. By doing this, you are effecting positive change and implementing new ways of thinking based on your employees' experiences in a reality laboratory.

Yet another benefit of role reversal is that it enables employees to empathize with the other side. Empathy is defined as understanding what somebody else is feeling, or appreciating the circumstances that another individual is in. You can't empathize with another person unless you've shared his or her experiences in a comparable way. Thus, by asking that your employees see things from their customers' perspectives, you are asking that they empathize with them. You are asking, in effect, that they translate this empathy and new understanding into a better product or service via better performances on their parts.

And lastly, any kind of role reversal sharpens self-awareness. When you put your employees into their customers' worlds, you're asking them to look into their own lives and explore what they do as customers—what does and does not satisfy them, and why.

All for One, One for All

At certain times in our lives, whether in our personal or our collective lives as Americans, we need to rally together, united in a common purpose. This "we're all in this together" mentality is so important in the workplace, too. But you've got to do more than enunciate it; you've got to make it come alive in all of your coaching methods and decisions.

It's human nature to be skeptical of our fellow man and woman. That is, we want to see the proof, for instance, that "we're all in this together" before consenting to pull our full weight as part of a team. This means that you, as coach and manager, must never allow yourself to be seen as imperiously above your staff. You've got to lead, but not condescend to any of your people. Your job is to tap into the human potential of your employees and turn it into harnessed energy, leading to stellar performances and, yes, customer satisfaction.

CHAPTER 16

Enhancing Profitability

This chapter shows you why and how particular coaching and mentoring methods make companies—even large corporations—more profitable and, in the process, enhance corporate reputations, which are often labeled inhuman, detached, and cold. Coaching and mentoring reverse this trend while still boosting profits.

The Coaching and Mentoring
Shock Absorber

We've got the global economy, the Internet, and downsizing and restructuring all coming together in a furious business blend. It's a fact of life we'd all better get used to. In this frenzied setting, unprepared managers and apprehensive employees alike are fearful about what the future holds. The future, however, is daunting only for those who don't understand that these tumultuous twenty-first-century business realities can in fact be tamed. Tamed by this thing called coaching, which acts as something of a shock absorber in the modern workplace.

ESSENTIALS

Coaching and mentoring's tools and techniques aim to tame the harsh realities of conducting business in the new millennium. By making employees more resilient, self-confident, and better prepared to handle the stress of today's work climate, a coach lessens the fear of the unknown tomorrow in the workplace.

As a coach and mentor, you're transforming yourself into a living, breathing shock absorber. Did you know that? You're equipping yourself to manage in the new millennium and ward off the inescapable shocks of the present workplace. There's nothing you can't handle if you've got coaching and mentoring's tools and techniques close at hand.

The big-shot companies are usually out in front of so many business trends. Hence, they understand that by putting coaching in their operations they're prepared for the inevitable breakneck changes that come with the territory of conducting business today. They also know full well that those companies who view learning as a finite experience will in short order be blown away by the winds of change.

Flexible Fliers

You're expected to be very flexible in your daily managing efforts—flexible in dealing with your diverse employees and flexible in your planning, based on the multiple factors associated with the faster-than-fast business realities of the present.

Flexible in dealing with people? You better believe it. Employees laboring in corporate America today will vote with their feet if their needs aren't met. They will leave their jobs for better opportunities and more satisfying places to work. And because working people are voting in great numbers, the companies that offer the most stimulating work and career advancement potential will get their votes. It stands to reason then that the companies with coaches and coaching programs in place are coming out on top in the vote counts.

Sound Investments

Because companies' initial training and orientation costs are more substantial than ever, it's in their interests to get a premium return on their investments. Translation: They must invest their time and money in employees who will do a good job for them and not their competitors. The highly competitive business world of today is aggressively competing for the cream-of-the-crop employees. And so, authoritarianism in the managerial hierarchy is breaking apart like a powdered donut dunked in a cup of coffee. Who wants to work for an ogre these days when there are so many more pleasing alternatives?

FACTS

Many big corporations have sullied reputations in the area of caring for their employees' on-the-job well-being. Coaching and mentoring in management are striving to overhaul these frosty reputations, and endeavoring to give these distant corporate faces human faces.

And, on the other end of the spectrum, managers who rely on managing via e-mail are not about to inspire commitment from their staffs. Neither authoritarian nor indifferent managers are going to keep the best and the brightest working in their folds. They're not going to extract the maximum human potential from their people because they're not allowing their employees to boldly go forward, or, in the case of mad e-mailer managers, they're not there in the flesh and blood to poke and prod them to perform. Wise companies see this and are consciously training, and in some cases retraining, their managers to be teachers and counselors—coaches.

Human potential is limitless. But it needs to be tapped like a keg of foamy beer. Companies with adroit management can actively mine human potential! But they need teams of schooled coaches and wise mentors to get the job done. Otherwise all that latent talent and great possibility will remain dormant and unrealized like buried treasure. People are brimming with ideas, including ideas on how better to do their jobs and perform at higher levels. They're chock full of skills and know-how that can easily go undetected if there's no coach around operating as the company store detective searching for all of this percolating productivity.

The Coach as Detective

Leave it to corporate bigwigs to view their managers as detectives on a diligent search for getting the best possible results. After all, it's common sense. Successful businesses don't run on autopilot, because their employees don't run on autopilot. Employees need to be turned on. We touched upon this subject matter in Chapter 14, when we talk about using coachable moments to spur self-motivation. Yes, it's up to employees to ultimately do the work, but coaches have to turn them on sometimes and adjust the controls now and again. No big surprise here. You've seen throughout the book that you've got to wear many hats in your coaching duties. And one of them is a detective's fedora. So put it on and get ready for some intriguing detective work in the office.

Let's say, for argument's sake, that you're a fusion of detectives Jim Rockford and Lt. Theo Kojak. Rockford is a private investigator on the West Coast, known for his unorthodox approaches in doing his job. You might say that he pushes the envelope on occasion. Kojak, on the East Coast, works within the confines of the New York City Police Department rules and regulations, but falls back on his vast experiences and lessons learned in his regular detective work.

Coaching by its very nature is unorthodox as it tries new ways of doing things all the time. Decisions are often based on the individual employee's personality and skill level. This focus on the individual is well outside traditional management parameters. By the same token, as a coach you must never forget that you work for a particular company with a particular vision. The *Fortune* 500 companies, for instance, are vigilant in guarding their reputations. Thus, you are expected to be unorthodox, yet work within certain guidelines as a coach.

You determine what works best for you. You ascertain what you've got to work with—that is, the people, their knowledge base, and their levels of skills. You detect in them what they can do and, essentially, set them to doing it. It's very important to project a can-do spirit; however, this confident spirit maximizes performance results only when it's paired with can-do employees. Otherwise, it's a hot-air spirit, which doesn't accomplish much in business or in life in general.

Stormy Weather: Brainstorming

From employees' perspectives, coaching means—among so many positive things—that their managers listen to them and afford them ample say in both defining and navigating their jobs. In your accepting presence, brainstorming permits your employees to sound off in a freewheeling, candid setting. That is, your employees express themselves without fear of the office thought police coming down on them.

As a coach, you have to promote the can-do spirit. You do this by exhibiting enthusiasm and setting bold but attainable goals. You must, however, make certain that you match your can-do spirit with can-do employees.

Your coaching methods and the overall office ambience can't be patterned after a totalitarian state. It can't be a place where "oppositionists" are thrown into prisons or gulags. Admittedly, you don't want oppositionists working for you who rail against your coaching program and all that you're trying to accomplish. But you don't want yes-men and yes-women, either. You want your people to freely speak their minds and go against the grain now and then.

Brainstorming sessions are, in many ways, microcosms of the relationships between coaches and their employees, because they represent communication without boundaries. And creative people relish this rhetorical freedom. They enjoy contributing their ideas and suggestions without fear of being ridiculed if their verbal offerings don't pass intellectual muster. When word gets out that you lend an ear to your employees' ideas, people of talent and ambition will be viscerally attracted to your work setting, and employees will want to stay in such a warm and nurturing business environment. This is yet another reason why big and small businesses alike are welcoming coaching and mentoring and their bold approach in letting employees have their say. Companies recognize that letting employees have their say often means that they want to stay.

Guidance Counselors

Because the biggest companies are big—really big—it is not surprising that a commonly heard employee gripe is that advice and counsel from management is hard to come by. And this is a big—really big—reason why coaching is being ushered into the various levels of many of these sprawling companies.

FACTS

A coach's workplace is not patterned after totalitarian governments. And don't forget that freedom of expression is a specially guarded right that coaches will defend to their deaths—as coaches.

In all levels of schooling, there are guidance counselors. In grade school, high school, and college, they are there and ready, willing, and able. What are they ready, willing, and able to do? Ideally, to answer students' questions and lend them support when needed. Grade school counselors' advice, however, is somewhat different from that of their high school counterparts. And college counselors, of course, dispense a different brand of advice altogether.

Creating a Pliable System

This chapter illustrates the importance of replacing an unbending managerial hierarchy with a more pliable support system. And this means placing the equivalent of guidance counselors—coaches and mentors—at all levels of the company.

Supplying Answers

Employees up and down the corporate ladder have questions and concerns. They want and deserve to know so many things, from what is expected of them, first and foremost, in their jobs, to what's in their futures in their respective companies. It's totally disheartening for employees in an organization to have a plethora of questions, but nary a soul to ask. So, yes, you're an answer man or answer woman as a coach. The company paying your salary is relying on you to thoroughly answer your employees' job-related questions and assuage any of their career concerns. Putting this aspect of coaching in the forefront of the support system is rudimentary if once faceless companies are to be given a human face. For it is this human face that will rescue reputations. It is the human face that'll also maximize employee performance results in today's business climate.

The Human Face of Corporations

While on the subject of putting a more human face on big companies, let's own up to the fact that many people are skeptical that it can be done. For the many doubting Thomases out there, let's look at it this way. How many of today's medical students are choosing to specialize in the fields of cosmetic doctoring? Many more than in years past, that's for sure. But putting a human face on a company is a lot easier than performing plastic surgery!

Changing the Corporate Face

Advancing technology in plastic surgery, coupled with runaway vanity, has made face makeovers the in thing. From the hair atop the head to the point on the chin, people are opting to change their looks by rearranging their faces. In the same vein, many businesses, courtesy of today's rapid technological growth, want to change their faces—their reputations—by rearranging the ways they manage their people. True, the technological advances in business are somewhat different in nature from those in medical science, but what they have in common is that they make what was impossible yesterday very possible today. Many businesses, big and small alike, are afforded very few choices when it comes to the survival game. And depending on their product or service, and the stiffness of the competition, a face-lift is more often a necessity than a luxury.

ESSENTIALS

Among the many hats that you wear as a coach is that of guidance counselor. You must have lots of answers at your disposal to the many questions and concerns of your employees. There is nothing more deflating than having questions and nobody to pose them to.

Despite the analogy, coaching can never be perceived as a mere cosmetic change if it is to work effectively, both in the short term and in the long term. In businesses where coaching and mentoring are seen as more cosmetic than real, businesses don't produce the results they should. Many businesses take bits and pieces of what they believe is coaching, but don't lay the proper foundation of management with integrity, which earns the respect and trust of their employees.

Some companies spout slogans such as: "Coaching begins with an attitude of helpfulness"; "Coaching is asking the right questions, not supplying the answers"; "Coaching requires commitment." And that's nice. But if they don't back up the words with credible actions, their attempts at inspiring employees to commitment are seen as laughable.

Making the Face-Lift Permanent

The coaching and mentoring methodology is anything but cosmetic. It is flexible and varied—always a work in progress—but it represents a permanent managerial face-lift. It's a face-lift that takes tired and worn-out traditional management approaches and turns them into young and sexy management styles befitting the new century and new millennium.

FACTS

For many corporations, coaching and mentoring represent a managerial face-lift. But this face-lift needs to be more than cosmetic if it's to achieve positive results. It must not resemble a human face-lift gone awry—bizarre or weird. It should appear young and sexy—alluring to employees.

As a coach, you want to appear "young" and "sexy" in managing your team. (Of course this is a metaphor, because coaching and mentoring don't discriminate against chronological age or physical attractiveness.) It's about being vigorous and attractive in your managerial practices and outlook. It's about challenging your employees without appearing overbearing and expecting the impossible.

It's worth repeating that both you, as a coach or mentor, and your employees or mentees can substantially benefit from a company's new face in so many positive ways.

The Benefits of Coaching

We've touched on many of these benefits already. It's nevertheless important to view the breadth and scope of this list. By so doing, you'll appreciate and understand why coaching and mentoring are not only increasingly popular, but also why they're not cosmetic at all when they are fully embraced and supported up and down organizational hierarchies. You'll see in this list, too, not only what you are responsible for imparting to your employees as a coach, but also what you, as a coach and manager, learn in your tireless efforts in leading people.

We've also looked at outside coaches coming into organizations to work on specific shortcomings of managers and employees both, or being brought aboard to introduce the methods of coaching to those unfamiliar with them.

Corporate executives work one-on-one with coaches, as do middle managers, supervisors, and career-oriented low-level employees. So, really, coaching and coaches are everywhere you look on the corporate ladder these days. They are employed for many diverging purposes. There is, however, one overriding aim that transcends all coaches and coaching maneuvers, and that's to better people as productive entities and, in so doing, make them better human beings in a variety of ways.

Here's a list summarizing the vast and varied benefits the practice of coaching and mentoring offers:

- Provides assistance in developing a personal vision that coexists with a company's business vision
- Sets into motion the attitudes and actions necessary in seeing this vision to fruition
- Emphasizes expanding knowledge and growing skills
- Offers guidance and regular counsel in overcoming negative personality traits or skill deficits that imperil career growth
- Increases self-awareness leading to better, more authentic relationships with coworkers, customers, and—yes—those outside of professional life
- Balances work life and personal life so that they are a harmonious one
- Develops business and working relationships far and wide through networking, thus broadening influence and career opportunity
- Accentuates learning the paths to achieving breakthrough performance results
- Engages in genuine dialogue and offers constructive feedback, and welcomes it in return
- Transforms negative organizational politics into positive working relationships
- Tempers work-related stress with routine and open communication
- Makes career self-reliance both a top priority and doable
- Asks open-ended questions and gives open-ended answers

- Understands the importance of strong communication skills, both written and oral
- Marries performance growth with personal growth
- Builds confidence in dealing with conflict situations
- Works with performance planning and functioning within them
- Sets aggressive but attainable goals
- Strengthens problem-solving skills
- Makes finding solutions to any and all problems job one
- Seeks positive outcomes in all work situations—big or small
- Grasps the importance of self-motivation and commitment to doing the job
- Recognizes commitment to today's job as relevant to tomorrow's job
- Imparts business acumen and the abilities to think entrepreneurial
- Overcomes personal limitations by embracing continued learning

As you can see in perusing this lengthy list of coaching and mentoring benefits, the practice of coaching and mentoring guarantees success in overcoming deficiencies and broadening horizons. Now the question: How do all these benefits help a company's bottom line?

The list of benefits notes obstacles that both you and your employees can overcome. You overcome these obstacles by gaining confidence in your own abilities and by becoming more aware of your strengths and limitations and how others perceive you. You plug up the gaps in your deficiencies and never pass up an opportunity to learn and to grow. By staying focused, you chart your own career. But your career isn't the be-all and end-all. That's why coaching and mentoring talk about the importance of balancing work and home life.

CHAPTER 17

Managing
Diversity

Diversity is a hot-potato issue as it relates to coaching and mentoring's roles in managing distinct female, minority, ethnic, and cultural concerns. Coaching and mentoring's tools and techniques are tailor-made to deal with employees as unique individuals with unique temperaments and talents. By avoiding the one-size-fits-all approach of traditional managing, coaching and mentoring are equipped to meet diversity challenges.

The Glass Ceiling

A look at corporate middle management reveals that the numbers of women and minorities in managerial positions are at a record high. And this is quite an accomplishment! But above middle management, the numbers of women and minorities are not particularly impressive. This phenomenon is sometimes referred to as hitting the glass ceiling. The glass ceiling is not an illusion, but an ingrained reality, even in the twenty-first century.

QUESTIONS?

What is the glass ceiling?
The glass ceiling is the term applied to the obstacles that women and minorities face in breaking into the senior management of corporations. Historic gains have been realized in middle management, but nothing quite as impressive above this level.

The logical question for us to consider now is "Why aren't women and minorities making the same positive strides into senior management as they are in middle management?" It's the answer to this profound query that defines coaching and mentoring's posture in countering the glass ceiling and the so-called diversity issues in the workplace.

The Invisible Hand

Is overt sexism and racism the reason for the glass ceiling's existence? Maybe thirty, forty, or fifty years ago, the answer would have been a resounding "yes!" But it's a vastly different day. There are strict laws in place now that prohibit discrimination based on gender, race, and any number of things. This isn't to suggest that there aren't some biased souls in the corporate sphere. Sure there are. But these folks are not the chief custodians of the glass ceiling.

Instead, we need to look at the invisible hand that's holding back so many women and minorities. Many mentoring and mini-mentoring relationships are in the invisible hand's tight grasp. By and large, senior managers groom people to work alongside them or succeed them, and they choose people they feel most comfortable with and trust. And who do you feel most comfortable with and trust? People who share your background, interests, life's reference points, and the like. That is, people who are most like you. This cultural connection can't be minimized in the understanding of why white males tap mostly white males to be their on-the-job peers and heirs. This isn't necessarily sexism, racism, or xenophobia. In fact, it has more to do with sociology. Generally speaking, people tend to socialize with friends and acquaintances most like them.

This is a roundabout way of saying that the old boy network exists because old boys prefer to play with other old boys. Today's political correctness often encourages us to jump to sinister conclusions and to frame everything in terms of discrimination. And the politically correct straitjacket we find ourselves in regularly has us clamoring for more government intervention in hiring laws, and so on, compelling corporations to get with the program—programs that give people a leg up based on gender or race, and not on talents and abilities.

FACTS

The invisible hand in many mentoring and mini-mentoring relationships is a big reason why the glass ceiling still exists. That is, white males in senior management tap other white males to work alongside them and succeed them. They do this based on the familiarity factor—common backgrounds, interests, and reference points.

No matter what benign labels politicians and the media minions apply to these policies, they are nevertheless unfair and counterproductive. Selecting employees based solely on gender or race was wrong fifty years ago, and it's just as wrong today. Opinion polls show that most everybody agrees it's wrong, regardless of race, gender, or ethnicity. Fortunately, the coaching and mentoring managerial approach is geared to forthrightly deal with genuine gender, race, ethnic, and cultural concerns, while not sacrificing the all-important meritocracy that is the bedrock of a fair and productive work environment.

Equal Opportunity Means Just That

Remember that "opportunity" is always your trump card. That's what you offer your employees from day one on the job; that's how you attract new talent to come work for you. The word "opportunity," as a matter of fact, is sprinkled all over this book's pages because opportunity is a valued principle of coaching and mentoring. In such a people-intensive approach to managing, opportunities for learning, new challenges, and, of course, advancement in the company, have to always be available to your employees. But the opportunity bell rings hollow if it doesn't mean genuine opportunity for everybody, regardless of gender, race, or ethnicity.

You can talk the opportunity talk all you want, but if Beth sees Sean, Will, and Christopher advancing at a faster clip than she is, even though she's equally or more qualified than all of them, then you've got a lot of explaining to do. Similarly, if Fred, Eugene, and Donald find themselves passed over for a promotion in favor of Ellen, who hasn't earned her on-the-job performance stripes, you've simultaneously got a credibility and a morale problem on your hands. So, what do you do to ensure that your talk of equal opportunity means just that? How do you factor in the sober reality of the glass ceiling? How do you ensure that women and minorities aren't excluded from those special relationships (mentoring and mini-mentoring) that play a considerable part in the opportunity equation?

Understanding the Role of Affirmative Action

Affirmative action is a much debated public policy issue. We'll leave the issue debate to a book on politics and public referendums, but the history of affirmative action reveals that it was originally crafted as a government access program, not a giveaway deal. Your job as a coach is to practice affirmative action in the workplace as it was originally and very nobly conceived. That is, you've got to make certain that women and minorities are apprised of all the advancement opportunities in the workplace and are given a sincere shot at competing for them.

Leveling the Playing Field

In the office environs—and it doesn't matter if you're a man or a woman—you've got to level the playing field, not the results. A level playing field doesn't mean different standards for people based on gender, race, or ethnicity. Rather, it means you're fully aware of and understand the roles of the invisible hands in your workplace, and that you make compensatory allowances for them. When mentors are assigned to employees, for instance, it is often the case that women and minorities bear the brunt here based on an entrenched and long-standing pecking order. Mentoring (see Chapter 4 for a full discussion on the role of the mentor) often refers to higher-ups in an organization advising and offering career counseling to employees on lower rungs of the corporate ladder. And, yes, as we previously noted, there is a propensity for male bonding in these relationships that perpetuates a shortage of diversity in high places. There is a mentality of "These are the kinds of guys I hang around with, live next door to, and talk to about all things. Naturally, these are the kinds of guys I want to work with and place my trust in."

ESSENTIALS

In order for you to promote diversity without inappropriate set-asides, you've got to understand the difference between equality and equivalence. Equality of office standards and performance expectations that everybody must abide by and meet are a must. Equivalence in individual employee treatment, however, is not in the coaching and mentoring playbook.

Okay, let's get specific in how you level the playing field without losing your credibility and authority as a coach and manager. First and foremost, you need to grasp and fully understand the difference between equality and equivalence. They are not one and the same when it comes to managing. This shouldn't be too difficult for you to fathom, because your coach's toolbox is crammed with tools and techniques designed for making such distinctions.

Upholding Equality

Equality is the principle in your office that everybody is expected to uphold by abiding by certain rules of conduct, ethical boundaries, and, of course, meeting performance expectations. Equivalence, on the other hand, is not part and parcel of coaching. In fact, it runs completely counter to it. Every employee in your charge is considered a special individual. Therefore, equivalence in treatment doesn't ever wash.

FACTS

Performance standards don't ever need to be lowered to accommodate diversity. You need only afford opportunities to those who fall under the diversity umbrella and allow them to meet those standards and advance based on merit and merit alone.

Now comes the hard part. Sure, you accept your responsibility in handling all the behavioral challenges and skill deficiencies in your employees that come down the pike. After all, you're a coach, and that's what coaches do. But now you're being asked to handle differences that are very apparent (gender, race, and ethnicity), but also very complex. Far-ranging variances in employees' temperaments, attitudes, and skills are challenging enough to manage, but now you must add another difference to the mix.

Keeping Firm Standards

Managing diversity is the kind of challenge you address with the firm standards you already have in place—standards that all of your employees are measured against. When involved in events concerning those standards, you deal with your employees on a one-on-one basis, yes, but you never alter your bedrock principles or lower your performance expectations—for anybody or for any reason. But diversity issues are ambiguous. You've got to look at gender, race, ethnicity, and other cultural differences in a manner quite different from the way you judge bad attitudes or skill deficiencies.

The obvious question that springs to mind by now is "Doesn't all this talk boil down to lowering or adjusting standards to accommodate diversity?" The answer is a resounding "No!" If you buttress both the company's expectations and your own expectations, you are always on solid ground. The problem of a lack of diversity atop the corporate managerial hierarchy is not that standards need to be lowered to assist diversity, but that diverse people need to be afforded the opportunities to meet those standards and move upward.

Putting a Premium on Skills

In your day-to-day coaching, you make opportunity a reality for everyone because you conduct business in a continuous learning environment, which puts a premium on growing employees' skills. And this means, too, that you're growing diversity because your staff of employees is no doubt a diverse lot. If you assiduously navigate your coaching course, you most certainly will be grooming star pupils from all walks of life. Hence, your employee pool of bright stars will be diverse, not because of a quota system, but because you devote your regular, everyday coaching activities to building up people—all people, regardless of gender, race, or ethnicity. You can uplift people by taking into account all aspects of their personality makeup, including diversity, and not ever run counter to your doctrine of equality.

Gender and Ethnicity Do Matter

Managing as a wise coach (that's what this book is all about) will automatically guarantee more women and minorities will get mentors and take advantage of other career-boosting opportunities. When you're managing as a confident coach, you won't hesitate to assign mentors to any of your performing employees regardless of race, gender, or ethnicity. You won't hesitate to groom them for promotions and offer them greater and greater challenges. You won't refrain from promoting employees of all stripes because you will be absolutely sure that your coaching methods are the right ones in developing highly competent, temperamentally suited, and peak-performing employees.

FACTS

A coach need not be color-blind nor gender-blind. On the contrary, a coach sees everything, evaluates everything, and considers nothing inconsequential with regard to decision-making, finding solutions, and seeking positive outcomes to any and all situations in the workplace.

Remember That Nothing Is Inconsequential

While gender, race, or ethnicity shouldn't be factors in hiring or promoting people, don't believe these factors don't matter in the workplace. When you sit down with a highly sensitive employee for one of your many coaching sessions, be it a get-to-know-you-better meeting, a performance planning session, a performance review, or a problem situation, you have to treat your sensitive employee different from the way you interact with the more thick-skinned employees in your ranks. And the same reasoning applies to diversity matters.

Coaches, for example, have to acknowledge that foreign-born employees who work for them have distinct customs and see the world from perspectives quite different from the native-born. So, when you coach employees from unfamiliar backgrounds, you can't disregard these cultural realities. This doesn't mean you bend your workplace standards to accommodate foreign workers in any way. It merely means that you consider everything in the makeup of the unique individuals on your team.

Avoid Extremes

Managing diversity is a very challenging affair for some coaches. But it's not something that should ever intimidate you. It's the managers who are intimidated in this area who tend to create more problems for themselves than need be. They either err on the side of condescending to diversity, for fear of getting branded an obstructionist or worse; or they preclude diversity because they don't know how to deal with it, and think that it's more trouble than it's worth. Both of these improper stances invariably explode in their practitioners' faces. If you don't manage diversity as you manage everything else, with calm and consistent assuredness, you will have a mutiny on your hands.

If you seem to be twisting your standards and moving away from the all-important workplace meritocracy, you will lose your credibility. If you show favoritism on the other end of the spectrum, you will similarly be viewed as not living up to your own words and principles. The bottom line is, you must allow everybody to play the game on your coaching field. That is, you must let every employee progress based on merit. You must not construct any roadblocks based on gender, race, or ethnicity.

ESSENTIALS   In your coaching, it is imperative that you avoid the polar extremes of managing diversity issues. That is, don't condescend to diversity by giving special privileges based on gender, race, or ethnicity. Conversely, don't ever impede diversity based on unfounded fears or prejudices.

If you always coach with a wise and understanding hand, you will see that it is in fact an even hand and that diversity will occur naturally and without any bending of your principles. And there will be no cloud hanging over your coaching efforts and raining down on what you've accomplished. There will also be no stigmas attached to those who are conferred more challenging job responsibilities, and those who get promoted and move on up in their careers.

Avoiding the Assumption Function

To keep you on the straight and narrow, there are a few things you must avoid doing. Stereotyping your employees based on gender, race, or ethnicity, for one, is a big no-no. Remove stereotyping from your thought process if you want to see diversity come to pass. Coaches never work with the assumption function that everybody from a particular group does things in a particular way.

Take George, a department manager, who assumed a lot of things that just weren't so. He managed quite a diverse brood. But he tended to give the greatest responsibilities and biggest challenges in jobs to the male members of his team. And when a highly able female in his employ, Laurie, questioned him on her perceptions that something was rotten in Denmark, George informed her that he couldn't afford any interruptions in the important job projects that stretched out over many months. Laurie couldn't quite figure out where George was coming from with such an explanation. What did "interruptions" in job projects over a period of time have to do with gender?

Upon further pressing of her concern, George admitted that in his last job, he managed a team with an employee who left on maternity leave in the middle of an important job that was very dependent on her knowledge and skills. From that moment on, stereotyping consumed George's mind as he assumed that every woman in his sights was poised to start or increase a family, cutting him adrift and causing overall performance to lag.

Laurie apprised him in no uncertain terms that he was managing with a sexist stereotype and discriminating in the process. She made it clear that his stereotyping was not only far off base but against the law as well. Laurie told him to clear his head and thinking process and she would avoid lodging a formal complaint against him. Suffice it to say, George heaved a sigh of relief at the offer.

ALERT

Coaches don't work with the assumption function. That is, they don't assume that everybody from a particular gender, race, or ethnicity does things in the same way. Similarly, they do not assume that a group doesn't possess particular skills or can't do certain jobs.

If you assume that employees cannot do certain jobs or learn particular skills based on gender, race, or ethnicity, you're very silly and not coaching timber. You're also asking for a mess of trouble on numerous fronts. Discrimination lawsuits in the workplace are routine these days and nothing to sniff at. This is something you've always got to be aware of while managing in the twenty-first century. Even if you view certain lawsuits as frivolous and without merit—and some of them are—it doesn't mean that they're not going to cause you and the company a lot of heartache—and, perhaps, a lot of money, too. But beyond the threat of lawsuits—and most important for you as a coach—is the maximization of performance and positive results. Don't let a thick head rob you of maximizing the talents and abilities of your employees and hence their performances, by stereotyping employees and assuming they can't do certain jobs.

ESSENTIALS In your workplace, you must adopt a zero tolerance policy toward off-color humor, abusive language, and exclusionary practices of any of your employees based on gender, race, or ethnicity. Such a strict policy in place—and enforced—will make the office environs a better place in which to work.

Communicating with and getting to know your employees is the building block that makes coaching, the managerial art, rise like a colossus. If you permit assumptions based on gender, race, or ethnicity to preclude you from digging deeper and finding out what your employees can do, you're being very shortsighted and foolish. And foolish folks with blinders on and silly prejudices don't make the coaching grade.

Make sure you respect the differences in your employees and set the right tone immediately in this sometimes touchy area. This means that you don't tolerate any disrespect in the office based on gender, race, and ethnicity. The glass ceiling is not a figment of people's imaginations. It hovers up above and does so because of exclusionary practices—conscious or unconscious—but exclusionary nonetheless. No employees, for any reason, should be excluded from any of the opportunities to do their jobs and do them well.

Eradicating Unhealthy Behaviors

There is a whole roster of behaviors that you'd be wise to eradicate from the office environs sooner rather than later. In order to preside over a healthy work atmosphere, you've got to make it a civil one, and that means that you must enforce zero tolerance for the following practices.

A Joke Too Far

This covers a lot of ground. Insult comedian Don Rickles is an entertaining performer, but a Don Rickles employee is altogether something else, and not someone you can tolerate on the job. Even if an employee is "only joking," those on the receiving end of the "joke," or within earshot of it, are the ones who make that determination. There are plenty of comedy clubs to go to and comedy channels to watch, and that's where put-down, sardonic, and off-color humor can flourish. The corridors and cubicles of the office aren't the places for edgy comedy.

Abusive Language

You also should be eternally vigilant in stamping out foul and abusive language of any kind. The workplace isn't the Howard Stern Show. And some people find working in a bleeping environment to be bleeping unpleasant and bad for bleeping productivity.

Risk Takers

Okay, you've opened up all the opportunity doors and everybody is welcome. You've done your job well. But it's ultimately up to the individuals themselves to walk through open doors, and sometimes that involves taking risks. There are various lessons that you can impart to those diverse members of your staff who might otherwise feel intimidated in moving into uncharted territories and opening doors. Many people in the workplace are averse to taking risks, particularly women and minorities who have been shut out from reaching certain levels. Indeed, it's human nature to allow cautiousness to take over when boldness is called for. Indeed, the fear of striking out, which cuts across a wide swath of all workers—men, women, all races, all nationalities—often precludes many home runs from being hit.

In baseball, to avoid striking out, a batter will sometimes choke up on the bat. This gives him more bat control and a quicker response time to swing at the ball. But it also cuts down on his power, because the shorter swing is calculated to hit the pitch and make contact. A bigger swing, on the other hand, is more likely to miss a pitch, but is also more likely, when contact is made, to send the baseball flying greater distances. The baseball player's choice is to play it safe or to go for it.

The same choices apply to moving up in the business world. Choking up on the job amounts to being cautious, which, in many circumstances, is a wise posture to take in business. Caution embraces thoughtful and deliberate thinking and a strong attention to detail. These are admirable traits and work effectively in certain jobs—but caution can also hold people back. Sometimes boldness, or risk taking, is required to reach the highest levels of management in an organization. Risk taking is something you as a coach should always welcome, and you need to pass this principle on to your employees, particularly those who will be charting areas where their gender, race, or ethnicity is underrepresented. Trailblazing in any area involves throwing caution to the wind.

Thinking Long-Term

Another important lesson that you should convey to all of your employees—but again, especially those under the glass ceiling—is to look at job- and career-related matters in the long term as well as in the short term. As we've seen time and again, coaching and mentoring try to bridge the short- and long-term goals of the workplace. Coaching pays very close attention to the job at hand and ties the lessons learned to employees' long-term goals.

FACTS

Coaching is uniquely qualified to deal with diversity issues because it is the mosaic of managing. That is, it is a work in progress that celebrates individuality. It places minimal restrictions on its coaches and is open and malleable.

Women and minorities who believe they must work harder to move up sometimes devote all their time and energy to succeeding beyond their wildest imaginations in the present, and give short shrift to planning in the longer term. This is understandable behavior that your coaching can more properly align, leading, of course, to greater opportunities. But just how is working hard in the present properly aligned with career movement? That's the next lesson.

Being Objective

The final lesson that you should transmit to your employees on the diversity front is that they should keep a sober eye on improving themselves, and view their career goals objectively and with dispassion, making the best decisions now for their long-term future. At the same time they need to work passionately at whatever jobs they are doing in the present, all the while learning and growing their skills.

CHAPTER 18

Retail and Service Industries

This chapter takes coaching and mentoring and their methodologies into the retail and service industries, charting a new frontier in the process. Here you'll discover that most of your coaching and mentoring tools and techniques can be applied to managing walk-in retail or service-oriented businesses.

Seeing How Retail and Service Are Different

Really, there are few places on the business landscape that clamor for a people approach to managing more than the customer-intensive businesses of retail and service. Why? Because, first of all, the atmospheres in many of these work settings are often unhappy and unhealthy for employees, and, most of all, employees deal face-to-face with their customers. These industries cry out for a fresh kind of leadership that looks out for employees' needs and wants, but also holds them to high standards of on-the-job professionalism.

ESSENTIALS In retail and service businesses, because you face the public, you've got to make clear—even more so than in office jobs—the importance of learning, growing skills, and gaining experience. You've got to extract lessons from every job and every situation and point them out to your employees so they present their best faces to your customers.

Remember, the Customer Is King

Long before the terms "coaching" and "mentoring" wound their way into business circles, you, as a customer yourself, experienced some kind of noteworthy treatment at a retail or service business—noteworthy, in that it was either especially good or especially bad. Sometimes the red carpet was rolled out for you; sometimes you were treated with a detached indifference; still other times you were made to feel unwelcome, as if you were an intruder.

The companies that roll out the red carpet for you are the ones showing their principles in action—principles that are instilled in all of their employees. They accentuate and practice good customer service. And considering that businesses live and die based on satisfying their customers, this "customer is king" mantra isn't exactly a bad idea, nor revolutionary thinking.

Some coaches prefer to work with the slogan "the customer is always right even when he isn't." This catch phrase exemplifies the great latitude that must be given to the very customers who make or break businesses every day.

You'd think sometimes today that granting the customer basic respect is in fact revolutionary, because respect seems to be getting rarer with each passing day. Is there hope of reversing this trend? Can coaching and mentoring's latticework wind its way down into these retail and service businesses that so often get overlooked for being too dirty and unworthy of so contemplative a managerial approach? Ironically, it's in these very retail and service businesses where the greatest numbers of people can reap the benefits of coaching and mentoring and their positive principles put into action.

Motivating Service and Retail Employees

We've all patronized places of business where a clerk or cashier delivers a set spiel: "Hello and welcome to Happy Burger. If you have any questions regarding our vast and varied menu, please do not hesitate to ask. Today's special is the double Swiss-cheese burger with our own special barbecue sauce. How may I assist you today?" Now, what's your reaction to these robotic renditions of common courtesy? For some people, it's very annoying, and they liken the experience to being serviced by an army of humanoids. For others, however, this android kind of courtesy is better than the alternative—no courtesy at all.

The reality is that this indoctrination of a short "welcoming the customer" speech is at least a start. It's what managers attempt to do first and foremost with a workforce of men and women who need a heap of training, particularly in the soft skills of interpersonal communication. Indeed, when you're confronted with employees who lack even the most basic social and professional skills, it's generally prudent to ask them to commit to memory a few sentences of civility and regurgitate them on cue. And then you can take it from there.

Motivate with Few Motivators

In addition to the lack of social skills, perhaps the most difficult hurdles that managers must leap over in retail and service businesses are associated with employee commitment and self-motivation. If you're managing in a busy restaurant or big chain store, for example, you're more than likely expected to work many long and hard hours. You're asked to motivate yourself to commit to a tough job, and to instill that same push and determination in your employees. This isn't an easy task in the office place, and it's a more difficult one, as you might imagine, in a retail or service business environment.

ESSENTIALS

Respect throughout the workplace is key. This means you must be respected and respect others. It is particularly important in retail and service businesses to elevate respect to its highest level, as many employees don't respect their jobs or feel respected in doing them.

For starters, the paycheck in most of these types of jobs is not as fleshy as in corporate office jobs. And when the pay is on the lower end of the scale, it's very hard to preach about the many benefits of going all out in the job. Another problem is that the range of opportunities for advancement in these businesses is often limited. Yes, it's tough for you to convince people that the sky's the limit while working in a coffee shop or a sneaker store.

Be Truthful

So, what you must do first in any kind of retail or service management position is tell the truth, as you would anywhere else. That is, don't make promises that you can't keep—or that nobody believes—and don't manufacture promotion opportunities that exist only in people's imaginations: "If you work your buns off here, you've got a chance to be the next Ronald McDonald and make personal appearances all across the country. You could be earning a six-figure income in no time flat." The fact is, most people aren't stupid enough to believe that.

Create Learning Opportunities

Since you can't always offer better job opportunities, your coaching stance must place the emphasis on where it properly belongs—on continuous learning on the job, and the growing of skills wherever and whenever possible. At first glance you might think that the notion of a continuous learning environment thriving in a fast-paced retail or service setting is some kind of joke. You might also conclude that you'd play the fool if you opined on growing skills and career advancement to a group of low-paid and overworked employees.

Well, you'd be greatly mistaken if you accepted this negative scenario as inevitable. Let's say, for example, that you're managing in a busy restaurant. You could assume that your staff—waiters, waitresses, et al.— would turn a deaf ear to your preaching about acquiring knowledge and growing skills on the job. But why assume this? Really, your success here boils down to your communication abilities and the bond of trust that you establish between yourself and your staff.

Many managers in high turnover retail and service businesses opt to sugarcoat reality. They paint rosy pictures at odds with reality and promise things that will never see the light of day. They view this as the only way to raise the performance level of their employees. It's an approach that usually gets them nowhere fast. If, on the other hand, you make the case that learning on the job—any job—transcends the job itself; if you make the case that growing skills—any skills—encompasses more than meets the eye, you will witness performance progress.

Back to you in the restaurant as a coach instead of a traditional manager. In these particular circumstances, you'd be charged with making a convincing case that beyond waiting tables—a skill in itself—lies a steep learning curve with copious learning opportunities. Your responsibility as a coach would be to illustrate the many lessons learned in waiting tables. For instance, successful waiters and waitresses will absorb valuable people skills in abundance while ministering to hungry customers. In the fast-paced environment of a restaurant they will also learn conflict resolution, which is a valuable, highly coveted skill that waiters and waitresses often master with time.

ESSENTIALS Experience is priceless. Coaches in retail and service management positions need to emphasize this time and again. They need to show how learning and growing important skills, such as responsibility, following directions, and overall work ethic, are invaluable in any kind of job.

And how about coaching in a fast-food chicken joint? Deep-frying chicken fingers may seem like a dead-end job—and it is to some people—but believe it or not, there's a lot of learning and growth potential downdraft of that hot oil. Coaching in this particular situation asks that you turn the chicken fingers into chicken cordon bleu. If you identify learning opportunities as more than just completing a task competently (frying chicken fingers to perfection), you go beyond the narrow parameters of the job and take in such important job skills as responsibility, ability to follow directions, and the overall work ethic. You thus make every task that you assign your workers a multilayered affair with lessons to be learned and a potential for growth.

If, in your coaching exertions, you can convince your staff that what they do today—no matter what their jobs—matters, you'll have upgraded a work environment that sorely needs upgrading. You'll have upgraded a group of people who sorely need upgrading. You'll have changed a job culture.

Start Coaching and Mentoring— as Soon as Possible!

To further expand on the most conspicuous problem in many retail and service businesses—that by and large the labor pool doesn't know how to properly service customers—we have to assess managers and employees alike. As the old adage goes, "The fish rots from the head down."

We know this customer service problem is real because we've all received poor treatment from managers and employees alike at some point while shopping, eating out, and such. We've experienced managers looking on in stony silence while their employees run amok. Worse still, sometimes we've gotten lousy treatment from the men and women who called themselves managers—at least that's what their name badges said—but they weren't coaches, that's for sure.

If circumstances like these don't cry out for coaching and mentoring—a specialized retail and service business version of it—then nothing does. When these types of businesses care enough to commit themselves to bettering both their employees' satisfaction and customer service at the same time, a coaching approach will be welcomed into management. And soon thereafter, just as in the corporate office, the retail and service businesses that go down this managerial pike will get noticed for offering not only a better product, but top-notch service as well. But, as we've noted previously, companies have to commit themselves from top to bottom to a managerial methodology like coaching and mentoring, or it's not going to work its magic.

FACTS

The best-foot-forward doctrine is something all coaches keep in mind. It says that employees attempt to make the best first impression possible by giving their all in interviews and during their first days and weeks on the job. If they violate this doctrine, you don't want them around.

In franchise operations or department store chains, for instance, coaching and mentoring need to be welcomed aboard, yes, but also rigorously placed into management from top to bottom. Senior management in these businesses has got to take the lead and insist upon this new managerial methodology, funneling it all the way down to in-store managers. They've then got to diligently search for the right people to put into these managerial slots—men and women who could assimilate the basics of coaching—and give them the absolute authority to manage as coaches.

Coaching in the retail and service sector is poised to make the many jobs available there more appealing to employees and would-be employees alike. And better customer service will be the natural by-product of overall job satisfaction and a more healthy work environment. It's a win-win proposition.

The Way We Were

If you're old enough to remember the good old days, you remember when you walked into a store—from the small mom-and-pop sort to the huge department store—and the help was actually helpful. Not too long ago, it was the rule that employees were expected to behave in a particular way and do certain things in waiting on customers. And if they didn't cut the mustard, they were shown the door. And, all the while, managers meticulously enforced the customer service curriculum. So wait a minute! What happened? Did a coaching-style management exist in the past and vanish as the dinosaurs did? No, not quite. There was no conscious coaching and mentoring style of managing in the past.

The Texaco guys, who would emerge from the interior of the gas station the moment customers pulled up to the pump to check their oil, tire pressure, clean their windshields, and service them with a smile, were not being managed by a 1950s version of a coach. Yes, their actions mirrored the high expectations that Texaco had for all of its service station owners and employees. But the real reason the Texaco guys served customers so well was because the cultural mores of yesteryear were very different from today's. Simply put, people back then treated each other better and had more respect for their jobs.

This isn't to suggest that all was hunky-dory for the Texaco guys and for employees at five-and-dime stores, malt shops, and the like. It surely wasn't. But if you talk with folks who worked their first jobs in the 1950s, 1960s, and 1970s, they more often than not express a certain nostalgia about them. They admit to having learned a lot while working behind the counter of a drugstore or clerking in the stereo section of a local department store.

The Retail Coaching Moment

Years ago in retail and other service industries, employees learned and valued the importance of responsibility—showing up for work on time, practicing good oral hygiene, wearing clean clothes, and functioning in a job with the best possible attitude. Today, these simple rules of conduct are often missing in action. For many entrepreneurs, their most depressing duties involve staffing their businesses. They find it well-nigh impossible sometimes to find competent and reliable employees to work for them. The pickings are often are very slim, and the prospective employees' attitudes are customarily negative.

FACTS

There are few coaching and mentoring tools and techniques that can't be applied to retail and service business managing, whether you manage a restaurant, department store, fast-food chain, meat market—the basic principles remain the same for any business.

It is a long-held and generally accepted view that people want to put their best feet forward in their job interviews. This makes perfect sense. Likewise, upon getting hired, they want to be on their best behaviors and make the best possible impressions during the first few days and weeks on the job. This again makes perfect sense. As a coach, you're conscious of this in interviews (see Chapter 11 for the basics of interviewing) and in the infancy of the relationships with your new employees. But ask around and you'll hear—if you haven't seen it up close and personal yourself—that many managers are witnessing new employees making very bad impressions immediately. They're making bad first impressions, not because they're trying too hard and are hopelessly inept, but because they aren't even making an effort to look good.

Strange as this may sound, it's not even on employees' things-to-do list. These employees are not even entertaining the thought that it's important to make good impressions at work, particularly when starting new jobs. Bad first impressions turn up in the offices of corporate America, but they're epidemic in retail and service jobs. For the small businessperson or manager on the retail and service front lines, the Best Foot Forward Doctrine, once inviolable, is regularly breached by today's employees. New employees arrive late on their first day of work with the excuse that they overslept. New employees call in sick a couple of days during their first week on the job. New employees complain about their jobs from the get-go, and some talk about retaining a labor lawyer and pass the word around to coworkers.

So just why would you want to coach in an environment like this? Why not? It's a coaching moment if ever there was one. We've talked at great length about challenges being one of the cornerstones of a coach's agenda. Challenges for you, the coach, coupled with many challenges for your employees.

Managing on Two Levels

Actually, you coach retail and service employees on two levels. You manage employees on the conventional level of assigned jobs, performance expectations, and the like, but you also manage them on another level, too—dealing with customers. In many ways, it's the ultimate coaching and mentoring challenge for the retail and service industries. That's the dirty secret that hopefully will be revealed to a wider audience. But until that occurs and coaching and mentoring become company policy on the larger corporate retail and service business fronts, you can implement coaching methods anywhere and anytime and achieve positive results. You see it happening in some of these businesses already. It's very noticeable, in fact, because good management in retail and service businesses stands out like never before.

Virtually every coaching and mentoring tool and technique can be transferred out of the office and onto the retail and service front lines. With some modifications, of course, but with the core principles intact.

Planning for Performance

Even though you might not be able to plan too far in advance because of the high turnover in the retail and service industries, you still must draw up performance plans, even if only for the short term. You can set goals with your employees and utilize action plans. And you can measure your employees' progress on a recurring basis. You've got to get good performances out of your people no matter where you are—at IBM or Tony's Pizzeria, it makes no difference.

Developing Trust and Integrity

The trust you develop with your employees, and the integrity that you personify, loom larger than ever in the retail and service world, because the leeway your employees will afford you is decidedly less than in the confines of the office. Why? Because most of these employees know they can walk down the street and get another job in the same sector tomorrow. So, what you've got to do is underscore trust and expand the field of learning. Talk faithfully about the value of gathering experiences and pride in successfully working at any job. Make your instruction plausible and cite examples from your own job experiences and the incalculable lessons that you have learned along the way.

Coaching and mentoring in managerial positions are desperately needed in retail and service settings, where poor employee morale is the rule and lousy customer service commonplace. Coaching in retail and service environments would touch countless people—from employees to customers—in a very positive and visible way.

Curbing Bad Attitudes

Bad attitude in retail and service jobs is the in thing these days among employees. It's hip to be negative. Indeed, this is the roughest road managers in these kinds of businesses must traverse if they are to succeed. Unhappily, for many managers of these disgruntled employees, the result of their efforts is failure. We've mentioned the myriad reasons for the poor attitudes in retail and service jobs—low pay, restricted job roles, general resentment, and, yes, dealing with Mr. and Mrs. John Q. Public.

Working Face to Face with Customers Isn't Easy

Mr. and Mrs. John Q. Public can be tough customers. In fact, it's in the area of customer relations where you, the coach, must work diligently to turn employees' bad attitudes into good ones. The learning environment that we've talked at length about in this chapter is so often grounded in relating to customers and satisfying their needs.

For those of you who have never worked with the general public, you've missed out on the learning experience of a lifetime. Catering to walk-in customers is a never-ending challenge because you never know what to expect. The smooth work road invariably hits a bump, and sometimes even a crater, without any warning at all. However, if you instruct your employees in how to deal with the public, carefully preparing them for the inevitable obstacles that come with the territory of customer service, you'll see a more resilient group of people developing before your eyes, and an increasingly more relaxed bunch over time. And this will translate into better customer service. You don't necessarily need to roll out the red carpet for customers, but you've got to remove the path of hot coals that often greets customers in so many businesses today.

Customers Aren't the Plague—They're the Paycheck!

You must disabuse your employees of the notion that customers are something of a plague. There are employees whose jobs require them to stock shelves and they go at it with an artist's aplomb. The problem is that some of these same employees testily bristle when customers come along and purchase things off the shelves, thus messing up their works of art. In this example, you've got to get the point across to your employees that the reason for packing shelves up to the hilt is so the buying public will buy the very things packed on them. And, further, that if the awe-inspiring packed shelves remained so, you and your employees both would be out of jobs.

The Customer Is Always Right

Everybody's familiar with the business maxim that "the customer is always right." This sentiment is both far-reaching and long-standing and is loaded with meaning. While it boldly declares that customers are always right, it's not meant to be taken completely literally. Those who toil in retail work would agree without hesitation.

What "the customer is always right" motto asks of managers and employees alike is that they accord their customers a tremendous amount of leeway. Pleasing customers has to be at the top of the agenda of any business and not just a mere afterthought.

One of the most dogged problems in customer relations today is that employees are not taught to understand, let alone respect, the meaning of "the customer is always right." In fact, many retail and service business managers set the inappropriate and counterproductive tone of criticizing or mocking customers behind the scenes, and sometimes even engaging them in antagonistic skirmishes for all to see.

This negative tone-setting creates the unfortunate ripple effect of marring the customer relations landscape. Predictably, employees join the fray with the imprimatur of their bosses.

ALERT

The popular adage, "the customer is always right," has to be ingrained in your employees' thinking. Not to be taken literally, its meaning must be understood. That is, customers need to be afforded lots of leeway because they're why businesses and, yes, jobs exist.

Your coaching, on the other hand, should set a decidedly different tone—a positive one—where you instill in your employees the mantra that the "customer is indeed always right, until proven otherwise—and even then sometimes." As a coach you must make sure that the inescapable bad apples in the customer barrel aren't permitted to spoil the whole bunch.

The daily grind of working with a constant flow of customers often causes employees to lose sight of an important fact: The vast majority of customers who shop, eat out, and the like are decent people. Remember that we are all customers sometimes.

Indeed, most shoppers and diners don't cause any grief at all; most people just want to buy their pound of seedless grapes, order their breakfast omelets, get their bags of chunky dog food, pay their tabs, and go home.

Dealing with Bad-Apple Customers

Unfortunately, it's the silent majority of good customers who bear the brunt of the minority of problem makers. It's the handful of griping customers who cause managers and employees to see and treat all customers as the enemy. As a wise coach, you've got to act as an aggressive iconoclast and destroy any false and destructive impressions, because the customer mischief-makers are the exceptions and not the rule. This important lesson is where you begin cleaning up the customer's tarnished image, and start putting your employees' heads on straight.

If you highlight repeatedly the positive transactions between your employees and customers, you will be accenting the true reality—dealing with the public is predominantly a positive experience, and shouldn't be viewed as a negative one. When the problem customer does come along, you position the interaction as a learning opportunity in the reality laboratory. You also emphasize that these bad experiences with customers are quite rare in the larger picture. If you can make the retail or service setting a positive place, you will see that your employees respond favorably and handle confrontational moments more professionally. You will see that you've got a more contented group of people in your employ who won't get sidetracked by a handful of complaining customers.

Respect Is Key

Retail and service businesses are joined at the hip with confrontational moments. We've made this abundantly clear. You can't have one without the other. Confrontations not only between employees, but managers versus employees, and—yes—employees versus customers. And this dicey multidimension is what makes managing in these types of businesses a very formidable undertaking. Respect is often in short supply. Employees often feel diminished from so many different angles. There is, in fact, an aura of smugness that surrounds many white-collar office folks. They are apt to look down upon retail and service workers, and couldn't possibly envision coaching and mentoring's tools and techniques applied in such rough-and-tumble business trenches. But, as we've laid out in this chapter, coaching and mentoring not only belong in retail and service businesses, but could provide a necessary uplift for countless disheartened employees and so many battle-weary customers, too.

In companies in business to serve people, respect is key to both employees and customers. Admittedly certain nightmare customers grumble about everything or treat employees as if they were servants, but here's your chance to use coaching and mentoring to uplift your employees, and in so doing, improve customer service, even to the worst of customers.

CHAPTER 19

The Role of a Lifetime—a Script for Mentoring

Explore how good mentoring follows a careful script—particularly in the relationships between adult mentors and their younger mentees. These relationships can be either inside the company or outside the workplace, and are part of many companies and their community programs designed to enhance social responsibility.

Being Careful with Words

The words "mentor" and "mentoring" are loaded. That is, they are infused with lots of high hopes, blue skies, and all things positive. All of us agree that the onus on a mentor is to pass on wisdom of some kind to a mentee. All of this good stuff, however, assumes that three very important factors exist and come together:

- A mentor with wisdom to spare and pass on
- A mentor with knowledge and understanding on how to deliver wisdom to a mentee
- A mentee receptive to a mentor

Ideally, a mentor is a teacher who should teach a mentee a thing or two. But a wisdom and knowledge transfer occurs only if certain mentoring guidelines are mastered and intelligently applied. Mentoring is not a casual or haphazard affair. Not-for-profit mentoring organizations treat the entire mentoring process with the utmost solemnity. Prospective mentors are screened, and those who make the cut are assigned mentees that best match up with their backgrounds. In this one regard, it's similar to a dating service trying to find a compatible fit. Similarly, a mentor in business is not assigned to anyone and everyone in the workplace. A mentor-mentee relationship on the job is established only when it is believed that something significant and positive for the company—and, yes, for the mentee's career growth—can come out of the pairing.

In parenting, too, there are particular modes of behavior that work better than others in imparting important life lessons and instilling solid values in their children. In order to be accepted as positive role models, parents must first connect with their children.

The Evolution of Mentoring Relationships

All mentoring relationships are about evolution. Mentors are charged with the responsibilities of evolving their mentees in many different ways. They are not expected to achieve positive results in a heartbeat. They are, however, counted on to move forward in these relationships, making progress all the time. However, making progress doesn't preclude the inevitable setback or two—it goes with the territory.

In most instances, the very concept of mentoring implies that you're dealing with complicated cases. That is, you're mentoring individuals in need of guidance, knowledge, and skills of so many kinds. Mentees outside of business circles usually require a complete change in the direction of their lives. And the truth is that negative to positive direction shifts aren't always easy to pull off. This is why we place the emphasis on the evolutionary nature of mentoring and why it is so primary to remain focused on forward movement.

FACTS

Many business leaders promote mentoring relationships by getting their employees involved with at-risk young people. These acts of social responsibility on their parts enhance their images and help disadvantaged youngsters in need of a helping hand; in need of tutelage in becoming the business leaders of tomorrow.

Stagnant mentor-mentee relationships fall apart because movement is absolutely essential in the relationship. Sometimes the movement won't be as swift and as smooth as you would like, but that's okay. A mentor-mentee relationship is not like running a 100-yard dash. It is a marathon—a lengthy, always forward-moving, supportive marathon.

The Mentoring Play in Four Acts

Whether a successful mentor-mentee relationship develops between employees in the workplace or out in the community with troubled teens, it unfolds in four acts. Act I is devoted to getting acquainted. Act II is a period of goal setting. Act III is all about seeing these goals through and meeting expectations. Act IV marks the closure of the mentor-mentee relationship.

Act I: Getting Acquainted

So much is made about first impressions in life. Some people swear that first impressions tell them all they need to know about another person. Others say that getting to know someone gradually over time is the only way to really get to know a person. There's some merit in both opinions. First impressions can make or break a relationship on the spot. Nowhere is this truer than in a mentoring relationship. This is precisely why it's so key that you move slowly at first. Early on in your relationship is not the time to come on strong with your mentee. The infancy of the relationship is the time when you informally acquaint yourself with your mentee. It's the time to put him or her at ease.

The initial meeting between you and your mentee may be somewhat awkward. Getting to know someone usually is. Don't jump to hasty conclusions. Don't allow any negative first impressions to cloud your hopes for the future. "How am I ever going to work with this punk?" "I don't see how I'll ever get through to a kid with such an attitude!" Hold on! Nobody ever said that mentoring was easy. It's not. It requires patience and sincere commitment. And in Act I of the mentor-mentee relationship, both patience and commitment are sometimes sorely tested.

ESSENTIALS

When setting career goals with your mentee, make sure they're your mentee's goals and not yours. Respect your mentee's interests and hopes about the future even though they may be very different from what you might choose.

Use your first few mentoring get-togethers to establish a bond of trust between you and your mentee. And there's only one way to do this. You've got to get to know your mentee as an individual. You've got to explore the personality and interests of your mentee while withholding any value judgments. Similarly, your mentee's got to get to know you. Two people getting to know one another gradually over time is the best path to establishing rapport. And rapport equals straightforward communication, which is essential in all successful mentoring relationships.

In Act I of the mentor-mentee relationship, you must secure a solid hold on your mentee's personality and temperament, and then determine the approach you're going to take to get the best out of him or her over time. For instance, you may be a person who talks about your personal feelings at the drop of a hat. Don't, however, assume that everybody else does. Don't assume that your mentee shares your penchant for getting in touch with "good stuff." The surest way to scare off mentees is to put them on the spot right away by asking them a barrage of therapist-style questions. Take it slow—evolve.

Pay special heed to the reasons behind the goals you set. Make sure that the mentee really wants to reach the goal and that it's not what he or she thinks you or a member of his or her family wants.

Your role as a mentor is not as a therapist. You're not a morning talk show host either. You're not looking for a big score in finding something juicy in your mentee's personal life. You're a mentor trying to help another human being. The bottom line is, when you bond with your mentee, you'll know how he or she feels about so many different things soon enough.

Make it your short-term goal to get to know your mentee slowly but surely. Then, when you emerge from your initial mentoring meetings, you'll have achieved your short-term objective and can move with confidence into Act II of your relationship.

Act II: Setting Goals

Once you've cemented your mentor-mentee relationship in the get-to-know-one-another phase of Act I, it's time to move to the goals stage. If the mentor-mentee relationship is on solid ground, as the discovery process evolves, so will expectations.

During Act II of the mentoring relationship both you and your mentee should talk about expectations for both of you and work closely together in establishing real, measurable expectations—goals—that both of you have for the relationship. Keep the goals doable and sharply focused. Put them in writing if you have to. Encourage your mentee to talk about the expectations that he or she has for you as a mentor beyond such high-sounding abstractions as "make a positive difference" and "provide direction." Make Act II in your mentor-mentee relationship the beginning of your intimate journey. That is, trust one another and commit to seeing the relationship through to real results—expectations realized and goals met.

ESSENTIALS

Be prepared in your scheduled meetings with your mentees. That is, keep your get-togethers focused and meaningful. Know where you're headed at all times. Don't fill in the time with fluff. Come overprepared—never underprepared—and you'll stave off any boredom on your mentee's part.

Act III: Meeting Goals and Expectations

In Act III, after you've set goals and established the level of expectations that you have for your mentee and that your mentee has for you, it's time to perform—to do. It's in this phase of the mentoring relationship where you can take more liberties with your mentee, without the risk of souring or ending the relationship. It's now when you must start taking your mentee to task, if necessary, for not living up to promises, upholding your standards, and strictly abiding by your mutually agreed-upon rules for the relationship.

Act III is the results-oriented phase of mentoring. It's at once a time of great acceptance between you and your mentee, and a time of change. And in successful mentor-mentee relationships, we're talking about positive changes and growth as human beings. You might, for example, have extracted a goal from your mentee to do better in school during the current semester. Within the goal are expectations of better study habits and preparation for exams. Thus, you ask and expect that your mentee practice self-discipline in making the necessary changes in his or her life to accommodate the added study and overall commitment to schoolwork.

In this example, the Day of Reckoning comes with the report card. This is the ultimate measure of success. But along the way, you've got exams and essays to look over, and other samples to measure your mentee's progress in reaching his or her goal. Like a coach and an employee's performance plan, you are expected to keep tabs on your mentee's performance at all times. You don't set goals together and be done with it. You don't say you want to see grade improvement and not keep tabs on the road to the report card. Just as in the workplace, you don't wait until the deed is done to do the first checkup. There need to be many checkups en route. And with periodic checkups come many opportunities to offer advice and counsel in making corrections, overcoming obstacles, and just good old-fashioned encouragement.

Act IV: Concluding the Relationship

This is the final act in the mentor-mentee relationship. You've traveled the normal mentor-mentee path and navigated around its many bumps. First, you spent time getting to know one another, moving cautiously with both an open mind and an open heart. Once you bonded as a mentor-mentee pair and trusted and respected one another, you were able to sit down and talk about goals for the future and what each one of you wanted to get out of the relationship. With goals in place, you assisted your mentee in achieving them. You were there to poke and prod, to chastise when necessary, and to celebrate progress and growth together.

The ending of a mentor-mentee relationship often engenders an abandonment issue in a mentee. This is why you must celebrate the ending of the formal relationship as a beginning—a beginning of many successes to come.

The last act in a mentoring relationship is the moment you put it to bed. A mentor-mentee relationship is not meant to be a lifetime proposition. It's meant to help people help themselves. Ending the mentor-mentee relationship doesn't mean you end any contact between you and your mentee. It merely means that you've done all that you can, and your mentee has positively responded and is ready to move forward on his or her own without your mentoring hand. It's up to you, in concert with your mentee, to determine the new nature of your relationship. Remaining friends is a popular next step for a mentor and mentee who have shared real successes and growth.

QUESTIONS?

Is your mentee supposed to mentor you, too?
Not quite. Nevertheless, your mentee will teach you many lessons about yourself and your abilities. Courtesy of your mentee, you'll discover your aptitude in teaching, gain patience, and better understand and appreciate human nature in its infinite diversity.

The reason mentor-mentee relationships are finite is the same reason kids are expected to leave the parental nest when they become adults. Ideally, they've been taught many lessons, experienced ups and downs, and are ready to go it alone.

Method Acting

Throughout the mentor-mentee relationship, from Act I to Act IV, there are some very specific techniques you should always keep in mind and utilize frequently.

Give Feedback

Foremost, be generous with your feedback. That's what you're there for. Positive feedback is preferred, but even negative feedback when it's called for is helpful. However, avoid any harsh criticism of your mentee, particularly early in your relationship. Reinforce the positive time and again. Take note of even the minutiae in your mentee's growth and development and be sure to tell him or her about it.

Ask Open-Ended Questions

Another important technique to employ in your mentor-mentee relationship is open-ended questioning. While you're cementing rapport and, of course, after you assume a relaxed relationship, you want your conversations and get-togethers to be as productive as possible. A little small talk goes a long way. It's a good icebreaker, and in small doses—that's why it's called "small talk"—helps get the conversational ball rolling. But keep in mind that it's essential you make the best use of the time you have together.

ESSENTIALS Communication is what makes a mentor-mentee relationship work. You've got to connect with your mentee, and this entails asking a lot of open-ended questions and genuinely listening and hearing the answers to them.

With open-ended questioning, you encourage your mentee to reach deeper into him- or herself. You ask your mentee to think about important things like the consequences of decisions and actions. Peppering your mentee with questions such as, "Do you think you are progressing in your new job?" and then accepting a "yes" answer and moving on is not the way to go. Remember, you're more interested in the exposition responses to questions than you are in the anticipated first responses.

You don't get much out of "yes" and "no" answers to questions. You've got to explore your relationship and know where you stand at all times. And the only way to really know where you stand is by asking open-ended questions and getting real answers. "What things are you doing in your new job that you consider successes?" "Why do you feel better equipped on the job today than on your first day?" These types of questions allow mentees to expound their answers. You get the information you need and a true sense of the progress that you're making in your relationship. And what you gather about where you stand enables you to move forward from reality and not a perception of reality.

Forbid the Negative

Lastly, there's a firm rule in a mentoring relationship that you must decree. That is, you need to enforce a no negative zone. Guard it and don't permit your mentee to go near it. Don't allow your mentee to speak ill about members of his or her family, schoolmates, teachers, coworkers, and others. It's best that you always stress the positive whenever and wherever possible, and remove the negatives and the blame.

FACTS

A mentor-mentee relationship is finite and naturally runs its course. When it's time to end the relationship, some mentors like defining their new relationships with their mentees as "associates," "partners," or "friends."

Alas, even with the best of intentions, sometimes mentor-mentee relationships visit the negative zone. After all, you're working with people who need help. Naturally this means there are persons in their lives who have not done right by them. There's a lot of anger. And anger often creates a multiplier effect that lands mentees in the negative zone. When this happens, you've got to diffuse the anger by not permitting streams of negative references to other people. When you stamp out the negative talk early in the relationship, you set the proper tone for the long term. A tone that says, "Let's avoid playing the blame game and start looking to ourselves for answers to our own problems."

The Benefits of Mentoring

When the mentor-mentee relationship succeeds, behaviors and attitudes change for the better. That's how success is measured. When mentees part company with their mentors, they often are more:

• Articulate	• Skilled	• Focused	• Trustworthy
• Self-aware	• Resilient	• Positive	• Sensitive

They are also:

- More open to differences of opinions
- More able to trust others
- Better problem solvers
- Better able to recognize opportunities
- Better able to seize opportunities

CHAPTER 20

Ten Myths of Coaching and Mentoring

You may encounter people who subscribe to some of the more common myths lurking in the recesses of people's minds concerning coaching and mentoring. These myths are debunked by employing the most powerful tool known to humankind: the truth.

You Don't Need to Coach Capable People

Wrong. There are, in fact, coaching and mentoring gurus who give short shrift to the importance of screening prospective employees in the interview process. It's as if employees arrive on the job by some sleight of hand. Really, though, making a thorough effort to vet job applicants is job one of the coach and the beginning of the coaching journey. (See Chapter 11 for a comprehensive look at a coach's role in hiring staff.) You want to employ the best and brightest people, don't you? Down the road, it'll make your managing job a lot less complicated and a whole lot more successful, too.

Yes, it's a fact: One of your principal coaching duties is to find good men and women to fill any open job slots at your disposal. You want to pick the most capable people possible to work for you. But the truth is, you won't always pick perfect people, and even those employees of yours who are top-notch performers require direction to grow in their jobs and improve their overall skills. Coaching and mentoring views learning as an infinite journey—for anybody and everybody and anywhere and everywhere.

Each and every individual employee—irrespective of his or her level of knowledge and overall talents—requires a guiding hand of some kind on the job. The support of a wise manager is essential for the best and brightest to get better and brighter, just as it is for those struggling along to get tutored and upgraded.

ESSENTIALS

It's incumbent upon you in your coaching efforts to not only reward the successes of your employees, but also to see that they understand the reasons for it. Generally, success is the result of good skills and hard work, and not mere "luck" as some employees claim.

Coaches support all of their employees—without exception—by providing hands-on managing and special attention to them on an individual basis. Hands-on, remember, does not mean micromanaging. It's somewhat ironic, but the most capable people become even more capable under the smart and forward-moving leadership of coaching.

Your Employees Do Most of Your Work

You've encountered endless references throughout this book on how coaching is high on delegating more responsibilities and providing more challenges to employees in their jobs. So, does this must mean you just parcel out all the work that needs to be done, put your feet up on your desk, and hit the snooze button? Hardly. Yes, coaching advocates making employees more capable by providing them jobs of substance with more opportunities to showcase their talents and abilities. As a coach, you want to maximize employees' performances by getting them to push their potential envelopes to the limit. But you've got to do some of the pushing, too, so you delegate important jobs to the deserving. You challenge those you feel are up to it. And you give added responsibilities to those who have earned your trust. The bottom line is that coaches don't have the time to put their feet up on their desks, delegating or no delegating.

Don't ever find yourself in the guise of a managerial loomer. That is, don't ever smother your staff by your omnipresence in watching every move they make. Use your communicative abilities to set employee performance in motion, discreetly monitor it, and let your people get the job done.

You Must Be Easygoing to Coach People

If this were the case, there would be very few coaches in management. Coaching and mentoring expect many things from their stable of coaches, but being perfect isn't one of them. That's a relief. The beauty of coaching in managerial roles is its adaptability. Thus, you can take the best aspects of your personality and mold them into a leadership model that works for you in getting the best possible performance results from your employees. Coaching is essentially about influencing employees to achieve. And you can be an influential and positive leader of people without being a warm and fuzzy type.

Personalities can be fine-tuned. If you're always fair, candid, and communicate with your employees on a routine basis, a support system exists in the workplace. This is the map of success. This assertive and consistent approach to managing trumps personality quirks every time. Of course, it certainly helps to be thick-skinned, empathetic, and understanding by nature. But all sorts of personality types succeed in coaching if they embrace its core methodology and not its mythology.

Employees Are Intimidated by Constant Feedback and Direct Communication

Why should employees fear feedback on their performances? Who doesn't want to know where they stand in their jobs? Granted, there are a lot of people who get anxious at the notion of constant communication and regular one-on-one meetings with the boss. They get panicky in theory, but in practice it's usually another story. Coaching and mentoring's managerial ways are the antithesis of scary. They are in fact reassuring.

ESSENTIALS
As a coach, you're asked to build confidence in your employees. The more confident your employees feel about their abilities, the more willing they'll be to take risks and not be afraid of making mistakes.

This very direct, people-intensive approach to managing is frightening only to those who are accustomed to working alongside dinosaur managers who dole out work assignments and then close their office doors tighter than drums. And the only time employees ever see them is when they've done something wrong or are about to get the old heave-ho. The pleasant reality is that the more employees know about their jobs and status, the better they feel and the more productive they are. And coaching and mentoring put a premium on honesty and being up-front with employees at all times, rain or shine. This is nothing to be intimidated by. Quite the contrary. Employees one and all should welcome such an approach to managing with open arms.

Coaches Don't Need Technical Qualifications

Wrong! In fact, a key element in cementing a bond of respect between you and your employees is deeply rooted in your competence. There is this strange idea held by some misinformed souls that coaches are placed in managerial positions to inspire their workers to perform and to achieve at the highest levels possible, and that coaches—one and all— are interchangeable. These people believe that coaches are merely inspirational talkers put in place to deliver motivational speeches and offer "you can do it" encouragement to employees.

The truth is, coaches need to know all the ABCs of the function they're managing—and then some. This makes sense. Imagine working in an engineering department in a company with a manager whose technical competence lies in social work. Suffice it to say, there's not going to be a whole lot of respect and trust for their manager emanating from that group of engineers. How can they respect a manager who tells them what to do and grades their performances, but doesn't know squat about engineering?

Because coaching utilizes performance plans and regular measurement of performance, it's more than imperative that coaches showcase technical competence in the areas they manage. In fact, they should exhibit more than mere competence, but some expertise. They should have the capacity to fully comprehend all that's going on around them and all that defines the ultimate performance results of their employees.

Only Employees Who Want Coaching Are Coachable

Not true. Coaching and mentoring are comprehensive managerial methodologies that apply across the board to one and all. Of course you can bring in external and personal coaches to work one-on-one with people for specific reasons. But day-to-day managing as a coach means coaching everybody without exception.

You don't join a football team and tell the coach you don't desire any of his coaching. You don't tell him that you know all there is to know about the game and that you'd appreciate if he would leave you alone, refrain from telling you what to do, and just let you play. That's not how the football bounces. Your football coach coaches a team of individuals. And a team is about teamwork, where every single person's performance contributes to the final results. Ditto for the workplace. A coach on the football field or in the office doesn't wait for invitations to coach.

QUESTIONS?

Is a coach in business like a coach in sports?
There are many similarities. For starters, both are results-oriented. In fact, many coaching methods are universally applied, such as inspiring people to motivate themselves to perform. Good coaching everywhere recognizes the individual's importance to the team effort.

You want to get the best performance out of every one of your employees. And that means that you want to maximize the performances of the best performers just as much as you do the lesser performers. Coaching places no caps on performance or potential. This is why everybody is a candidate for coaching without exception. This doesn't mean that everybody will respond well to coaching. But more times than not, coaching gets more out of employees than other managerial approaches. Coaching and its uniquely personal touch gets more out of people both in job performance and in job satisfaction. And that's one winning combination.

Close Working Relationships Make Conflicts Impossible to Rectify

Just the opposite. To some people, a close working relationship with employees on an individual basis is a ticking time bomb waiting to explode when a tough problem or obstacle comes down the work pike. These folks view coaching and its support system as an employees' insurance program. They see coaches as union bosses who will defend their employees come hell or high water, and therefore gloss over problems and mitigate disagreements without righting things. This is as far from the reality of what coaches do as possible. The very fact that coaching asks of its coaches that they get to know their employees and candidly communicate with them on a regular basis means that all sorts of job snafus are likely to be caught early in their development and dealt with expeditiously and openly.

As a coach, you're not there to be your employees' best buddy. That's been established. You're their coach, which means that you're their manager in a work setting dependent on the bottom line of results. You're a professional who expects professionalism in the job performance of your employees. You expect that your employees will always be responsible for their words and actions, and do their jobs to the best of their abilities. With all of your expectations out in the open, coupled with performance goals set by your employees, you make problems—from performance breakdowns to employee-versus-employee conflict—easier to deal with because the atmosphere in your office is always aboveboard.

Coaching Works Only in Office Jobs

Coaching and mentoring know no boundaries. Their tools and techniques, with a little situational fine-tuning, of course, work in both the offices of the corporate world and in the retail and service business environments, too. In fact, the principles of coaching and mentoring are most welcome in the business venues with the poorest employee morale and the highest turnover. That is, in businesses perceived as offering drudge work, poor pay, and dead-end jobs, the need for an uplifting managerial approach is self-evident.

One of the key factors in the present business environment that's given rise to coaching and mentoring is the reality that today's jobs—and jobholders—are so often transient. That is, there's more voluntary and involuntary movement in the labor force than ever before. And coaching employees takes this fact of modern life into account by scrupulously working on the job at hand, yes, but simultaneously recognizing that tomorrow's job is also an important consideration. What this means is that coaching and mentoring want to fashion knowledgeable and better skilled workers, and hence employees who are more resilient and ready to move on to new and better jobs when the opportunities arise.

Even in seemingly unskilled jobs, good coaching extracts lessons to be learned and in so doing creates better prepared workers who are more apt to go on to bigger and better things based on their experiences working with coaches. Coaching and mentoring look at skills beyond hard technical skills and teach the softer skills involved with dealing with people, accepting responsibility, maintaining a good attitude, and practicing the work ethic. These key skills need to be taught and applied in the restaurant and the record store, just as much as in the office place.

A Coach Meets with Employees as a Therapist Meets with Patients

No way. In fact, you're not hired as a coach to be all-knowing and solve problems unrelated to the job. The time we live in sometimes brings psychotherapy into places it doesn't belong. And it doesn't belong in the workplace. Some companies refer employees with psychological or personal problems of a great magnitude to trained and licensed professionals. And this is good.

ESSENTIALS
Coaches maximize the performance of their employees by, among other things, maximizing the use of their time. A coach works with the belief that office hours are finite and that time spent in the office needs to be quality time—no wasted minutes from morning bagel to evening yawn.

That said, coaches nevertheless are expected to have a good handle on human nature and how people motivate themselves. But this isn't something you have to sport a degree in to know the score. For coaches, it's often a matter of being more patient and empathetic that ratchets up their employees' performances. You need to approach each one of your employees in a distinct manner to spur them on to perform. This isn't therapy by any stretch of the imagination. It's being thoughtful and wise. Parents know that their children are unique individuals with different personalities. And the best parents don't raise their children in a restrictive, one-size-fits-all mold. Well, the best coaches look at their employees in much the same light. You don't have to be a psychologist to be a good parent, or a good coach.

Coaches Make All Decisions in Concert with Employees

Yes, it's true that coaching and mentoring encourage coaches to extensively consult with their employees on job-related matters. But, no, coaches aren't bound by making consensus decisions with their employees. Nevertheless, there is this pervasive myth that portrays coaches as somewhat impotent leaders presiding over something more akin to focus groups than a staff of employees.

The confusion here rests in the reality of employees playing key parts in shaping their jobs and—by extension—their future careers. And this is what coaching and mentoring bring into management—a partnership of sorts between coaches and employees. But this partnership doesn't relegate the coach to merely a titular head of a staff of people. There must always be one leader who sets the tone and direction of the office. There must be one leader who monitors what's going on in the office by measuring performance and doing what it takes to remain productive and forward-moving. Coaches, in fact, are asked to be more informed, more understanding, and more aware of the work in progress in the office than other managers. It's true. And we are not talking about micromanaging every detail and looking over every employee's shoulder all day long.

Appendix A
Cases in Point

This appendix shares case studies from the business world that show how coaching and mentoring played a positive role (or could have played such a role) in avoiding an unhealthy work situation.

Food for Thought

NEIGHBORHOOD DINERS ARE SCATTERED all across the American landscape. We might say they are as American as the apple pie they serve. And the food and customer service that we receive in them varies widely. The particular diner we will patronize for our case study is a poorly managed mid-sized eatery. This once popular diner, with a long, prosperous history in the neighborhood that it served for many years, changed ownership for the first time in its lifetime. The move immediately generated the usual problems that such a stark and sudden change brings to customer-intensive businesses. A cozy, neighborhood diner embodies more than food; it's a meeting place akin to a local bar, but with food the chief nourishment and not liquid spirits.

When the new management team took over, they made the colossal mistake so many businesspersons do: They incorrectly evaluated their market standing and disregarded the loyal customer base already in place. They operated with the mind-set that the previous owners didn't know what they were doing all across the board, including lagging behind the times as far as updating their equipment and menu (no cappuccino maker) into the modern era. Tangled within this dismissive mind-set was the sentiment that the legions of old customers were a bunch of yahoos.

Wise management, however, doesn't throw the baby out with the bathwater, or, in a diner's case, their industrial refrigerator out with the rancid rice pudding. Yes, it was wise to upgrade equipment and add a few yuppie dishes to the menu, but very unwise to neglect employee satisfaction and customer service both, which is what they did. The new diner management, in fact, replaced all the wait staff with their own people, even though many of the waiters and waitresses let go had worked in the diner for many years, and were well-known and liked by the customers. The new management reasoned that they wanted their own people—men and women who could be instructed in the new ways of doing things and not inflexible holdovers used to doing things "the old way." A common business posture for sure, and one that makes a great deal of sense, but only if the new ways are a marked improvement of the old ways.

The new help was first and foremost instructed to put a premium on getting people in and out of the diner posthaste, and that rapid customer turnover was essential in generating more business at the brisk breakfast, lunch, and dinner hours. Management, in fact, instituted all sorts of employee rules and regulations, including directives regarding coffee cup refills—only one and then only when requested. The diner's once-upon-a-time bottomless coffee cup was stopped, much to the dismay of caffeine-needy patrons. In addition, strict codes regarding fraternizing with customers were also enforced. No personal conversations of any sort were permitted with customers at the dining room's booths and tables outside of "hello" and "goodbye." Waiters and waitresses were advised—in written policy, by the way—to take customers' orders and deliver their food—period.

Predictably, the entire diner staff felt smothered. And the icing on the chocolate layer cake was that they were compelled to listen to increasing numbers of customer complaints they couldn't rectify because most of the protests were aimed at the new management policies. The staff could only remain silent and smile through it all, if they wanted to keep their jobs.

The newly managed diner was not a healthy environment by any measurement. And that's leaving the quality of the food out of the equation. Customers were unhappy. Employees labored in the antithesis of a learning atmosphere. Predictably, the constrictive work conditions manifested themselves in constant employee turnover. And in a diner setting, revolving-door employees are regular customers' worst nightmares. Needless to say, the diner management refrained from anything resembling coaching its employees. It desired maximizing employee performance—yes—but not by respecting its employees. On the contrary, it put them in a job straightjacket and asked that they maximize diner profits by strictly adhering to a surplus of rules and regulations. The result was that there was no personal approach to service, and—surprise—no maximization of profits. Management viewed the diner business only in terms of dollars and cents and superimposed this bloodless posture onto their employees. They didn't see the human potential of their workforce, nor did they try to tap into it, because it never occurred to them that it existed.

The bottom line is that the bottom line suffered. It suffered because the purported farsightedness in upgrading equipment, menu, and so on, and bringing the eatery into the twenty-first century was not commingled with farsightedness in the key areas that the coaching and mentoring managerial methodology addresses. The diner desperately needed a people approach to managing with strong communication between management and employees and, on the other end of the spectrum, strong communication between employees and customers.

Stagnant Waters

FOR HER ANNUAL PERFORMANCE ASSESSMENT, Martha reported to her immediate superior, Ken, who told her without any hesitation that he thought she was stagnating in her position as a team leader. Ken didn't mince his words, telling Martha that she managed with a detached, almost haughty style that was turning off members of her team left and right. He concluded that the result of this disconnect between manager and employees was that overall performance suffered.

Ken further explained to Martha that she was perceived as unap-proach-able, and that this aloofness presented a serious problem. In her position in the organization (a large insurance company), she needed to convey information to and upgrade the skills of her staff on a regular basis. And because of her standoffishness, a wall separated her and members of her team, making the necessary flow of information and the upgrading of skills slow and incomplete.

Martha wasn't surprised in the least by her performance review. Deep down she knew her remote persona had caused a rift to develop between herself and her employees. She readily agreed to make some necessary adjustments to her style of managing. She didn't tell Ken exactly how she planned on undergoing the metamorphosis, only that she was going to communicate better and forge a stronger relationship with those working for her. Martha didn't reveal to Ken that she intended to work with an external coaching consultant who specialized in managerial behavior modifications. She hired a personal coach and paid for the service out her own pocket, initiating a coaching relationship via the telephone. Not an uncommon arrangement, by the way.

Martha found that she could unburden herself to her coach. She laid out all the pertinent details of her job situation. In return, she was given advice and counsel on behavioral adjustments that put her on the road to being a better, more accessible person and manager. The external coaching sessions enabled Martha to experiment with her new approaches to managing and then check with her coach to see how she was doing.

Martha's coach advised her in a whole host of areas, including mode of dress. Yes, her coach told her, there are certain styles and colors of clothing that are more open and less forbidding. "Start at the beginning," her coach told her, by putting the right clothes on in the morning. In Martha's managerial makeover, she met with her employees on a one-on-one basis and began leaving her office door open during the workday. This is the literal interpretation of the open door policy. Symbolic, yes, but very effective in Martha's particular situation. It had been said previously that her door had been so tightly shut that employees needed a crowbar to get it open! The change in managerial style assumed by Martha didn't go unnoticed. Not only did her team feel more comfortable with the new Martha as their superior, but others in similar management positions throughout the organization noted the improvement in Martha's approach and the inevitable better performance results from her people.

In Martha's particular situation, she worked for an organization that didn't have coaching in its management—either internal or external. So she took it upon herself to hire a personal coach to improve her managerial skills. By doing this, she also—over time—enhanced her employees' skills, job satisfaction, and performance levels.

In addition, by getting this outside coaching help, Martha not only bolstered her position in her current job, but also made her career shine brighter. The knowledge and skills that she picked up from her coach and, more importantly, that she experimented with in the reality laboratory called the workplace, made a positive difference for her today and for her tomorrow, too. And that's what good coaching is all about. It's always a continuum.

Two-Headed Monster

TWO MANAGERS, Jeff and Andrea, were on the same level in the organ-izational hierarchy. They had different managerial roles but encoun-tered some overlap in their job responsibilities. In one peculiar instance, they even shared the same employee for a time. Having two managers to report to was the unusual dilemma that confronted Pat, who served as an assistant to both Jeff and Andrea.

Pat generally liked working for both his superiors at the beginning of his job stint. Jeff and Andrea, on the other hand, didn't care for one another. Their distaste was both personal and professional, and they made no bones about it. Their cross working relationship was competitive and contentious. In essence, Pat was compelled to serve two masters at odds with one another much of the time.

Jeff thought very highly of Pat. He believed that his employee's future was bright. He hoped to groom him for an important sales rep position in the company. Jeff felt Pat possessed the strong verbal communication skills necessary for success in such a position. He saw in him a vast reservoir of human potential and hoped to tap into it over time. Jeff, in effect, assumed the role as Pat's more experienced mentor.

Andrea, on the other hand, saw Pat in a decidedly different light. To her, he was a capable assistant and not much more than that. She didn't view him as a man with great potential beyond his rather ordinary office tasks. Yes, she considered Pat highly intelligent, a witty conversationalist, and a treasure trove of knowledge. But in her opinion, he sorely lacked what she considered to be the key to success—an ambitious soul married to a robust work ethic as the engine of career advancement.

When Jeff informed Andrea of his plans for Pat, she vetoed the idea with great alacrity. This only worsened the already strong antipathy the two managers felt toward one another. And, naturally, this impasse did nothing to uplift Pat's on-the-job spirits. Jeff's mentoring of Pat ran headfirst into an impenetrable roadblock. Coaching and mentoring in management put no such obstacles in employees' ways. And while coaching champions a meritocracy, it never consigns employees to fixed jobs and doesn't impede, in any way, their forward movement. The job circumstances that confronted Pat violated these core principles.

Of course, Pat was not working for a company with a formal coaching apparatus in place. And although Jeff adopted bits and pieces of the coaching and mentoring methodology, it needs to be wholly embraced and supported to get the best possible results. The rancorous relationship between Jeff and his colleague in management, Andrea, imploded what was a good-faith attempt on his part to grow the skills of the employee who worked for both of them.

Pat, meanwhile, was caught in the crossfire and saw the handwriting on his cubicle wall. He concluded that he was in a dead-end job and wrote a strongly worded memo to both of his superiors—Jeff and Andrea—citing his inert position as beneath his talents and abilities. He eloquently grumbled that he was not being afforded opportunities for growth and development in his current job.

Jeff, immediately upon receiving his copy of the memo, raced over to Andrea's mailbox like a gazelle. He wanted to spare Pat, whom he still liked and maintained high hopes for, the wrath of boss number two, Andrea. Jeff was looking out for Pat the whole time, and viewed Pat's no-holds-barred memo as counterproductive in the big picture. Jeff saw it as injurious to both Pat's present job status and future possibilities.

Unfortunately, the fleet feet of Jeff were no match for Andrea's attention to detail, as she was already reading Pat's memo when he arrived to intercept it. Pat's memo, among many things, compared his job tasks to that of a houseboy—i.e., making power lunch reservations, travel arrangements, and even picking up his boss's laundry. Andrea didn't appreciate the tone of her employee's missive, nor did she accept its pessimistic premise. She promptly put her disgruntled employee on a ninety-day probation, telling him that he either ratchet up his increasingly lackluster work habits and realign his attitude, or face termination. Jeff, meanwhile, was powerless to intercede. He encouraged Pat to pick up his work pace to placate Andrea. And although he continued to believe in Pat's overall intellect and potential, he couldn't in good conscience defend Pat's increasingly lifeless work ethic and poor attitude.

In the end, Pat looked at the probation period as the last straw and decided he had no future in the company. He deliberately didn't do what was necessary to save his job, figuring that termination would get him an unemployment check while he looked for another, more challenging position.

The Calling

KATHY CONSIDERED HERSELF A BURN-OUT case in the making. Courtesy of her many years in the increasingly dog-eat-dog corporate world in which she labored, she was developing stomach ulcers. Kathy had long heard whispers of this new approach to managing called "coaching" and started to look into what all the fuss was about. In her research, she concluded that coaching methods in managing were just what the doctor ordered. She wanted to incorporate the many tools and techniques of coaching in her own day-to-day managing. For her own psychological and physical well-being and the benefit of her employees and the company's bottom line, she felt coaching was worth trying.

A product manager, Kathy took her coaching idea to the head of her division. She explained what kinds of changes in managerial methods she envisioned. She said she anticipated that such new-fashioned approaches would obtain significantly better results than she was getting. Kathy's superior considered her idea and got back to her with the good news. She had the okay to proceed in what was dubbed a "pilot project." That is, if her trailblazing coaching methods got the results she anticipated, the company would consider adapting coaching throughout its entire organization.

With the green light, Kathy immediately set about changing the way things worked in her office. Communicating on a one-on-one basis was the first change she inaugurated. She brought each of her employees individually into her office for a chat. She wanted to get a fix on where they felt they stood in their jobs and what they thought could improve their job performances and overall satisfaction with their work. She queried them on whether they felt challenged in their jobs, what their future plans included, and if they tied their present jobs together with their long-term careers.

By undertaking this thorough personnel inventory of her employees, Kathy culled many useful things. She learned that some of her employees were unhappy in their jobs, feeling that they were being underutilized or, in some cases, had responsibilities altogether mismatched with their talents and abilities. With this wealth of information now at her disposal, Kathy made personnel shifts in job responsibilities and roles, putting the right people in the right jobs as never before. It was like piecing together a puzzle.

In a short span of time, the results Kathy got out of her team were demonstrably positive. The overall aura of the office also changed for the better. The regular communication that Kathy instituted as office policy not only improved the morale and productivity of her team, but she herself felt less stress in her own life. She was a happier camper all around and kept her blossoming ulcers at bay. The new rapport she generated with her employees was a real eye-opener. She described this new relationship as a revelation—life-changing in so many ways. Because her huge workload was previously bringing her down—both on the job and in her personal life—she discovered that coaching tools and techniques were totally effective in removing a lot of anxiety from her life.

By developing a bond of trust between her and her employees that didn't exist before, Kathy gave her employees real wings for the first time. Wings to do the jobs that they were most capable of doing. And wings to do them better than ever before because of the new support system in the office. Prior to coaching, Kathy was a worrywart extraordinaire, who never felt comfortable delegating responsibilities to her employees. And when she did delegate, she did not feel confident that all would turn out well. In her coach's role, however, Kathy felt that because she was armed with so much more information about her people and what they could do, she could delegate with confidence and bring her employees into the planning process of their own jobs.

The pièce de résistance, as far as Kathy was concerned, was that her coaching pilot project was considered a resounding success throughout the company. She was thus promoted and given the important job of converting the entire organization into the coaching mode. This was the ultimate in jobs as far as she was concerned because she believed in what she was doing like never before. She believed that teaching the ways and means of coaching and mentoring was more than just important, but apocalyptic in altering business environments for the better, in a time when such changes were desperately needed.

Table Talk

THE FIRST THING JEN NOTICED when she assumed her "desk" in her new job was that she was afforded little privacy. In fact, everybody in her particular department of the company worked at the same long table. They worked in the same large room taking and executing real-time stock trades via the telephone. Jen compared the look of the office to a cafeteria. However, her job wasn't about a sandwich and cup of coffee, but high finance.

When Jen accepted the job, she did so with some trepidation. It wasn't the type of job that she wanted. It was work unlike anything she'd ever done before, but she was—in the common parlance—"desperate" and had "bills to pay." Jen was unnerved when she saw the office setup for the first time. She had been apprised of her job tasks and role, but nobody had told her about the long table and constantly ringing telephones, with everybody aware of what everybody else was doing. It looked very frenetic and intimidating. Jen would have preferred to work behind a cubicle wall while getting her feet wet. Nevertheless, she kept her apprehension to herself.

Steve, her manager, oriented her as best he could. He was warm and reassuring, Jen thought, and she appreciated the way he highlighted— without her having to say anything—the office setup and seemingly stress-filled, scary atmosphere. Because of Steve's openness, Jen began her first day on the job nervous, but not nearly as nervous as she thought she might be. Steve told her to remain calm at all times and expect to make some initial mistakes. He told her never to hesitate coming to him with any questions about job-related issues and concerns.

Steve, in fact, made himself highly visible beyond the reality that everyone worked in one big room. He managed the place like a seasoned performer, making everyone feel a part of something important; making everyone feel that they were contributing to a final product. And this was no small accomplishment, considering that the work they were doing involved busily answering telephones and typing in stock orders for people with a lot of dollars and very little patience. This type of work was ripe for resentment and meltdown, as many employees dealt with snippy, condescending customers who didn't have much use for them beyond their fingers typing in the right numbers and right away.

Almost to a person in the office, though, there were few complaints about the frenzied work. Steve managed to make his staff take the work seriously—because it was serious business—but not take to heart some of the gruffness and curtness of the phone callers. By separating the two things, Steve fashioned remarkable loyalty from his troops. He was respected and liked because he was always aware, always fair, and always there for his employees.

After a period of only a few days on the job, Jen's high anxiety was a thing of the past. She was also pleasantly surprised that she enjoyed the fast-paced work. The big long table in the open office now appeared welcoming and nurturing. However, one fateful day, a major faux pas on Jen's part tested the mettle of both her and her manager. During her transcribing of the order information from one caller, she somehow missed an important zero in a keystroke. A $100,000,000 stock trade typed in as $10,000,000 may be one keystroke off, but it's also $90,000,000 off. Not chump change!

Jen was not only embarrassed, but a little frightened, too. It's not everyday that $90,000,000 goes missing and you're the guilty party. Steve, although alarmed, maintained calm, and set to rectify the situation by retracing the steps leading up to the transaction gone awry and locating the missing money. Thanks to Steve's diligence and equanimity, the error was found and fortunately no long-term damage was done. It was a happy ending for all concerned. Jen thought that she might get the boot for her $90,000,0000 blunder, but Steve took her aside and explained exactly what went wrong, and how such a mistake was to be avoided in the future. Jen described the meeting with her boss as amiable but firm, with Steve telling her with something of a smile, "Don't do that again." Steve didn't gloss over the momentousness of what had happened. Yes, he said, everybody would make mistakes from time to time, but there are mistakes and then there are Mistakes!

Steve proved himself a fine coach-manager. He presided over a healthy and productive workplace. The people who worked for him learned a lot on the job. They learned how to work under extreme pressure—so much so that after a short span of time, it didn't seem like so much pressure at all. And, as for Jen's mistake, Steve followed the coaching script. He didn't bawl out Jen or fire her on the spot to set an example for others, but he expected her to learn from the mistake and not make anything resembling such a big blunder again.

Double Life

SHEILA MANAGED AN OFFICE WITH FIFTEEN EMPLOYEES. Because Sheila was a coach, she always made it a point to get to know her people inside and out, including tidbits of their personal lives. No, she wasn't a busybody who wanted to excavate all of the dirt from their closets. She merely wanted to know what made her employees the people they were and what motivated them to behave as they did.

One of her best employees was a man named Michael, who since he joined her team had significantly elevated its overall performance. Sheila knew that Michael was married with two kids. By all indications, he had a very happy home life, and he never tired of pulling out his wallet full of snapshots of his young boy and girl doing everything from trick-or-treating on Halloween to learning to ride a bicycle. After about eight months on the job, however, Michael's cheery demeanor changed. At first, his coworkers noticed only subtle differences in the way he went about his work. Then more overt changes became evident, as Michael began snapping at his colleagues. He even looked unkempt on occasion. Eventually, his performance slowed, impacting everyone on his team who depended on him.

Sheila met regularly with all of her employees, including Michael. At first she was unable to get anything out of him. He said that all was well and she didn't press him any further. When his performance slipped, she could no longer accept the "everything is fine" line, because she knew it wasn't. So, Sheila pressed on, expressing her disappointment at his on-the-job regressing. She also noted the changes in his temperament and even in his appearance. Why was this formerly easygoing, neatly dressed, and punctilious fellow no longer any of these things? There had to be a reason or reasons behind the transformation.

With patient but persistent questioning, Sheila finally got Michael to unburden himself. He told her that his little daughter had been diagnosed with a serious, possibly life-threatening illness, and that he and his wife had been spending much of their time running back and forth to doctors and hospitals, getting very little sleep, and sometimes not even changing out of their clothes from one day to the next. Surprised, Sheila offered her complete sympathy, and wondered why Michael hadn't told her or any of his coworkers sooner. He said that he considered it a personal matter and didn't want to bring his problems from home into the workplace.

Sheila informed him that many of his coworkers were worried about him and had expressed their concerns to her. She offered him time off if he needed it. Michael said that he thought it was best that he keep working, but appreciated the offer and Sheila's understanding. He did, however, accept Sheila's offer to rearrange his work schedule to accommodate his home needs, which she insisted must always take precedence.

She further suggested that he tell his colleagues what was going on in his life. First, she told him it would be better if he got it off his chest. After all, his coworkers were asking him time and again if anything was wrong, and his snippy responses were only exacerbating things. Second, Sheila felt that teamwork required openness, and if his work schedule and job assignments were adjusted to balance his home situation, it was important that his coworkers knew the reason why. If they didn't know the explanation behind the changes, they might feel he was getting special treatment and resent it, leading to morale problems. And, of course, it would create a leadership problem, with Sheila being seen as favoring one employee above all the others.

Sheila always preached that it was in the team's best interests if everybody's cards were on the table. She firmly believed that Michael would get support from his coworkers that would help him get through his trying personal crisis, and assist him, too, in doing his job better under difficult circumstances.

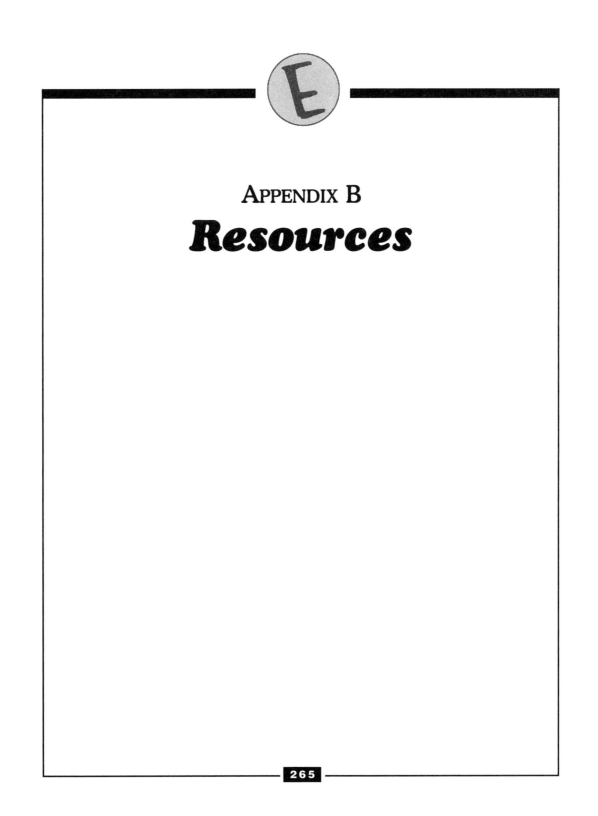

APPENDIX B

Resources

📖 Books

Ambrose, Larry. *A Mentor's Companion.* (Perrone-Ambrose Associates, Ltd., 1998)

Berry, Donna. *Fifty Activities for Coaching/Mentoring.* (Human Resource Development Press, 1993)

Cook, Marshall J. *Effective Coaching.* (McGraw-Hill Professional Publishing, 1998)

Cullen, Jack and Len D'Innocenzo. *The Agile Manager's Guide to Coaching to Maximize Performance.* (Velocity Pub, 2001)

Dotlich, David L. and Peter C. Cairo. *Action Coaching: How to Leverage Individual Performance for Company Success.* (Jossey-Bass, 1999)

Flaherty, James. *Coaching: Evoking Excellence in Others.* (Butterworth-Heinemann, 1998)

Gilley, Jerry W. and Nathaniel W. Boughton. *Stop Managing, Start Coaching! How Performance Coaching Can Enhance Commitment and Improve Productivity.* (McGraw-Hill Professional Publishing, 1995)

Goldsmith, Marshall, Laurence Lyons, and Alyssa Freas, Eds. *Coaching for Leadership: How the World's Greatest Coaches Help Leaders Learn.* (Jossey-Bass, 2000)

Holliday, Micki. *Coaching, Mentoring, and Managing: Breakthrough Strategies to Solve Performance Problems and Build Winning Teams.* (Career Press, 2001)

Hudson, Frederic M. *The Handbook of Coaching: A Comprehensive Resource Guide for Managers, Executives, Consultants, and HR.* (Jossey-Bass, 1999)

Logan, David, Ph.D., and John King. *The Coaching Revolution: How Visionary Managers Are Using Coaching to Empower People and Unlock Their Full Potential.* (Adams Media Corporation, 2001)

Peterson, David B. and Mary Dee Hicks. *Leader as Coach: Strategies for Coaching and Developing Others.* (Personnel Decisions International, 1996)

Stone, Florence M. *Coaching, Counseling, & Mentoring: How to Choose & Use the Right Tool to Boost Employee Performance.* (AMACOM, 1998)

Whiteworth, Laura, Henry House, and Phil Sandahl. *Co-Active Coaching: New Skills for Coaching People Toward Success in Work and Life.* (Davies Black, 1998)

✑ Web Sites

The Center for Coaching and Mentoring:
www.coachingandmentoring.com

The Coaching and Mentoring Network:
www.coachingnetwork.org.uk

The Oxford School of Coaching and Mentoring:
www.oscm.co.uk

The Coaching and Mentoring Bookstore:
www.topresults.com

Employee Coaching and Mentoring
Training Products:
www.ideasandtraining.com/Employee

Coaching and Mentoring for Small Business
Owners:
www.annstrong.com/coaching.htm

Coaching and Mentoring Training Videos:
www.publicdoman.com/Coaching-Mentoring.html

Manager's Forum:
www.managersforum.com/services/coaching.htm

Coaching and Mentoring Careers:
www.fillyourpractice.com/coach.htm

Peer Resources:
www.mentors.ca/peer.html

Coaching and Mentoring Training:
www.rctm.com/CoachingDirectory.html

32 Activities on Coaching and Mentoring:
www.therapeuticresources.com/60-6text.html

Mentorship University:
www.mentorshipu.com

APPENDIX C

Glossary of Terms

action plans: The plans within a plan. Clearly defined directions inserted in all performance plans detailing what employees literally must do—the actions that they have to take—to reach their goals and meet their standard of performance. There are usually several action plans within each performance plan.

advocacy: The posture of support assumed by coaches and mentors in relation to their employees and mentees, whereby they identify opportunities for and assist them in their career development and in other aspects of their lives.

anticipated first response: An answer to a question that is both expected and unenlightening. Coaches are more interested in the illuminating exposition response.

assumption function: The inaccurate deduction that each individual from a particular group does things the same way. This mode of thinking is often related to employment discrimination and runs completely counter to coaching and mentoring.

attitude: The embodiment of an individual's overall thought process and the precursor of actions. Thus, attitude is usually the harbinger of performance on the job.

attitudinally disabled employees: Individuals who possess unfavorable attitudes 24/7.

avenues to positive outcomes: A firm coaching tenet fixed in locating the best possible ways to solve any and all problems and obstacles in the workplace.

blame game: The practice of managers and/or employees not accepting responsibilities for their own actions and shifting the accountability onto others. Sometimes referred to as passing the buck.

boredom bomb: Work that's not challenging, intellectually fulfilling, or interesting that is poised to detonate and explode into employee performance drop-offs, general discontent, and personnel turnover.

brainstorming sessions: A tried-and-true coaching and mentoring technique of permitting employees or mentees to express themselves and offer ideas and suggestions without fear of ridicule or worse.

close-ended questions: Queries posed to provoke definitive, short, often "yes" or "no" responses.

coach: A manager in a business setting who shapes an optimum work environment by emphasizing the continual growth and development of employee knowledge and skills. A coach communicates with and encourages employees on a one-on-one basis to maximize their job performances and to realize their full potential both personally as well as professionally.

coach pickup line: An utterance by an employee that doesn't jibe with the reality of the workplace situation, thus causing a coach to spring into action in an attempt to extract the truth through open-ended questioning and robust, give-and-take dialogue.

coachable moments: Workplace situations that are tailor-made for coaching efforts to correct problems, grow employee skills, and maximize employee performances.

coaching: The managerial methodology that seeks to maximize employee performance by conscientiously considering individuals and their unique talents and abilities. Coaching is rooted in consistent and honest communication between coaches and employees, is solution-oriented, is collaborative, and seeks positive outcomes to any and all situations relating to the job and job performance.

commitment: The spirit a coach inspires in employees to get the most out of their performances. This is realized by making a plausible connection between a job well done today and a better on-the-job tomorrow and long-term career.

compartmentalization: The conscious act of individuals completely separating one set of circumstances or attitude in their lives from another set of circumstances or attitude in order to focus on a goal and/or make forward progress.

continuous learning: The dynamic workplace atmosphere fashioned by coaches emphasizing the never-ending expansion of knowledge and growing of skills for all involved.

corrective coaching: A designation applied to particular coaching efforts in situations where employee attitudes and behaviors point to serious problems and workplace disruptions unless rectified.

delegating: An essential coaching technique that affords deserving employees more responsible and challenging jobs.

dinosaur managers: The old-style, doer, directive-style, more traditional managers who do not work with employees on a personal level, and do not collaborate with them in defining their jobs and futures.

disruption: An employee's performance slowdown, or bad performance, that initiates the ripple effect in the office—a more widespread slowdown or halt in the overall work of a team or group.

doghouse: A popular punitive technique employed by dinosaur managers—not coaches—that puts certain employees on notice by giving them the cold shoulder, a cut in pay, poor job assignments, and so on. All of these in lieu of open communication and confronting the problem forthrightly.

elevate respect: A highly valued coaching technique of taking any job situation—in the office or in a walk-in retail business—and upgrading the entire work atmosphere to one where respect runs deep. This elevation enables any job in any situation to be a learning environment.

empathetic: Describes a caring coaching posture that connects coaches with their employees on a level of understanding that transcends their jobs and touches them in a very personal way.

empowerment: A coach's charge in forging a work environment that puts a premium on the growth and development of the individual employee, leading to a more contented and productive work force.

equality doctrine: Office standards that every individual—with no exceptions—is expected to uphold by abiding by established rules of conduct, ethical boundaries, and performance level expectations. Equivalence of employee treatment is, however, not part of coaching, which views employees as individuals—with their unique temperaments and backgrounds—and adjusts coaching methods accordingly and as needed on a one-on-one basis.

evolution: The forward movement of all successful mentoring relationships in business and outside of business. This progression is indispensable for mentor-mentee relationships to succeed.

exacting control: The special mode that coaches switch on when dealing with highly sensitive and thin-skinned employees. This, in effect, puts coaches on high alert to remain even-tempered and matter-of-fact in presentation at all times.

expectations: Real goals, beyond noble and high-sounding words, established by mentors and mentees at a phase in the relationship when the two parties have fashioned strong rapport. The next phase consists of measuring and evaluating the results achieved on the way to fulfilling the goals.

exposition response: An answer to an open-ended question that is generally more enlightening than an anticipated or rehearsed answer. Coaches rely heavily on communication with their staff members, and on understanding what they are actually thinking and how they are truly feeling.

external coach: A consultant from outside the company brought in to troubleshoot particular problems and remove workplace obstacles by working intimately with individuals or groups and utilizing the tools and techniques of coaching. This brand of coaching is not day-to-day managing, but specialized and usually short-term.

feedback/constructive feedback: A fundamental coaching and mentoring communication technique and information dispenser utilized every day to pass on observations on employee performance and other workplace concerns. It's either positive or negative in nature, but it's neither praise nor criticism. It is wholly constructive in practice. That is, it is meant to find solutions and foster positive outcomes to all situations. In addition, it is recommended that coaches and mentors, too, solicit feedback on their performances from their employees and mentees.

five points of professionalism: Honesty and integrity, learning and initiative, resilience, positive attitude, and teamwork.

glass ceiling: The term used to characterize the conceptual barrier preventing women and minorities from breaking into corporate senior management positions in numbers commensurate with their percentages in lower positions in the workforce at large.

goals: Performance aims established in collaboration between coaches and employees in the first phase of performance plans. Also called objectives. Goals are also important outside of performance planning in the workplace, and in mentor-mentee relationships away from the job.

grooming: Special coaching provided to employees who are ripe for promotions or responsibilities over and above other members of their team or group.

hard skills: Knowledge and technical skills that are measurable in aptitude and performance. Hands-on skills.

high-octane coaching: An appellation applied to coaching efforts in situations where special employee training is required, such as when welcoming a new employee, teaching new skills, grooming a staff member for promotion, and so on.

interior journey: The betterment of the individual—the employee—as a human being beyond the job and work career.

internal coaching: Managing as a coach on a regular, everyday basis within a company. This is in contrast to external coaching, which is brought into organizations from the outside for specific problem solving, skills upgrading, and so on.

invisible hand: The term given to the ambiguous cultural reasons keeping women and minorities from cracking into senior management positions in large numbers. It refers to the practice of people selecting those with whom they feel most comfortable to mentor and groom as their successors, perpetuating a cycle of exclusion.

lead by example: To model the professional behavior you expect from your employees.

learning: The acquiring and organizing of information and placing it in both a useful context and sound perspective.

listen and hear: A key coaching duo that requires coaches, when communicating with their employees, to absorb what they are being told and respond to it in some substantive way.

listening tours: An overriding coaching communication principle that asks that coaches continually dialogue with their employees, hear what they have to say on all job-related matters, and make more fair and sound decisions because of these efforts.

look-out-for-them principle: The doctrine that coaches live by in providing perpetual on-the-job and career development opportunities for their employees.

magnet for talent: What coaches are expected to make the workplace courtesy of their shaping a positive work environment rich in opportunity that is appealing to the best and brightest in the labor pool.

measures: The standards by which performance is judged. Periodic monitoring and verification of performance plans via mutually agreed upon (coach-employee) methods ensure that standards are being meet. Examples of ways to report how standards are being met include audits, status reports, physical observation, and so on.

mentor: An individual in a business setting who assumes a relationship with an employee on a lower rung of the organizational hierarchy for the purpose of grooming the employee for job and career growth and development. This is accomplished by imparting useful lessons learned, offering pertinent advice and counsel, and listening. Also, an adult individual who tutors a younger person in need of guidance.

mentoring: A more informal relationship than coaching, rooted in passing on wisdom and know-how from one person to another, mentor to mentee. Applicable in business settings and on the outside, including in organizations devoted to helping at-risk young persons.

mini-mentoring: An appellation affixed to in-house helping relationships, usually between two employees. A coach often initiates this relationship by having one employee with stellar knowledge and skills tutor another in need of improvement in particular areas.

mini-vision: A coach's microcosmic goals for the particular niche of the company that he or she manages. A mini-vision is transposed from the company's broader, long-term vision, and it is more intimate and meaningful for employees in the here and now.

mirroring feelings: An empathetic coaching technique involving coaches observing and understanding an employee's state of mind, and adjusting to it accordingly in any conversation or meetings.

natural mentoring: Mentoring relationships that occur by birth, by chance, or by a twist of fate, such as parenting, friendships, teachers, and the like.

no negative zone: The dictum enunciated by mentors that precludes them from speaking ill of family members, schoolmates, teachers, coworkers, and others.

objective ear: An unbiased stance assumed by both coaches and mentors who need to be fair and honest at all times with their employees or mentees. This posture is in stark contrast to being sycophantic cheerleaders, which is not the role of coaches and mentors, on or away from the job.

open-ended questions: Queries regularly posed by coaches and mentors to draw out extended, thoughtful responses from employees or mentees. There are no right and wrong answers attached to these questions.

paraphrasing: An essential listening skill in coaching whereby coaches let their employees know that they are hearing what is being said to them by repeating the sum and substance of it in their own words.

performance plans: A coach's tool and the centerpiece of each employee's work life. These plans, crafted by the coach in concert with the employee, consist of goals/objectives, standards of performance, action plans, and measures. Employees usually work with several performance plans simultaneously. Sometimes called work plans.

performance review: A coaching tool prepared for employees on an individual basis to document their job performances. Contained in these reviews are specific details of each employee's efforts—solid or otherwise—and their achievements or lack thereof.

personal detachment: A necessary bulwark in coach-employee relationships eschewing personal friendships and romantic liaisons.

planned mentoring: Mentoring in business circumstances whereby a higher-up in an organization is paired with an employee being groomed for new job responsibilities or a promotion. Also refers to the not-for-profit programs in which adult mentors are matched with young mentees.

positive outcome philosophy: A coaching and mentoring canon that holds that every problem or conflict in the workplace has a positive solution.

positive reinforcement: A coaching and mentoring technique that identifies and lauds the right behaviors of employees and mentees on the spot, leading to more of the same.

potential envelopes: Employees' and mentees' vast supply of unique talents and abilities that wise coaches and mentors tirelessly work to push to the surface, as in "push the envelope" or stretch to the limit.

power to the people: A coaching and mentoring catch phrase that means respecting individual initiative, and thus tapping into employees' unique talents and abilities one person at a time.

principled coherence: The coaching and mentoring standard that asks coaches and mentors to do what they say they're going to do, when they say they're going to do it.

productive confrontation: Conflicts in the workplace converted into positive lessons learned and forward movement.

professionalism: The conscientious behaviors expected of individuals in the workplace. Encompasses how the job is done, not the results.

quality time: Making the best and most productive use of a finite amount of time.

reality chasm: What employees believe they can do versus what they actually can do. It is essential that coaches understand that this gap sometimes exists and carefully evaluate what are their employees' genuine talents and abilities versus what is hot air.

reality laboratory: The place where employees metaphorically go when they engage in role reversal. It's a place where experimentation leads employees to think as entrepreneurs, empathize with the other side, fashion flexibility, and sharpen self-awareness.

role: A group of work responsibilities and job expectations; i.e., the position the employee is hired to undertake.

self-motivation: An individual's embracing of commitment to the job coupled with the personal desire to perform well and move forward. Applicable outside the work force in many other circumstances, but always with the same principles in place—commitment and a desire to move forward.

sensitivity plus: A coaching communication technique for handling thin-skinned, overly sensitive employees, which entails coaches modulating their tone to suit the circumstances. Often applied when passing on negative feedback to employees to soften the delivery of the content, but still get through to them without generating a defensive, antagonistic response.

skills: Special competencies in particular fields, including technical skills and soft skills such as people skills.

social responsibility: The general principle adopted by many business organizations that leads to their participation in not-for-profit mentoring organizations and other acts beneficial to the community at large.

soda pop rule: From the old 7-Up ad, "You Like It, It Likes You." A coaching technique called into action to temper employee versus employee conflict. Its "you like your job; your job likes you" theme importunes combative employees to amend their rancorous relationship and solve job performance problems to save their jobs.

soft skills: Communication and interpersonal skills that are behavioral and abstract in nature, but nevertheless essential to performing in most jobs.

solution orientation: The irrevocable coaching tenet of being focused on finding solutions to any and all problems and obstacles in the workplace.

sponge for learning: Managers and employees who unceasingly soak up knowledge and skills.

standards bar: A coach's clearly enunciated level of achievement and professionalism that all employees are expected to reach or surpass.

standards of performance: The expectations of the quality of results in performance plans. Sometimes shortened to standards.

taking stock: A regular inventory that all coaches take of their own successes and failures.

talk up: A verbal coaching technique of elevating employees by respecting them and never talking down to them.

task: A particular activity within a job.

three As of mentoring: Advice, access, and advocacy.

three Bs of coaching and mentoring: Be aware, be fair, and be there.

three C triangle: Coach, communication, and coordination. A coach relies on regular communication with his or her employees, leading to solid coordination of efforts in the workplace.

three Ps of coaching and mentoring: People, performance, and positive outcomes.

tone setting: A coach's words and actions establishing the conduct of the workplace and the nature of all on-the-job relationships. An offshoot of leadership by example.

vision: Noble, aggressive goals for a company's short-term and long-term future.

work ethic: The overall work habits of men and women on the job.

zero tolerance: A wise workplace policy in this litigious age that prohibits such things as insult humor, profanity, and personal animus between or among employees leading to the shunning of others. Rigorously enforced by coaches.

Index

THE EVERYTHING LEADERSHIP BOOK

Trade paperback,
$12.95 ($19.95 CAN)
1-58062-513-4, 320 pages

By Bob Adams

In order for any group to run smoothly, it needs a strong, capable individual at the helm. Whether you are a senior executive or the captain of your softball team, *The Everything® Leadership Book* teaches you how to effectively direct and manage people. The book includes practical advice on leadership techniques and how to maintain professional composure, as well as tips on what separates the leaders from the followers. You'll learn to exude self-confidence, become a role model, and make a difference at work and in your community.

OTHER *EVERYTHING*® BOOKS BY ADAMS MEDIA CORPORATION

BUSINESS

Everything® **Business Planning Book**
Everything® **Coaching & Mentoring Book**
Everything® **Home-Based Business Book**
Everything® **Leadership Book**
Everything® **Managing People Book**
Everything® **Network Marketing Book**
Everything® **Online Business Book**
Everything® **Project Management Book**
Everything® **Selling Book**
Everything® **Start Your Own Business Book**
Everything® **Time Management Book**

COMPUTERS

Everything® **Build Your Own Home Page Book**
Everything® **Computer Book**

Everything® **Internet Book**
Everything® **Microsoft® Word 2000 Book**

COOKING

Everything® **Barbecue Cookbook**
Everything® **Bartender's Book, $9.95**
Everything® **Chocolate Cookbook**
Everything® **Cookbook**
Everything® **Dessert Cookbook**
Everything® **Diabetes Cookbook**
Everything® **Low-Carb Cookbook**
Everything® **Low-Fat High-Flavor Cookbook**
Everything® **Mediterranean Cookbook**
Everything® **One-Pot Cookbook**
Everything® **Pasta Book**
Everything® **Quick Meals Cookbook**
Everything® **Slow Cooker Cookbook**

Everything® **Soup Cookbook**
Everything® **Thai Cookbook**
Everything® **Vegetarian Cookbook**
Everything® **Wine Book**

HEALTH

Everything® **Anti-Aging Book**
Everything® **Dieting Book**
Everything® **Herbal Remedies Book**
Everything® **Hypnosis Book**
Everything® **Menopause Book**
Everything® **Nutrition Book**
Everything® **Stress Management Book**
Everything® **Vitamins, Minerals, and Nutritional Supplements Book**

HISTORY

Everything® **American History Book**

All Everything® books are priced at $12.95 or $14.95, unless otherwise stated. Prices subject to change without notice.
Canadian prices range from $11.95–$22.95 and are subject to change without notice.

Everything® **Civil War Book**
Everything® **World War II Book**

HOBBIES

Everything® **Bridge Book**
Everything® **Candlemaking Book**
Everything® **Casino Gambling Book**
Everything® **Chess Basics Book**
Everything® **Collectibles Book**
Everything® **Crossword and Puzzle Book**
Everything® **Digital Photography Book**
Everything® **Drums Book (with CD),**
  $19.95, ($31.95 CAN)
Everything® **Family Tree Book**
Everything® **Games Book**
Everything® **Guitar Book**
Everything® **Knitting Book**
Everything® **Magic Book**
Everything® **Motorcycle Book**
Everything® **Online Genealogy Book**
Everything® **Playing Piano and**
  Keyboards Book
Everything® **Rock & Blues Guitar**
  Book (with CD), $19.95,
  ($31.95 CAN)
Everything® **Scrapbooking Book**

HOME IMPROVEMENT

Everything® **Feng Shui Book**
Everything® **Gardening Book**
Everything® **Home Decorating Book**
Everything® **Landscaping Book**
Everything® **Lawn Care Book**
Everything® **Organize Your Home Book**

KIDS' STORY BOOKS

Everything® **Bedtime Story Book**
Everything® **Bible Stories Book**
Everything® **Fairy Tales Book**
Everything® **Mother Goose Book**

NEW AGE

Everything® **Astrology Book**

Everything® **Divining the Future Book**
Everything® **Dreams Book**
Everything® **Ghost Book**
Everything® **Meditation Book**
Everything® **Numerology Book**
Everything® **Palmistry Book**
Everything® **Spells and Charms Book**
Everything® **Tarot Book**
Everything® **Wicca and Witchcraft Book**

PARENTING

Everything® **Baby Names Book**
Everything® **Baby Shower Book**
Everything® **Baby's First Food Book**
Everything® **Baby's First Year Book**
Everything® **Breastfeeding Book**
Everything® **Get Ready for Baby Book**
Everything® **Homeschooling Book**
Everything® **Potty Training Book,**
  $9.95, ($15.95 CAN)
Everything® **Pregnancy Book**
Everything® **Pregnancy Organizer,**
  $15.00, ($22.95 CAN)
Everything® **Toddler Book**
Everything® **Tween Book**

PERSONAL FINANCE

Everything® **Budgeting Book**
Everything® **Get Out of Debt Book**
Everything® **Get Rich Book**
Everything® **Investing Book**
Everything® **Homebuying Book, 2nd Ed.**
Everything® **Homeselling Book**
Everything® **Money Book**
Everything® **Mutual Funds Book**
Everything® **Online Investing Book**
Everything® **Personal Finance Book**

PETS

Everything® **Cat Book**
Everything® **Dog Book**
Everything® **Dog Training and Tricks**
Everything® **Horse Book**
Everything® **Puppy Book**
Everything® **Tropical Fish Book**

REFERENCE

Everything® **Astronomy Book**
Everything® **Car Care Book**
Everything® **Christmas Book, $15.00,**
  ($21.95 CAN)
Everything® **Classical Mythology Book**
Everything® **Divorce Book**
Everything® **Etiquette Book**
Everything® **Great Thinkers Book**
Everything® **Learning French Book**
Everything® **Learning German Book**
Everything® **Learning Italian Book**
Everything® **Learning Latin Book**
Everything® **Learning Spanish Book**
Everything® **Mafia Book**
Everything® **Philosophy Book**
Everything® **Shakespeare Book**
Everything® **Tall Tales, Legends, &**
  Other Outrageous Lies Book
Everything® **Toasts Book**
Everything® **Trivia Book**
Everything® **Weather Book**
Everything® **Wills & Estate Planning**
  Book

RELIGION

Everything® **Angels Book**
Everything® **Buddhism Book**
Everything® **Catholicism Book**
Everything® **Judaism Book**
Everything® **Saints Book**
Everything® **World's Religions Book**
Everything® **Understanding Islam Book**

SCHOOL & CAREERS

Everything® **After College Book**
Everything® **College Survival Book**
Everything® **Cover Letter Book**
Everything® **Get-a-Job Book**
Everything® **Hot Careers Book**
Everything® **Job Interview Book**
Everything® **Online Job Search Book**
Everything® **Resume Book, 2nd Ed.**
Everything® **Study Book**

All Everything® books are priced at $12.95 or $14.95, unless otherwise stated. Prices subject to change without notice.
Canadian prices range from $11.95–$22.95 and are subject to change without notice.

WE HAVE EVERYTHING . . . .

SPORTS/FITNESS

Everything® **Bicycle Book**
Everything® **Fishing Book**
Everything® **Fly-Fishing Book**
Everything® **Golf Book**
Everything® **Golf Instruction Book**
Everything® **Pilates Book**
Everything® **Running Book**
Everything® **Sailing Book, 2nd Ed.**
Everything® **T'ai Chi and QiGong Book**
Everything® **Total Fitness Book**
Everything® **Weight Training Book**
Everything® **Yoga Book**

TRAVEL

Everything® **Guide to Las Vegas**
Everything® **Guide to New England**
Everything® **Guide to New York City**
Everything® **Guide to Washington D.C.**

Everything® **Travel Guide to The Disneyland Resort®, California Adventure®, Universal Studios®, and the Anaheim Area**
Everything® **Travel Guide to the Walt Disney World® Resort, Universal Studios®, and Greater Orlando, 3rd Ed.**

WEDDINGS & ROMANCE

Everything® **Creative Wedding Ideas Book**
Everything® **Dating Book**
Everything® **Jewish Wedding Book**
Everything® **Romance Book**
Everything® **Wedding Book, 2nd Ed.**
Everything® **Wedding Organizer, $15.00** ($22.95 CAN)

Everything® **Wedding Checklist,** $7.95 ($11.95 CAN)
Everything® **Wedding Etiquette Book,** $7.95 ($11.95 CAN)
Everything® **Wedding Shower Book,** $7.95 ($12.95 CAN)
Everything® **Wedding Vows Book,** $7.95 ($11.95 CAN)
Everything® **Weddings on a Budget Book, $9.95** ($15.95 CAN)

WRITING

Everything® **Creative Writing Book**
Everything® **Get Published Book**
Everything® **Grammar and Style Book**
Everything® **Grant Writing Book**
Everything® **Guide to Writing Children's Books**
Everything® **Writing Well Book**

ALSO AVAILABLE:

THE EVERYTHING® **KIDS'** SERIES!

Each book is 8" x 9¼", 144 pages, and two-color throughout.

Everything® **Kids' Baseball Book, 2nd Edition, $6.95** ($10.95 CAN)
Everything® **Kids' Bugs Book, $6.95** ($10.95 CAN)
Everything® **Kids' Cookbook, $6.95** ($10.95 CAN)
Everything® **Kids' Joke Book, $6.95** ($10.95 CAN)
Everything® **Kids' Math Puzzles Book, $6.95** ($10.95 CAN)
Everything® **Kids' Mazes Book, $6.95** ($10.95 CAN)
Everything® **Kids' Money Book, $6.95** ($11.95 CAN)

Everything® **Kids' Monsters Book, $6.95** ($10.95 CAN)
Everything® **Kids' Nature Book, $6.95** ($11.95 CAN)
Everything® **Kids' Puzzle Book $6.95,** ($10.95 CAN)
Everything® **Kids' Science Experiments Book, $6.95** ($10.95 CAN)
Everything® **Kids' Soccer Book, $6.95** ($10.95 CAN)
Everything® **Kids' Travel Activity Book, $6.95** ($10.95 CAN)

Available wherever books are sold!
To order, call 800-872-5627, or visit us at everything.com

Everything® is a registered trademark of Adams Media Corporation.